Memorial candles

The Holocaust has had a deep effect on the children of survivors, with parents who were irreparably damaged, both physically and psychologically. They grew up in the shadow of psychic conflicts stemming from bereavement, mourning, guilt feelings and anxiety, which often resulted in overprotection and overexpectation. Dina Wardi has worked for the last twenty years as a psychotherapist in Israel with the second generation of Holocaust survivors and her remarkable book describes the impact of trauma over the generations.

As the children of Holocaust survivors reach adulthood, they often need professional help in establishing a new identity and self-esteem. During their childhood their parents have unconsciously transmitted to them much of their own trauma, investing them with all their memories and hopes, so that they become 'memorial candles' to those who did not survive. The book combines verbatim transcriptions of dialogues in individual and group psychotherapy sessions with analyses of dreams, fantasies and childhood memories. Dina Wardi traces the emotional history of her patients, accompanying them on a painful and moving journey into their inner world. She describes the children's infancy in the guilt-laden atmosphere of survivor families, through to their difficult separation from their parents in maturity. She also traces in detail the therapeutic process, which culminates in the patients' separation from the role of 'memorial candles'.

Memorial Candles will be of great value to all those whose work brings them face-to-face with the traumatic effects of the Holocaust upon survivors of all nationalities and their children. It will also be of special interest to those involved in the study of post-traumatic stress in general and inter-generation trauma transmission in particular.

Born in Italy in 1938, **Dina Wardi** was taken to Israel by her Zionist parents at the age of one year and thus escaped the fate of her people in the Holocaust. She lives in Jerusalem, where she conducts her psychotherapeutic practice.

The International Library of Group Psychotherapy and Group Process

General Editor

Dr Malcolm Pines
Institute of Group-Analysis, London, and formerly of the Tavistock Clinic, London.

The International Library of Group Psychotherapy and Group Process is published in association with the Institute of Group-Analysis (London) and is devoted to the systematic study and exploration of group psychotherapy.

Memorial candles:
Children of the Holocaust

by Dina Wardi

Translated by
Naomi Goldblum

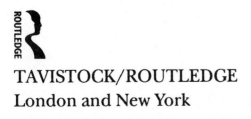

TAVISTOCK/ROUTLEDGE
London and New York

First published 1992
by Routledge
11 New Fetter Lane, London EC4P 4EE

Simultaneously published in the USA and Canada
by Routledge
a division of Routledge, Chapman and Hall, Inc.
29 West 35th Street, New York, NY 10001

© 1990 Hebrew Edition Maxwell-Macmillan-Keter

© 1992 English Translation Dina Wardi

Typeset by LaserScript, Mitcham, Surrey
Printed and bound in Great Britain by
Biddles Ltd, Guildford and King's Lynn

British Library Cataloguing in Publication Data
Wardi, Dina
Memorial candles: children of the holocaust. –
(International library of group psychotherapy)
I. Title II. Series
940.5318

Library of Congress Cataloging in Publication Data
Wardi, Dina, 1938–
[Nos 'e ha-hotam. English]
Memorial candles: children of the Holocaust/by Dina Wardi;
translated by Naomi Goldblum.
p. cm. – (International library of group psychotherapy and
group process)
Translations of: Nos 'e ha-hotam.
Includes bibliographical references.
1. Children of Holocaust survivors – Interviews. 2. Holocaust,
Jewish (1939–1945) – Psychological aspects. 3. Children of Holocaust
survivors – Psychology. 4. Holocaust survivors – Psychology.
I. Title. II. Series.
[DNLM: 1. Jews – psychology. 2. Parent–Child Relations.
3. Psychotherapy. 4. Self Concept. 5. Stress Disorders,
Post-Traumatic – psychology. 6. War Crimes. WM 170 W265m]
D804.3.W3613 1992
940.53'18 – dc20
DNLM/DLC
for Library of Congress   91-847
                                                                      CIP

ISBN 0–415–06098–2
    0–415–06099–0 (pbk)

To my parents.
To my late father, from whose artistic soul I inherited sensitivity and vision.
To my mother, who gave me courage and esteem for the written word.

Contents

Foreword

The author of this book, Dina Wardi, was born to an Italian Jewish family and grew up in Palestine-Israel, far from the terrors of the Holocaust. After World War II, in 1946, she visited her family in Italy for the first time. Her grandmother took her to the nunnery in which she had hidden from the Germans during the war. This visit left an impression on the little girl, and it seems that it was then that seeds of the intergeneration memory were planted in her heart, which were to sprout many years later in her professional work.

Dina Wardi graduated from the School of Social Work at the Hebrew University of Jerusalem. After completing her studies she worked in the Youth Probation Service. Later she went to the United States and changed her field of specialization to clinical psychotherapy, in which she obtained her MSW degree; she studied family therapy, group therapy and gestalt therapy, the latter with the founder of the method, Fritz Perls. Upon returning to Israel she taught group therapy and later opened a private practice.

Dina Wardi is one of the first psychotherapists in Israel to use group therapy in the treatment of the second generation of Holocaust survivors. After the 1973 War she began doing intensive group therapy with young people, and she found that many of the patients were the children of Holocaust survivors, and that all of them had experiences, emotional burdens and methods of expressions that were common and unique to this group.

During the same period the children of Holocaust survivors in other countries as well were beginning to find one another, and they realized that they spoke a common language about experiences that they also had in common. Both in Israel and abroad it was discovered that sensitivity to separation, feelings of mourning and guilt, the burden of their parents' exaggerated tendencies to worry, the desire to protect their parents and suffering people in general – all of these are common threads running through the fabric of the lives of the survivors' children.

Indeed, the Holocaust impressed its stamp on the children of the survivors. They grew up in the shadow of psychic conflicts stemming from bereavement, mourning, guilt feelings, excessive anxiety, over-protection and overexpectation – with parents who were irreparably damaged, both physically and psychologically. But in the psyches of the children a struggle for an independent identity developed – including personal, social and even historical identity. The survivors' children are bent almost double under the weight of the burden placed on their shoulders, yet at the same time – due precisely to this burden itself, but also due to their therapy – they are becoming stronger. For what are involved here are not only emotional load, conflicts and the need for therapy, but also psychological strength, stamina, and the ability to identify with others. Indeed, many of the children of survivors chose careers such as social work, teaching, psychology, medicine and psychiatry.

The metaphor 'memorial candles' has great power. Candles are a Jewish symbol replete with feelings and invested with great signi-ficance, and memorial candles, even if they express an emotional burden, are also a source of light and hope.

The Holocaust has affected all of us, and in truth we are all its survivors or the children of its survivors. But the children of those who were actually there have an intimate knowledge of the signi-ficance of being both victim and winner. Thanks to the author of this book, we can listen to the stories of the survivors' children, acquire some of this knowledge, and find out about the details of their emotional lives, their dreams and the mutual relationships existing in their families. And since the topic concerns all of us, and is so laden with significance, a unique professional approach is required on the part of the therapists.

Memorial Candles touched me deeply. After reading it I under-stood many things that had been unclear before, and new thera-peutic perspectives were revealed to me. Lay readers, on the other hand, will find in this journey into the past, into the intimacy of the family and the intricacies of the soul, the richness of people's psychological resources and the infinity of hope.

Professor Haim Dasburg, Administrator
Ezrat Nashim Psychiatric Hospital, Jerusalem

Acknowledgements

My thanks are given first of all to my family: to my daughters Sharon and Orit and my sister Dafna, who were patient with me, supported me and encouraged me during the process of writing the book; and to my husband, Emannuel, for his willingness to invest many hours in editing the first draft of the manuscript.

Mrs Judy Friedgut deserves special thanks for her patience and for the effort she put into the typing of the manuscript.

Thanks to the late Professor Hillel Klein and the late Dr Shamai Davidson for supervision and guidance, and for sharing with me their deep knowledge and understanding of the traumas and effects of the Holocaust.

Special thanks go to my colleagues Dr Shalom Littman and Ms Tamar Shoshan, with whom I shared many hours of work in the guidance of groups of second-generation Holocaust survivors; together we dealt with the difficulties and doubts, and together we enjoyed great satisfaction.

Thanks to Professor Haim Dasburg, who was an active partner in my theoretical and clinical deliberations. His comments on what I had written were of great help to me.

We thank the authors Aharon Appelfeld, David Grossman and Nava Semel and the publishers Am Oved, Hakibbutz Hameuhad and Sifriat Poalim for permission to quote sections from their books; also E.P. Dutton for the translation of *Tzili: The Story of a Life* and Farrar Straus & Giroux for the translation of *See Under: Love*.

Finally, I owe my deepest thanks to the survivors' children who allowed me to accompany them on their painful and moving journey into their inner world. Many of them followed the writing of the book with great interest and even encouraged me; perhaps this is their contribution to all the survivors' children whose world is still enshrouded in the mists.

The patients quoted in the book have been given fictitious names.

Introduction

During the past fifteen years, in my work as a psychotherapist combining individual and group therapy, I treated dozens of the sons and daughters of Holocaust survivors. In this book I have reported my impressions from the many dialogues that took place between them and me in individual therapy sessions, and between them and their fellow members in group therapy sessions. I have also reported my impressions from many discussions I held over the years with members of the second generation of Holocaust survivors in professional workshops and meetings and at lectures, not necessarily in a therapeutic setting.

The course of therapy combines individual and group sessions, and generally takes about four years. The groups are composed of 10–12 young adults of both sexes, from 25 to 35 years old, and are homogeneous with respect to the educational and socioeconomic level of their members, and as far as possible also with respect to the strength of their ego forces and the types of conflicts they have. On the other hand, the groups are heterogeneous with respect to the present family status and the family background of the members; the same group might include single, married and divorced people – some of them the children of survivors and others from families with different backgrounds. This was meant to prevent the formation of excessive defensive merging which might affect the normal progress of therapy. Each patient met with the therapist twice a week: for two hours in the group setting and for one hour in an individual session. In the group setting we used the dynamic techniques that characterize analytic group therapy, such as dream analysis, reflection and interpretation of early experiences, and the analysis of interactions and processes taking place within the group; other, non-verbal techniques were also used occasionally.

Most of the survivors' children who go for therapy do so in their late twenties or early thirties, an age when young people are generally beginning to manage their own lives as independent adults. The transition to adult life generally involves the need to deal with physical and emotional separation from the family home. For most members of the second generation, this separation is especially difficult, and it is apparently one of the main reasons for their seeking therapy at this stage of their lives. Another reason is perhaps the difficulties and conflicts encountered by the survivors' children when they are faced with the task of forming a really intimate relationship with a partner. It seems that their inability to cope with these difficulties and to resolve their conflicts by themselves is what spurs them to seek therapy at precisely this stage.

As mentioned, I have been specializing in the therapy of children of survivors for many years. It is no wonder, then, that I have often been asked if I too belong to this category. I must admit that I do not have an unambiguous answer to this question. My parents are not actually Holocaust survivors, nor did any member of their extended families meet his death in the Holocaust, except for a distant relative of my father's, but the Holocaust nevertheless impressed its stamp upon various layers of my inner world, as it did for every Jew whose roots are in Europe. My personal connection with the Holocaust was formed in my early childhood, but I became aware of it only at a relatively late stage of my life, precisely because of my therapeutic work with the second generation. In retrospect I can identify four factors in the creation of this personal connection.

About a year before the outbreak of World War II, when I was still a baby, many refugees who had escaped from Germany because of the decrees of the Nazi regime began arriving in Italy. My parents, who were Zionists and were preparing to immigrate to Israel, could not stand idly by and so delayed their immigration. My father, an artist, left his work and joined a group of Italian Jews who did all they could to assist the persecuted refugees who had chanced to arrive in their country. Years later my father told me many stories about those days when he devoted all his time to the relief work. He would come home very late, tired and bothered, and when he would take me in his arms he would fall asleep. What did this baby absorb then of the thoughts and anxieties running through her father's head? Undoubtedly something was absorbed.

The second event occurred in Israel at the end of 1944, when I was already five years old. One day, when my mother was standing at the kitchen sink washing the dishes, I noticed tears running down her cheeks. I still remember how frightened I was, with what anxiety I asked her why she was crying. She answered that she had found out that her parents and her sister were still alive. She had found this out indirectly, and she did not yet know anything about the fate of the rest of her family. Obviously I could not grasp the full significance of her words at that time, as I did not actually know my grandparents or my aunt. Indeed, it was only years later that I gradually realized how great my mother's tension and anxiety must have been all those years, so that their relief by this sudden discovery simply melted her.

I lived through the first years of my childhood during World War II, while my parents were trying to be farmers at a cooperative village in the Sharon Valley. Among the orchards, chickens and anemones that filled our innocent, childish world my sister and I enjoyed the joy and peace of nature, and I doubt that we paid much attention to our parents' anxieties about the fate of their dear ones. But I have no doubt that in the deeper layers of our tender souls, we absorbed a bit of the terrible permanent worry that didn't leave them even for a moment.

The third event was my trip with my family to ruined postwar Italy, where, amid intense excitement, we met the many members of the family who had survived. My impression of the visit to the convent where my grandmother had been hidden, which had enabled her to survive, is one that I carry with me throughout my life.

My grandmother was a strong, proud woman, and despite the threat and fear involved in her hiding out in the convent she succeeded in maintaining her identity, her honour and even her beauty. She established strong bonds of friendship with the Mother Superior – who was the only person in the convent who knew that she was Jewish – and she used to play piano duets with her and tell her proudly about her granddaughters in Palestine. She acted like a Christian in every respect, and even participated regularly in the nuns' prayers at the church. Although I had grown up in a totally secular household, something in the story I heard from my grandmother disturbed me. I didn't hesitate for long, and in somewhat stammering Italian I asked my grandmother worriedly, 'What, grandma, did you say the Christian prayers with all of them?' My grandmother became serious and looked me right in the eyes, but suddenly she smiled and winked at me and said, 'Don't worry, Dina – actually, in a whisper, so no one could hear, I used to say our Jewish prayers.' I clearly remember my feeling of relief when she said that, and how I was filled with pride in this grandmother of mine at that moment, for her success in maintaining her honour and her Jewish identity even in the conditions of hiding. This feeling has not left me to this day, and I preserve it as a precious inner value that I inherited from my mother's family.

More than thirty years passed before I felt a personal sense of belonging to the Holocaust once again. When I began my therapeutic work with the children of survivors, my mother reminded me about her friendship with the writer Primo Levi, a relative of ours from Turin whom she had known from childhood. She described what had happened to him in the death camps during the war and she even gave me his book *Is This a Man?* to read.

When I read this book in Italian, the language of the author as well as my own native language, I was overwhelmed by intense emotion. I especially remember what I felt when I read one fragment in which the author describes how he was once standing in the yard at Auschwitz, as naked as the day he was born, in the middle of one of the selections. Suddenly I stopped reading, struck by a razor-sharp thought: instead of Primo, or at his side, could have stood my grandfather, my grandmother or some other member of my large family, who had been saved from this fate only by a miracle. At that moment of revelation I was overwhelmed by a strong wave of pain and sadness. I actually tried to force myself to return to the imaginary picture in which my grandfather and grandmother were standing naked in the snow in a queue of people marching to their death. The feeling of terrible humiliation and anxiety caused by this picture was so strong that I couldn't bear it, and I had to detach myself emotionally from the picture. Only after some time was I able to return to it. At these moments it seemed to me that I had experienced a tiny taste of the intense feelings and anxieties in the depths of the soul of every child of survivors.

When I finished reading the book I became aware of a feeling of pride, and I felt gratitude and admiration for Primo Levi, for his ability to continue being a 'man' and maintain his human image even in the heart of the 'other planet'. I therefore gathered my courage and wrote him a letter. I told him about my therapeutic work with the children of survivors, thanked him for the intense experience his book had given me, and explained its unique significance for me, both personally and professionally. Levi answered my letter, and from that time until his death we continued to correspond.

Thus I am not actually a daughter of survivors, but, like every member of European Jewry of that period, I too am a daughter of survivors in potential.

Indeed, which member of the Jewish nation is not a child of survivors in potential? It therefore seems to me that the problems raised in this book touch the essence of the Jewish nation in the post-Holocaust generation. The central topic of this book is none other than the intergenerational transmission of the traumas caused by exile and extermination, which have unfortunately been only too frequent throughout the generations and have not ceased even in our own generation. It is thus possible that my descriptions and explanations may be able to some extent to elucidate problems belonging to large groups of people throughout the generations in many different countries. Thus many people, both old and young, should find an interest in the problems discussed in this book, and the most sensitive of these may be able to use the book to gain a better understanding of their fellows.

In the literature dealing with the psychological problems of the children of Holocaust survivors the question repeatedly arises as to whether the unique syndromes discovered among them by psychologists should be attributed to the survivors' children in general or only to the clinical population, that is, to those survivors' children who seek psychotherapeutic assistance. This question has double force in view of the especially high achievements of the second generation of Holocaust survivors in both practical and theoretical areas, from politics and business to research in literature and the arts, without any significant distinction between those who did or did not require psychotherapeutic assistance. The question is thus very difficult, and the answers offered to it are controversial. Some people take the risk of making generalizations, while others limit the implications of their findings to the clinical population. It is clear, at any rate, that in order to give an adequate answer to this question it would be necessary to take into consideration many different variables, such as the age of the survivor parents during the war, their personal background before the war, and the type of traumas they underwent during the Holocaust; since all these, as well as the psychological strengths of each and every child of survivors, might be a significant factor in determining the character and intensity of the intergenerational transmission of the trauma. It seems to me that whenever the transmission occurs it generally takes on very similar forms, and I have concentrated on these forms in this book.

Moreover, as we shall see, in most of the survivors' families one of the children is designated as a 'memorial candle' for all of the relatives who perished in the Holocaust, and he is given the burden of participating in his parents' emotional world to a much greater extent than any of his brothers or sisters. He is also given the special mission of serving as the link which on the one hand preserves the past and on the other hand joins it to the present and the future. This role is generated out of the need to fill the enormous vacuum left behind by the Holocaust. The cutting off of the natural processes of intergenerational continuity has imposed on the second generation both the privilege and the obligation of being the connecting link that heals the trauma of the cutting off and fulfils the enormous expectations of their parents – and perhaps not theirs alone, but also, to some extent, those of the entire Jewish people. The burden of these expectations is simultaneously an activating and facilitative factor and an oppressive and retarding factor for the growth and functioning of the second generation. In my opinion, both of these inner forces exist among all the children of survivors, but the two forces have different weights on the internal balances in different people, and this affects their ability to cope and to function, as well as their need to seek therapeutic assistance.

Over the years I have attempted to locate the main foci of conflict disturbing the inner world of the 'memorial candles' – conflicts connected with the Holocaust, with their parents, and with the families they lost somewhere in Europe – to understand them and to resolve them, with the assistance and the active and moving participation of the 'memorial candles' themselves. I hope that our joint work – which was sometimes very difficult and painful, but also moving and satisfying – has indeed borne fruit.

Chapter 1

Survivor parents – uprooting and separation traumas

> Death in the Nazi concentration camps and forced labour camps requires no explanation. It is survival that requires explanation. It is the survivors of the destruction that astonish us.
>
> (Bluhm 1948, p. 25)

Survival was the supreme goal of the inmates of the ghettos, the forced labour camps, the concentration camps and the extermination camps. For the purpose of survival they marshalled all their powers, both physical and psychological, for months and years. Terrible bodily suffering, illnesses, incessant hunger, tiredness and feebleness – all these were the lot of the camp inmates. In order to exist they developed the ability to improvise quickly in situations of sudden threat and danger. The chances of survival were thus dependent in large measure on the person's age and physical stamina, but this was not enough. Ultimately, survival in the extermination camps was a matter of luck (Bettelheim 1960).

The camp inmate needed to preserve in his heart a feeling of autonomy, of dignity and of reality in order to be prepared at all times to take advantage of any situation that might be able to stave off the danger of death for even a short while. Among the factors leading to survival must therefore be counted the moods that created the inmate's psychological state, and the psychic energy he was able to marshal in the terrible conditions reigning in the kingdoms of death.

Many researchers who studied psychological aspects of the Holocaust focused on the changes that took place in the mental state of the survivors. It must be remembered that the primary purpose of the Nazi psychological warfare, which was the destruction of the Jewish people as a collective, was realized partly through the destruction of the identity and personality of each individual as a person and as a Jew. The traumatization at the time of the terrible transport to the camp, the first selection at the camp gates, the incessant violence within the camp, the isolation that did not permit any hope of a future – all these drove the inmates to regressive behaviour and ultimately led to the total breakdown of their individuality. Life in the camps was a protracted process of traumatization, which was intended to destroy all inner reality and all representations of the familiar world and what it stands for (H. Klein 1987).

Personal identity is the product of a system of identifications and processes that occur to the infant, the child and the adolescent in the course of their psychological growth. The system of identifications plays a central role in the person's ability to form object relations and in the learning processes that are with him all his life. Identification is also the central component of the internal structure of the ego and the superego. Therefore any interruption or damage to this process of identification has long-range effects.

The external reality that was forced upon the camp inmate was powerful enough to destroy their personal identity and sense of belonging. This loss had a great impact on the personality of many survivors and on their ability to function in their lives after the war, as well as on their children, the members of the second generation.

The changes that occurred to the psyche of the survivors were thus an effect of the traumatic experiences they had undergone, and the defence mechanisms required by the persecuted psyche to cope with these traumatic experiences. In order to adapt, the inmates needed to marshal defence mechanisms that caused changes in the internal structure of the ego and the superego. But a person's ability to preserve an independent and consolidated self-identity is dependent upon his ability to preserve the internal identifications that are vital for the preservation of the continuing internal sense of a stable and secure ego, as well as increasing perception of other objects. The continual psychological violence therefore damaged precisely the inmates' ability to preserve their personal identity in a consolidated and independent form.

One of the topics discussed in this book is the question of whether the Nazi system succeeded in arresting or completely eliminating the identification processes within the surviving inmates who had been children or adolescents at the time of their stay in the camps. To what extent did this system succeed in warping these identification processes, including the internalized representations of the parents, siblings and other relatives that had been consolidated in the children's psyches before the war began? This question is very important for the transition between the generations, from the survivors to their sons and daughters, in the areas of identity and identification.

Separation from one's family

'The last time I saw my parents and sisters going further and further away from me, in the direction of the camp, comes back to me again and again, day and night. Their last glance at me at that moment will be with me for the rest of my life. I think that from then on nothing more happened to me.'

Fania, who is about fifty years old, a married woman with four children, was about eleven when she was separated from her family in one of the camps. On the surface she seems to be living a full life. She got married, she bore and raised four children, but in reality she carries within herself since that day the heavy burden expressed in her last sentence: 'from then on nothing more happened to me.'

The fact that survivors say very little about their separation from their parents, siblings and other family members can be misleading. The topic of separation is indeed often omitted from the story of what happened to them during the Holocaust, or drowned in a sea of events that seem more important. Sometimes, after many years have passed, some of them are ready to talk about the separation from their families (generally in answer to their own children's direct questions), but even then their descriptions are usually short and narrated in a monotonous voice. However, this appearance is misleading. A deeper look shows that the trauma accompanying the survivors' separation from their families is very deep – perhaps the most difficult trauma to cure.

The separation from their families left residues of pain, anger, guilt feelings, and feelings of loss and emptiness in the psyches of the survivors. It remained a wound in their souls, which may seem to have been covered over by a scab, but still gives them no rest.

This 'unfinished business' generally takes the form of nightmares, dreams and fantasies. But for some of the survivors the trauma was so great that it was completely repressed, and it is expressed only indirectly, in ways that seem inexplicable, such as psychosomatic symptoms and other mental disturbances. Separation from their family, especially from their parents, during childhood or youth, caused the formation of a break in their identity, which led to the formation of a zone of apathy in their personal identity. Among survivors who were adults at the time of the Holocaust the damage was different and somewhat less.

Krystal (1968), and later J.S. Kestenberg (1972), emphasize the point that if one takes into account the regressions that took place among the survivors – both those due to the sharp break between them and their dear ones, and those due to the fact that the adults became entirely dependent on other people, and were forced to give up their status as adults and transfer it to their Nazi persecutors – then the distinction between childhood traumas and the traumas of adults becomes less clear.

The fact that the camp inmates became totally dependent on their captors, and that the parents were humiliated in front of their children, could not but lead to the destruction of their children's image of them as parents who could love and defend them.

Elie Wiesel (1972) claims that when the two generations of a family were permitted to stay together, a very deep psychological conflict was often created for the children. The deterioration of their physical and psychological state caused the parents to become dependent on the children, while the survival of the children was almost always dependent on their ability to abandon their parents. But not only children were trapped in a psychological conflict; even young adults who had grown up before the Holocaust in warm and loving families often regressed so severely as to lose all their faith in their parents. To this day many of them are still seesawing between two extreme positions – between idealization of their lost families and bitter accusation of these families for not finding any way to protect them.

Mina, fifty-five years old, married and the mother of a grown daughter, tells the following story:

'Nearly forty years have passed since then, and only now can I tell a little of what happened to me during all those months and years. The inability to express these horrors has severely affected my entire existence to this very day. Beneath my emotional apathy are hidden terrible traumatic experiences, human horrors, bodily torture, physical and psychological suffering that cannot be repaired. During dozens of miles of death marches, countless hours of backbreaking labour, from a certain moment a person loses himself. He is abandoned because he has become apathetic. People are not built to live alone, neither when things are bad nor when they are good.'

'When I heard the echo of the shot at my mother, who was marching behind us in that death march, I was stricken dumb. I couldn't utter a sound. For more than a month I was unable to speak.'

'When I returned from the camps no one was able to understand me. I felt a hundred years old, ancient in my soul although my body was only sixteen years old. I no longer had any desire for a spiritual or social life, or for a marital life. Nothing interested me any more. Very slowly we returned to the cycle of ordinary life, but we never came back to ourselves. We did not remain embittered, we did not hate anyone, but we did not want to remember, we only wanted to forget.'

One senses very clearly the breaking point in Mina's story: the moment she heard the echo of the shot that ended her mother's life, and did not react in any way but continued on the death march and became frozen within herself. Her physical muteness lasted for a month, but her emotional muteness is still with her: 'we never came back to ourselves.' Lifton (1980) defines this muteness as the psychic closing-off that remains with the survivor throughout his life, while he remains incapable of freeing himself from it. The abandonment here was mutual – Mina's mother abandoned Mina by dying, and Mina abandoned her mother: she allowed her to die alone at the side of the road, and thus she lost her own self as well.

Mina's fragmentary sentences include feelings of abandonment, anger, sadness, pain and guilt, whose intensity is so great that the ego is forced to defend itself against them by excessive use of the mechanisms of repression and denial: 'we did not want to remember, we only wanted to forget.' The total repression of her traumatic separation from her mother undermined and cut off the natural process of identification with the mother which is so important for an adolescent girl. But feelings of anger and frustration are also characteristic of adolescence, and these feelings are entirely split off, including the feelings of anger at being abandoned. Their place is taken by harsh guilt feelings, alongside which there often develops an idealization of the parents, especially the figure of the mother.

Leah, who was born in Poland, was nine years old when the Germans captured the town in which her family lived. The family – including her parents and her two little sisters, as well as uncles, aunts and cousins – hid in the cellar of their house. Leah looked old for her age and also had an Aryan appearance, so she was delegated to leave the hideout, wearing a dress of her mother's, to find food for the whole family.

This continued for several weeks, until one day, when Leah returned to the cellar with two loaves of bread hidden in her bosom, she found it empty. From that day on she never saw any of the members of her family alive.

Leah's daughter said that her mother tended to repeat the story of this event compulsively, in a monotonous and emotionless voice. Here as well the moment of abandonment was transformed into a memory laden with rage, pain and guilt. The compulsive attempt to return in memory to that empty cellar apparently expresses the need to find a solution to an insoluble conflict: her inability to reactivate the terrifying feelings that filled her heart when she stood at the door of the cellar prevents her from filling the internal void in her psyche. The void of the empty cellar is also the void of her interior, which became a constant threat.

The destruction of her parents' image began even before Leah found herself alone in the world, when the burden of providing food for the entire family, including aunts, uncles and cousins, was placed on her shoulders. The normal identification based on continuity between the generations, which is a central element in the process of adolescence, was interrupted for her, as it was for many survivors who were children or adolescents at the time of the Holocaust. The changes in the attitude of the children and adolescents to their parents' image were not essentially different from those that occurred to adults, but among the adults there was a frequent tendency to idealization of the parents' images, which covered up the excess of guilt feelings. The feelings of guilt and pain at the loss of spouses and small children constitute another important factor, which will be discussed later.

The separation from the parents often occurred after a long period when the children and adolescents watched their parents undergoing a process of regression, during which the parents' ability to serve as a source of livelihood, defence and security for their children gradually diminished; the separation, which occurred at the end of this traumatic process, only put the final seal on the inner splits that warped the normal framework of identification between children and parents. These inner splits led to structural changes in the psyches of the children and adolescents, which were expressed in an accelerated process of growing-up, involving hasty learning and internalization of new legal and moral values which were entirely different from those they had known before.

We thus witness an excessive use of the mechanisms of defence, denial and compartmentalization, which had become vital for the preservation of some basic integrity of the ego. But the excessive use of these mechanisms necessarily leads to structural changes in the ego itself. Emotional experiences that flood and terrify the ego eventually bring about internal splits and rifts, which are expressed in the inactivation of the ego functions which previously served as agents and balancers of the psyche (A. Freud 1967).

It is against the background of the break in the sense of continuity of intergenerational identification that one must understand the centrality of the guilt feelings in the survivor's personality. The survivors' guilt feelings became an essential element intimately connected with the core of their identity, and they remained such for many years after the liberation (H. Klein 1987). These feelings not only preserved the centrality of the conscience, but also became an important factor in the preservation of the internal continuity of the ego and object representations that had been created within the survivors before the war, as well as in the preservation of the sense of time. That is, the element of continued identification with the images of the parents and the extended family was preserved covertly or indirectly, alongside the break in identification, precisely through the guilt feelings that continually recurred to the survivors during the course of their lives.

Nevertheless, there were times when the guilt feelings became obstacles to the survivors' capacity to adapt to the new world after their liberation, and to the possibility of reaching an integration of the two worlds – before and after the Holocaust.

We again witness the paradoxality of continuity: guilt feelings serve as a connecting element with the images of lost relatives, but at the same time they make it more difficult for the survivors to construct new ties with the families they established after the Holocaust.

Life in the death camps

The Holocaust's influence on the psyches of the survivors has been investigated extensively during the last few decades, and it has been documented in both the professional and general literature.

Niederland (1964) sees the death camps as a giant machine hammering incessantly, and systematically destroying the mental balance of the victims' personalities. Devoto and Martini (1981) compare certain aspects of the death camps with mental hospitals in their description of the death camp as a 'total institution'. The process of erasing the semblance of humanity from the victims began even before they reached the death camps. It began in the long journey in the cattle cars, which involved such profound humiliation that the semblance of humanity was lost; the acts of intimidation accompanying the journey played a crucial role in this process. Those who remained alive at the end of the 'selections' had to adapt to the 'total institution'. The process of adaptation necessitated the adoption of an entirely new value system, with the most important value being survival – how to manoeuvre between life and death, since after all the concentration camp was nothing but a huge kingdom of death. For most of the inmates, especially the children, the adoption of new values was completely impossible without a parallel process of psychic adaptation. In Frankl's (1947) words, an abnormal situation requires abnormal behaviour. There were several stages to this process of psychic adaptation, and each stage had different psychological dimensions, which are described below.

Robotization 'Everyone,' says Frankl, 'was pushed hither and thither with no clear thought or motive. Sometimes they were thrown together and sometimes they were violently separated from one another, like sheep in a herd.'

All Holocaust researchers agree that the ability to disappear into the crowd became one of the major commandments that had to be obeyed by anyone who wanted to survive; this is also apparent in the motto of the concentration camp inmates: 'Never stand out.' Those who succeeded in overcoming the initial shock adopted automatic reactions and behaviours that were directed solely at the value of survival; these were acquired at the price of the excessive repression of independent self-esteem and judgement, and the desire for self-expression.

The sense of emotional disconnection quickly led to the loss of personality, or 'robotization', that is, severe cognitive suppression involving the loss of all feeling of self-identity and even the loss of the sense of time and causality (Bettelheim 1960; Levi 1947; Krystal 1968, 1978; Krystal and Niederland 1971).

Without the ability to rely on the sign of anxiety for distinguishing potential danger, the inmate gradually went from a state of hyper-arousal and the continuous sense of mortal danger to a state of inhibition and suppression of sensitivity (Krystal 1968). Eventually the state of perpetual anxiety led to such severe shock to the normal functioning of the ego as to threaten its very existence. The blocking of the capacity to give verbal expression to feelings led to a diminishing or even total elimination of the capacity for symbolization; the power of imagination was affected and in most cases totally lost. The stabilization of a chronic traumatic state involves the dulling and deadening of the senses, and leads to the destruction of the feelings associated with self-identity, and the conscious suppression and noticeable weakening of the perception of time and reality.

Regression The psychological warfare waged by the SS against the camp inmates was intended to cancel the inmates' personalities. This was the purpose of the initial traumatization and the constant necessity for regressive, dependent behaviour, which was ceaselessly enforced.

The conditions of camp life contributed to the regressive state, as did the absolute dependence of the inmates on the SS commanders in matters of life and death. Some researchers even claim that the conditions of camp life actually demanded regressive behaviour and even rewarded it, as passive behaviour and total obedience helped preserve physical strength in particular and aided survival in general (Bettelheim 1960).

It is no wonder then that these behaviour patterns often continued to be an integral element of the survivors' personalities a long time after they were liberated from the camps.

With the loss of basic trust and healthy narcissism, the inmates' hostile feelings were turned against the self. The first signs of fragmentation and regression in the capacity for symbolization were accompanied by the loss of the vital ability of self-defence and constant awareness that was so necessary for survival. Sometimes this regressive process turned the person into a psychomotor organism whose automatic actions were the first signs of impending death.

Defence of the ego   Many inmates developed a 'false personality', made up entirely of rigid stereotypic conformity, which served as a barrier in the face of any spontaneous flow of true self-expression.

The true inner personality of many of these inmates was so repressed that from any practical viewpoint it could have been considered dead. Even after their liberation many of the survivors continued to use this false personality in their daily lives. The inmate constructed a kind of psychological armour whose purpose was to serve as a barrier between him and all feelings of pain. And thus, in order to protect himself from feeling anything, the inmate became rigid and closed. 'The disappearance of bravery,' writes Primo Levi (1947), 'turned us, under the oppressor's whip, into cowards indifferent to the pain of a tortured friend, and the incessant hunger focused all our feelings in our stomach' (p. 17).

As a result of the inability to relate to other people, the capacity for empathy was greatly reduced (Grubrich-Simits 1979), as was the capacity for the formation of emotional ties. And since the procedures of mourning had lost their meaning, the capacity for mourning lost relatives or friends was also lost. All mental activity, except of the most primitive kind, was totally destroyed. The inmate's personality was emptied of vital feelings until he finally felt that he did not exist at all.

'And a few days later,' relates Leah, 'when we arrived at the extermination camps, we knew no fear and we were punished without logical thoughts, without imagination and dreams, without illusions – we had turned into robots. Without a present and without a future and without memories of the good past, because we were immersed in ourselves and our immediate surroundings in order to live from moment to moment, from day to day. We didn't want anything. We didn't feel anything. Hope, human values, sounded strange. No one tried to encourage anyone else. It was only with difficulty that we saved our own selves. Occasionally, when we sat down to eat the bowl of soup and the slice of bread, we exchanged a living look in silence, from a distance, and we were happy that we were still alive so that we could fight against the current of extermination.'

The 'robotization' served as a defence mechanism during the years of terror, but it did not disappear with the liberation. Rather, it continued to leave its signs in the survivors even many years afterwards.

Changes in the superego The extensive exposure to excessive hostility and violence created internal pressure within the inmates, but they were forced to suppress their natural sadistic fantasies and the desires for revenge that were aroused in their minds. The signal function, which is meant to bring about self-organization for appropriate defence in the face of immediate danger or violence whose source is in the nearby environment, lost its capacity to function as a reliable warning sign. The normal functioning of the superego as a guard and protector became purposeless, and the psyche was left helpless, unprotected and unwilling to see.

The accepted ethical values became useless, as the constant terror of death diverted into a narrow channel all feelings whose source was in the outside world. A new system of expectations was created, entirely directed at survival.

The limited usefulness of verbal communication and symbolic functioning could not but steal from both the ego and the self – as well as from the internal reflection of external objects within the ego – all of their individuality, so that the borders between individual and universal were completely blurred. It is no wonder, then, that identification with the laws of the aggressors gradually replaced normal narcissism and all feelings of separate identity.

The capacity for adaptation that characterized all the camp inmates to one degree or another may be seen as 'emergency morality'. The giving-up of the self was a type of self-defence; it contained the advantage of creating a distance between the victim and the aggressor, as well as the ability to predict approaching disaster and even to escape from it. Some researchers believe that this emergency morality gradually turned into 'moral absolutism', which is based on the regression of the superego and on fears of external authority. In order to protect the essence of the psyche from harm the inmates needed primitive, magical and unrealistic identifications, which were utilized in a psychic framework that was becoming narrower and narrower.

Perhaps the atmosphere of danger and fear, stemming from the incessant violence, caused the victims to re-externalize the super-ego images that had been previously internalized. It is therefore not surprising that after the liberation the survivors' superegos remained weak and in danger of further regression and de-differentiation.

According to some researchers, for many years after the liberation of the camps many survivors still suffered from the syndrome called 'concentration camp syndrome'. This syndrome is characterized by the following symptoms:

1. Self-preoccupation. A depressive state; a state of unworked chronic mourning, accompanied by guilt feelings and a sense of emptiness.

2. Emotional dullness and inhibitions. A state of chronic anxiety stemming from the loss of basic trust and healthy narcissism. The anxiety floods the ego functions and threatens the person's emotional existence, while damaging the capacity for giving verbal expression to feelings and limiting the capacity for symbolization and the creation of fantasies.

3. Various physical and psychosomatic disturbances. Night-mares, drastic mood changes, and other symptoms.

4. Defective functioning of the superego. Splitting of the ego and of the objects reflected in the superego. The defects are caused by the conflict between identification with and denuncia-tion of Nazi morality.

5. The ego functions remain automatic. The ability to relate to other people is considerably weakened, together with the capacity for empathy, while the avoidance of mourning and of the internal processing of grief causes the loss of the capacity to form ties with others.

6. Damage to the bodily self-image is caused by the physical tortures and humiliations and the lack of intimacy. This is some-times accompanied by identification with the Nazi message concerning the Jewish image; this message was partially internal-ized by some of the survivors and became part of their world-view.

The methods of suppression used by the Nazis thus constituted a long process of intentional traumatization, whose purpose was to destroy the inmates' inner reality and their healthy representations of the familiar world. Denial, repression and emotional isolation therefore became appropriate and vital mechanisms.

In addition to the processes of destruction and distortion of the inmates' inner integration, psychic processes with an opposite tendency must also be isolated and emphasized – that is, those processes whose purpose was to preserve as far as possible the inner integration of the ego and the self, and to prevent total disintegration. In the most terrifying traumatic situations one can identify psychic processes leading to the narrowing of the ego and the loss of clear identity, while at the same time preserving some of the feelings of identity, selfhood and continuity.

At times the same elements (such as the extensive use of defence mechanisms) paradoxically served, at the same time, both of these tendencies – the narrowing and the preservation of the ego – which seem at first glance to be opposites. Denial and repression, for example, allowed the creation of fantasies which served as expressions of ego functioning, and the formation of a separation between the threatening and traumatic reality and the inner world constructed of memories and images.

Frankl (1947) describes how he would succeed from time to time in imagining the figure of his young, beloved wife, feeling longing for her, and remembering the experiences of joy and the wonderful moments of closeness and intimacy they had experienced together. He never tires of stressing the importance of these moments for him – they gave him the psychic strength to continue the struggle, not to fall apart and not to give in to weakness, hunger and torture.

H. Klein (1987) also sees the ability to arouse memories, to feel longing for beloved figures, and to live these feelings in the evil-saturated present as a victory of the inmates over their torturers. He adds the ability to write poetry in the very heart of the kingdom of death – poems of love and hope.

Collective songs and individual poetry are mentioned in many memoirs. The songs sung in the ghettos and the camps contain, according to Klein, unconscious reminiscences of the lullabies sung by mothers to their infants. Most lullabies contain clear primary elements of holding, which the mother provides for the infant during nursing. The ability to preserve the connection with these primary elements is a necessary condition for the continuation of the inner integration of the psyche and the ability to preserve – even if only partially – the sense of continued identity; without this the inmates would not have been able to marshal the energies that were vital for physical survival.

The return to 'the post-Holocaust world'

After the liberation the survivors left the extermination camps, the hideouts and the forests, and began to wander about. Most of them eventually reached the displaced-persons camps that had been set up in various parts of Europe. Many of them hoped to find lost family members and began to search for them, to ask about them, and to anticipate their arrival. This expectation generally ended in bitter disillusionment. Of their entire extended family, they realized, no one was left but themselves. Their dear ones had indeed perished and they would never see them again. This disillusionment brought with it a sense of unbearable loneliness, which was soon accompanied by the realization that they had lost not only their families but also their homeland. The knowledge that they would never return to their birthplace, and that their houses and communities had been destroyed, was no less harsh a blow than the loss of their families. Only psychic emptiness could continue to protect them from being flooded with feelings of loneliness that threatened their very existence.

Appelfeld (1971) describes the divided inner world of the displaced survivors:

> After the war a strange optimism seized people. The pain of separation was still fresh. People were incapable of evaluating what had happened to them, what had happened with them. The circulating blood knew more than the mind; nevertheless there was a kind of optimism...
>
> The circulating blood already knew: the wound can no longer be sewn up. We are dry, withered seeds, continuity will no longer come from us.
>
> (p. 82)

He goes on to describe the heroine of the book:

> Betty did not let go of her sleep, she was sunken deep in sleep. He understood: she was searching for the paths of her ancestors, without them she had no continuity. He was little

now at the side of her sleep. He also wanted to sleep, but he was alert, as after a disaster.

(pp. 82–3)

And in describing Gruzman, the hero of the book, he says:

Only now did he feel, after many years had passed, that they had all fallen off him like a hard shell, he had grown up without them. Even his father and mother had cut themselves off from him. The world had ejected him from one climate to another, from one language to another, as if carried on the backs of waves. . . He felt the lightness of his body as if after an extended walk. The feet continue to walk without the body. He felt that his roots were sprouting far from here, at the side of the Prut, where they were living without him.

(p. 82)

Appelfeld's description expresses the wave of loneliness and emptiness that flooded the survivors when they learned that the old world had disappeared. The process of splitting within their psyche, which had begun while they were still in the camps, could therefore not come to an end.

Part of the ego continued to live in the death camps, totally vulnerable, lacking protective armour and tied to the images of lost relatives. At its side was consolidated another part of the ego, which denied and repressed the trauma and the terrible pain stemming from the mutual abandonment and the realization of what had been the fate of their families. Only the repression of this pain could allow the ego to continue functioning and to begin to adapt to the new world after the Holocaust.

Appelfeld's Betty symbolizes that part of the ego that continued to preserve – even if only in sleep, in a state of blurred consciousness – the connection with a past that had been lost and sealed off forever, and with the images of the parents who had gone, never to return. For without this connection there is no inner continuity. There is only an unconscious inner struggle. In her sleep Betty preserves the sense of continuity, the connection and identification with the images of her dead parents.

In contrast, Gruzman, her husband, symbolizes the other part of the ego, the part that realizes the importance of continuity but nevertheless finds a way to cut itself off. This is a separation not only from the images of the relatives who had perished, but also from what might be called his roots. However, in the process his Jewish identity is undermined, as this identity is constructed from the sense of belonging to a family, a community and the Jewish people as a whole.

The break in Gruzman's identity is expressed in the undermining of his faith and the loss of his identification with the nation he belonged to. The language of the Jews was lost to him. He has not opened a religious book for years. The blood flowing in his veins is no longer his parents' blood, and his parents' voices no longer reach his ears, he no longer speaks their language. A deep rift has been created in his feeling of inner identity.

As is well-known, the mother's voice, which Gruzman no longer hears, is one of the most important elements of the archaic, preverbal world of the infant – a world composed of fantasies, images and voices. These voices, when part of a positive experience of motherhood, allay the infant's anxieties and give him primary feelings of calmness, warmth and security; the voices make the baby happy and calm, and when he has internalized them they become the foundation upon which are built feelings of security and belonging, which are such an important element in the shaping of the ego.

Appelfeld thus touches upon the breaking point of the basic feelings of security and belonging hidden in the archaic, unconscious world that serves as a foundation upon which one's identity is constructed. In essence, there is evidence here of changes that occurred in the survivors' psyches after they had already been liberated from the fear of death. Those primary, basic feelings of holding that the survivors had succeeded in preserving – perhaps, as Klein says, in virtue of the songs sung in the camps – represented the relationship and identification with the internalized images of close relatives. Thus the feelings of the wholeness of the ego and of continuity were maintained. But after the liberation – when all their internal energies were no longer directed at physical survival, and the intensity of their existential anxiety was attenuated – it was precisely then that the basis of these elements was undermined.

After the war, when the bitter disillusionment of the survivors' hopes that the old order would be restored undermined what little was left of their capacity for feeling security, belonging and continuity, nothing was left in their hearts but a sense of profound emptiness that engulfed them on all sides and filled their entire being (Davidson 1980).

Appelfeld (1971) goes even further:

All those who remembered were blown away afterwards like sawdust in the wind. Their brooding thoughts drove them insane, their memories drove them insane. Only those who had the ability to forget lived long. All those who possessed excellent memories died.

(p. 61)

In other words, all those who were unable to dissociate themselves from their memories – all those whose hearts did not turn to stone – did not survive. Only those who succeeded in dissociating themselves totally from their past were able to survive.

Lifton (1980) defines the state of dissociation as psychic closing-off, and he distinguishes among different degrees of depersonalization. The survivors' capacity for trusting other people and relying on them became very limited. To love again was for them not only a betrayal of the dead, but also taking a chance of losing their control over their feelings and being swept away into a whirlpool of emotion.

Nevertheless new relationships were formed – or more precisely, alliances – and many of the survivors married. However, these marriages generally took place after a hasty and superficial acquaintance, out of the longing to be dependent and the fierce desire to escape their loneliness and to allay their feelings of mourning, depression and fear of abandonment. Among the survivor couples no real emotional relationship was formed. Their alliances were often based on the ability of one member to provide the other with some sort of material security. But the choice of a partner was also influenced by other factors, including similar Holocaust experiences or some similarity, however feeble, to one of the beloved relatives who had perished.

Appelfeld (1983a) describes a meeting between two survivors:

He met Rosa on a beach in Italy, among the many confused refugees, between the huts and the water. . .
 . . .he said to her, 'Come', and she got up and followed him. And the same thing happened the next day. She didn't ask. . .

She didn't say, 'Do you love me?' Or 'When will you come back again?' She didn't even ask for his name. . .
. . . her silence enchanted him.

(pp. 94–5)

And that's how many alliances began: a chance encounter on a beach and nothing more; no courting, no extensive acquaintance-ship, no emotional encounter or intimate dialogue. On the contrary, the entire encounter is based on the absence of dialogue: it was Rosa's silence that enchanted him.

And what happened later? The absence of dialogue also characterizes a more intimate encounter:

They would make love for an hour or two. Afterwards he would leave her without even one word. The hour of love-making would send her into a very deep sleep. Only after some days did he notice that her face was expressionless. And when he brought her a box of candy for the first time she took it and said, 'It's good,' and ate some without offering him any.

(p. 95)

The same almost random choice of partner – based on a sense of basic, almost physical, existential security – reappears again and again in the descriptions given by many members of the second generation of Holocaust survivors about the way their parents met.

Shulamit, who was born in 1946, the daughter of two survivor parents, tells the following story:

'My mother was about nineteen when she left the camp. She had been through a lot and was completely broken. At the time of the liberation she found out that she was entirely alone in the world. None of her family had returned. My father, who was twenty years older than her, was somewhat better off. He had worked in an ammunitions factory during the war and so had got a little more food. When he left he managed to find a shack to live in and some work to do. When he met my mother he offered to share the shack with her. He took care of her and nursed her until she recovered, and then she just stayed in the shack. I don't know, but it seems to me that if he hadn't had the shack they might never have come to live together. A few months later I was born.'

Hava, who was also born in 1946, the daughter of two survivor parents, describes her parents' wedding:

'My father and mother met in Germany after the war. My mother was about sixteen, and except for one aunt none of her relatives had survived. My father, who originally came from the same town as my mother, did not have even one surviving relative in the entire world. When they met they clung to each other and were never separated again, even though my father was nearly twenty years older than my mother.'

'Their wedding took place in haste, and my mother once told me that she came to the wedding dressed in rags. She didn't have a single dress left. At the last moment one of the few friends that had come to the wedding noticed how she was dressed, and this friend took off her own dress, which was in somewhat better repair, and managed to fit it somehow to my mother's thin body using safety pins. I was born a few months later, still in Germany.'

The parents of Baruch, another 1946 child, both of whom were survivors, separated immediately after their marriage.

'After the war,' Baruch related, 'my mother and father left the extermination camps, wandered to Switzerland, and met each other there. A short while after they met my mother found herself pregnant, and this was the excuse for their wedding. My mother wanted to go to Israel at any cost, while my father insisted on going to the United States. He thought that it would be easier to get rich there. My mother refused to give up her Zionist aspirations and got to Israel by herself, in the last months of her pregnancy. I was born in Israel. My mother lived alone, and aside from a handful of friends she didn't know anyone. I saw my father for the first time when I was four years old. Only then were we reunited as a family, when I became critically ill.'

When the members of a couple are totally disoriented, confused and disintegrated within themselves, when a feeling of emptiness envelops them from the outside and fills them from within, their marriage cannot give rise to a mutual relationship built on dialogue and intimacy. Thus such a relationship never existed in most of the families of survivors, and this fact left its imprint on the children.

Chapter 2

Designating the children as 'memorial candles'

Many Holocaust researchers repeatedly stress that the spearhead of the Nazis' war against the Jewish people was directed against its continued existence, that is, against its potential for reproduction. It is therefore not surprising that many survivors considered the establishment of new families a response to this central element in the Nazis' plans.

One and a half million Jewish children were murdered in the Holocaust; now, after the liberation, the birth of new children became a symbol of victory over the Nazis.

Davidson (1980) and other researchers stress the supreme importance of the birth of children in the consciousness of the survivors. But nothing can compare to Appelfeld's (1971) description in its capacity to concretize the desire for children that seized the surviving remnants after the war was over:

> After the liberation, on the beaches, many children were born. They were wild and irresponsible. They were nourished by the sun, by the sand, by cans of food, they spoke a mixture of languages, they frequently wandered about in the abandoned military camps, many of them were abandoned. . .
>
> The people became wiser and realized that they were unable to be parents. They destroyed them in the forest and in the camps. They hated the instinct for existence that pulled them with ropes towards life. But each wave of refugees brought children with them, and every day children were born. Death withered in the people, in front of them a generation grew up.
>
> The people slept a lot, but the clown of existence did its work in secret. Even older women became pregnant and gave

birth. . .life was proud. No one had the power to stop them.

(pp. 60–1)

The generation of 1946 burst into the world half-alive, half-dead, born to parents filled with feelings of confusion and internal contradictions. Yet in spite of the intense emptiness they were imbued with, they were unable to avoid being seized by a certain sense of euphoria at the miracle of their very survival.

The actual physical existence of the babies that were born had the power to spread some light in the middle of the chaos. These little children were given the role of lifesavers for the confused souls of their parents. But the parents saw the children not only as lifesavers, but also as new content for their lives.

Sigal, Silver, Rakoff and Ellin (1973), Rakoff (1969), Trossman (1968) and others stress the intensity of the survivor parents' expectations from their children – that they would infuse content into their empty lives and serve as a compensation and a substitute for their relatives who had perished, their communities that had been wiped out and even for their own previous lives. For if they could not consider their new children a continuation of the loved ones they had lost, all their suffering and their efforts to survive would have seemed to them a worthless sacrifice.

The assumption that these expectations of the survivor parents would gradually disappear in the course of time proved false. Not only did they not disappear, but they became more demanding and more extreme in their intensity.

Psychologists dealing with the topic of children born immediately after the Holocaust agree among themselves on the place of these children in the consciousness of their survivor parents (Russel 1974). They were not perceived as separate individuals but as symbols of everything the parents had lost in the course of their lives.

Barocas and Barocas (1973), who agree with this thesis, nevertheless add that their own observations of the families of survivors they have treated taught them that the survivor parent tries to reconstruct his feeling of identity through his children. By relating to the children as a kind of offshoot of themselves, the parents satisfy their inner need for identity and identification, but this prevents the children from being able to individuate themselves and to create a unique identity. (This topic is discussed in detail in a later chapter.)

The descriptions given by many people of the second generation about the circumstances of their birth support the thesis
suggested here.

Arye, a man in his forties, the son of two survivor parents, tells
the following story:

'I was born in 1946, after my parents had found out that their
entire families had perished. I have three given names [the
meaning of the giving of multiple names is discussed in the next
chapter]: Arye, Zvi and Moshe, as well as three family names.
Yesterday, when I was at a party and someone asked me my
name, I suddenly became confused. I am actually carrying the
whole family around on my shoulders. My sister, who was born
a few years later, was given only one name, after one grandmother who had perished. My father always told me that if it
hadn't been for the war, and if my mother hadn't become
pregnant, he wouldn't have got married. It follows from this
that he didn't want me at all. When they piled on me all the
names of the dead relatives. I don't believe they were thinking
of me, they didn't try to balance the injustice for me. Now I have
no choice but to carry the dead on my back.'

The issue of multiple names arises in Hava's story as well:

'I was born in Poland in 1946. My mother, who was about eighteen
when I was born, was the only one left of her whole family. My
father was also alone, except for one distant cousin. Immediately after I was born my mother went out to work and I was
left for part of the time in the care of a neighbouring Christian
family and for much of the time by myself. It's not enough that
I have three names that my parents gave me, but the neighbours
called me by a Christian name of their own. I am named after
my two grandmothers and my mother's younger sister, who
perished when she was only a little girl. My sister was born only
about ten years later, when we were already living in Israel.'

Nehama, who was also born in 1946, the daughter of two survivor
parents, is not the first daughter in the family: she has an elder
sister who survived together with the parents, but her story is not
essentially different from the others:

'I was born in 1946. When the war ended my parents found out
that their entire families had perished. Later my mother dis-

covered that one aunt was still alive, but at the time she didn't know about this. My mother was already fairly old, over forty. My older sister was over ten when my parents decided to have another child, me. The birth was very difficult and my mother almost died in the process. She was in a very bad physical state and she was also very depressed. I think I was born to fill the enormous void that was suddenly created. For my father I was a continuation of his mother and his sisters, who I was named after, and also a continuation of his younger brother. I was a symbol for him of things with an uncomfortable and frightening significance that were also very important.'

Nehama, like many of the survivors' children, is well aware of the special role for which she was designated even before she was born. Her entire existence was intended only to fill the terrible emptiness left behind by the extended family that had perished and the community that had been destroyed.

We find again and again in the description of the survivors' children the sense of the terrible emptiness into which they were born and the role of substitute that was designated for them – symbols from the moment of their birth. But actually there is no essential difference here from what takes place in many families in difficult circumstances, which often tend to designate one member as a scapegoat, as an imagined solution to their problems. Everyone recognizes the roles that can be given to a particular child in a family – 'the stupid one', 'the bad one' or 'the problem child' – which often eventually turn the child into the family scapegoat; as a result of being given this role the child actually becomes more sensitive and vulnerable.

Titchener (1967) stresses the existence of conscious and unconscious communication channels in family experience. Through these channels are transmitted feelings that are repressed from the sender's awareness and totally cut off from the literal meaning of the message, so that the unconscious message circumvents the repressive barrier of the receiver.

Satir (1968), Jackson (1957), Bell and Vogel (1960) and others show how parents get their children to adopt their own conflicts and to fulfil their shared wishes, without being in any way aware of this. When the parents' hidden wishes are focused on one of their children in a dysfunctional way, this child becomes the 'identified patient' of the family. This process involves a considerable cognitive distortion of their perception of the child's true essence, a distortion whose purpose is to fit the child to the role of scapegoat or identified patient.

And indeed, one of the characteristic features of survivors' families is the placing of the role of scapegoat on one of the children. However, in the course of my years of treating the children of survivors I have seen that the role of scapegoat in these families has special characteristics, qualities and contents which are a direct result of the family history and of the traumatic past of the parents and of the relatives who perished.

It seems most probable that the survivor parents transmitted, through both conscious and unconscious communication channels, cognitive and emotional messages pertaining to the Holocaust in general, and to the history of certain relatives, whose fate was part of their personal Holocaust, in particular. For example, Hanna, the daughter of a survivor father, tells that on Passover, when everyone would get dressed up for the Seder, her father would put on a striped shirt he had left from Auschwitz.

The content of the messages transmitted by the survivors to their children was thus anchored in the traumatic inner imprint of the Holocaust on their tortured souls. They contain an ethical appeal, partly overt and partly covert, that can be summarized in a few sentences: you are the continuing generation. Behind us are ruin and death and infinite emotional emptiness. It is your obligation and your privilege to maintain the nation, to reestablish the vanished family and to fill the enormous physical and emotional void left by the Holocaust in our surroundings and in our hearts. That is, the main role of the scapegoat in ordinary families is the discharge of the intrapsychic and interpersonal conflicts in the family relationships, while in the families of survivors this role is only one of the tasks imposed on the scapegoat. Not only must they fill an enormous emotional void, but they must also construct the continuation of the entire family history all by themselves, and thus create a hidden connection with the objects that perished in the Holocaust. Therefore, because of the unique significance of the role the children were chosen to play, the word 'scapegoat' is not appropriate, and it would be better to call them 'memorial candles'.

In dealing with the history of families, it is well to remember that the nuclear family does not exist in a void; on the horizontal dimension it is at the heart of a number of concentric circles – the circles of the extended family, the community and the nation – while on the vertical dimension it is a link in the chain of generations which represents long-term family continuity.

Before the Holocaust the survivors' families were linked by chains of belonging and identification to their extended families, their communities, their surroundings and the entire Jewish people – and at the same time to the generations of parents and children. The Holocaust severed the links in these chains and nothing was left of them. Therefore the role of 'memorial candle' involves both the personal history of the parents during the Holocaust and the attempt to repair the broken links between the parents and their extended families and communities. Survivor parents generally tell their children very little about what happened to them because of the great pain involved. They give their 'memorial candles' the task of infusing content into the emptiness of their hearts and rearranging the broken and hidden pieces of the mosaic within it.

Meissner (1970) ascribes special importance to the timing of the birth of the child designated for the role of scapegoat. He claims that the family situation at the time of the child's birth has an extensive influence on the nature of the role given to the child within the family and on the relationship that develops accordingly between himself and his parents and siblings. Bowen (1960) adds that the choice of the specific role of each child in the family is influenced in part by the unconscious role being played by the mother in reality at the time of the child's birth. As an example he shows that the developing relationship between a mother and a child born around the time of the death of her own mother is totally different from her relationships with her other children. This can explain the choice of the children born in 1946 as 'memorial candles' – they were born around the time of the most traumatic period in the lives of their mothers and fathers.

But not all the 'memorial candles' were children born in 1946. Other factors often influenced this choice, among them physical resemblance to specific objects that had perished and the child's being of the same sex as an important figure that had perished.

According to Heller (1982), the survivors tended to choose girls more often than boys for the role of 'memorial candles', perhaps because the *halacha*[1] prescribes that it is the mother's religion rather than the father's that determines the religion of the child, and so a daughter with the role of 'memorial candle' can serve as a factor preserving the family's Jewishness as well. But this is not the only reason – another reason is that in Jewish families the role of taking care of emotional problems within the family is generally a feminine role.

As we have seen, many 'memorial candles' were named after one or several family members who had perished. Many researchers, including Axelrod, Schnipper and Rau (1980) and Barocas (1971), describe how the children unconsciously accepted the identity of objects who had passed away many years earlier. The acceptance of these identities constituted an attempt to solve their survivor parents' insoluble emotional conflicts. (This topic is discussed extensively in the next chapter.)

Heller (1982) has also found that the 'memorial candles' are more culturally sensitive than the members of control groups, and they are more concerned about their parents' feelings; the cultural sensitivity is expressed especially in matters concerning the Holocaust.

Since one of the children in the family has accepted the role of 'memorial candle' upon himself, his siblings are liberated, at least on a conscious level, from the emotional burden weighing down the family from the period of traumatization during the Holocaust. This finding is similar to those of Meissner (1970) and others, who investigated problem families and their division of roles. The behaviour patterns created in such families between the parents and the scapegoated child are quite different from those between the parents and their other children. Thus the other children are less involved in the family problem and are not so caught up in the emotional thicket as to be unable to separate themselves from the intensive dependency in the mother–father–child triangle.

A story related by Menahem, a son of two survivor parents, born in 1946, provides a concrete example of the involvement of the 'memorial candle' in his parents' problems. Menahem has two sisters, one older and one younger than he; he is the only son, named after both his uncle and his grandfather on his father's side and his grandfather on his mother's side. The session in which the following story was related took place at an advanced stage of therapy, when his awareness of the special content of the role of 'memorial candle' was already quite extensive.

'I had a dream last night that I want to tell you about,' Menahem began. 'In the dream I saw a piece of white paper. On one side there were some lines of writing, but the writing was unclear, incomplete, I knew it belonged to my mother. On the other side of the paper there was a strange symbol: a circle with a cross inside dividing it into four parts, with a dot in each part. I didn't know what it was, but I knew it belonged to my mother. But surely also to my father. Something associated with my relationship with them. My mother finally went with my sister to see a play related to the Holocaust. When I asked her how it was and how she reacted, she answered without any feeling that she was well acquainted with all that. But later she said something after all. For the first time in over thirty years she said: "You know, when we went through all this there, we were, I was, in a state of total numbness. I didn't know what I was feeling or what was happening." Actually, until this day she and my father are in this sensory fog. Thus, in the same fog, they also had me.'

'Actually, many families of survivors have only one child. My little sister, who was born several years after me, was actually an accident. My older sister already existed at the time of the war. The fact is that they had me when they didn't want children any more. One child is enough to continue the chain.'

'You understand, I think my parents' problem was that they couldn't go back and feel what they went through there. They also couldn't speak openly to their children about what happened there. So the only way was to secretly transfer the burden and the pressure of things to one of the children. This particular child is appointed to bear his parents' burden, a burden that they themselves are unable to bear. But let's come back to the dream. The circle with the cross is me, it's a kind of notation, and the unclear lines written by my parents are their message. Very misty. They have a text, but it isn't written clearly.'

Here Menahem fell silent, and a few moments later he continued:
'You know, the sign in the circle looked like a cross. . .almost like a swastika. This reminds me of the crusaders. They used to go and carry huge crosses in their hands. Sometimes they chose or were chosen to die for others, for the sake of the holy cause. We are somewhat similar to them, carrying the cross for our families.'

In his dream Menahem describes almost visually the unconscious message being transferred both through the symbol of the cross, which is later transformed into a swastika, and through the unclear text which becomes clearer in the course of the session.

Menahem is the 'memorial candle' in his family. On the one hand he preserves for the family the link with the past and the family identity, and on the other hand he bears the heavy burden of death and loss, of guilt and anger. The continuity of the family must be preserved, but when the family history is associated with feelings that are so threatening that the parents cannot cope with them consciously, then the coping falls on the shoulders of the 'memorial candles', the family cross-bearers.

On the other hand, precisely this emotional burden connected with the family's past and its loved ones who perished in the Holocaust is the dearest and most intimate element in the hearts of the survivor parents. Therefore the 'memorial candles' themselves eventually become the new bearers of their parents' love, very dear substitutes, making separation from them very difficult. It is thus not surprising that these sons and daughters, who sense their special place in their family and their value for their parents, also find it very difficult in the end to separate from their parents and to liberate themselves from their difficult task.

Nine-year-old Momik, the hero of Grossman's book (1986), is his parents' only son and his family's 'memorial candle'. He is aware of his task and of the almost messianic mission that has been given to him. He is entirely immersed in the topic of the Holocaust, both when consciously awake and in times of lowered consciousness or dreams, while the real world becomes entirely secondary to his mind. He attempts to find answers and solutions to all the questions and mysteries creeping around inside his house and in his neighborhood, which is mainly populated by Holocaust survivors who live in a ruined, frightening and confused world – just like his parents and grandfather.

> Over There everyone is covered in a very thin layer of glass that keeps them motionless, and you can't touch them, and they're sort of alive but sort of not, and there's only one person in the whole world who can save them and that's Momik. Momik is almost like Dr Herzl, only different. He made a blue and white flag for Over There, and between the two blue stripes he drew an enormous drumstick tied to the back of a Super Mystère, and below it he wrote the words 'If you will it, it is no fairy tale', but he knows he doesn't have the least idea yet about what he's supposed to do, and that kind of worries him.
>
> (p. 50)

Sometimes as Momik lies on his stomach in ambush, he sees the tall smokestack of the new building they just finished over on Mt Herzl, which they call Yad Vashem, a funny sort of name, and he pretends it's a ship sailing by, full of illegal immigrants from Over There that nobody wants to take in, like in the days of the British Mandate, those scoundrels, and he's going to have to rescue that ship somehow. . .

(p. 55)

Momik makes simulations of situations. He constructs his own 'Holocaust' in the basement of his home – a world crawling with frightening beasts symbolizing the Nazi beast. This emotional simulation helps Momik cope with the anxieties, wishes and fantasies that relate to the emotional messages and contents he has been absorbing since the day he was born.

Every time he goes down into the basement he renews his encounter with the Holocaust. And every time he comes out alive, even if he has wet his pants in fear, he wins a double victory: both in his unconscious striving to penetrate the secret places of his parents' inner world, and in his effort to free them from the thicket that the Holocaust left in their psyches. Momik is an eternal witness to everything that takes place in the nightmarish inner world of his parents and grandfather, but he is not a passive witness. On the contrary, he identifies with their pain and shares it.

Moreover, as an only child he bears the entire weight of the family tragedy on his shoulders, the narrow shoulders of a child that are too weak to carry such a heavy load. And so the emotions that are aroused within him are not always consistent, and sometimes they are ambivalent. Most of the time he is willing to carry the burden, and in his imagaination he devotes almost his entire life to rescuing the members of his family from the teeth of their memories. But

he's sort of exhausted all the time, he can hardly move or concentrate, and sometimes he has these not very nice thoughts, like what does he need this for, and why does he have to do all the fighting himself, and why does no one step in to help him or take notice of what's going on around here. . .

(ibid., p. 69)

The contradictory feelings in Momik's psyche are typical for 'memorial candles', and I discuss them extensively later.

In Menahem's dream, as in Momik's story, the sense of an

almost messianic mission stands out. To concretize this sense of mission, which is very common among 'memorial candles' and constitutes part of the interaction between the survivors and their children, Hazan (1987) makes use of a metaphorical comparison with the Israelites who wandered in the desert for forty years. He compares the survivors to the parent generation of freed slaves, the generation that left Egypt and wandered for forty years in the desert, but did not reach the Promised Land. Their children, who were born and grew up in the desert, were indeed born free in the technical sense, but the task of true inner liberation remained on their shoulders.

Devora, who was born in 1946, is her family's 'memorial candle'.

'It's very sad,' she says, 'it's suffocating. I think about my restlessness, my constant feeling of uneasiness, the emptiness and anxiety associated with all the symbols and tasks and meanings that the people who are close to me see in me.'

'For my mother I was something not particularly desired that came into the world when she was relatively old. A very difficult birth. And afterwards post-natal depression, an extra complication after the Holocaust. For my father I am a continuation. A continuation of his sister Devora, of his younger brother Shmulik, of his father, of his mother, of everyone. Something so loaded, so difficult, something that symbolizes frightening things. Not comfortable.'

'For my sister Miriam I was nothing but a complication of adolescence, something she associated with the grief and sorrow after the Holocaust, with the depressing atmosphere in the house she ran away from at the age of seventeen. She had three children right away and made herself a home. And I cry. I cry because no one has ever seen me as an ordinary human being whom one should relate to and perhaps even love. They buried me with the dead while I'm still alive. It's hard for me to drag their dead around with me all the time. They say: "Don't put them down, it's better for us that way." I want them to take their dead back, but they can't and they don't. I'm not the family hearse, yet after all that's what I am.'

'My father never talked about the Holocaust. Nothing. Not about any of his family. But often he would give me a long look, full of sadness and longing, and say: "You look like my sister Devora, only not as pretty as she was." That's his sister Devora, the one I'm named after.'

The father thus sees his sister in his daughter Devora and unconsciously transmits to her all the complexity of his unsolved feelings for her. But he doesn't see his daughter Devora at all, or any of what she feels, thinks, or needs. And as if this were not bad enough, he also hints that she will never be a satisfactory substitute for his sister, as even though she resembles her she's 'not as pretty as she was'. This multivalent statement teaches us about the ambivalent position of the 'memorial candles' in their parents' consciousness. In the face of the images of the perished objects, who were idealized after their death in the survivors' psyche, the 'memorial candles' have no chance. This confrontation is totally unfair, and the 'memorial candles' will always come out the losers.

Devora lives near her parents. She is not married and has no children, and has not yet succeeded in separating from her parents or attaining individuation and an identity of her own. For her father she is a symbol of everything significant in his life, but only a symbol. However, Devora is not only a symbol of the dead; she is also her family's healer on the emotional plane. With her birth she filled the terrible vacuum that had reigned in her parents' life; she pulls their hearse, but she also fulfils their childhood wishes that they were unable to realize. She is successful in her academic studies and is getting a degree in one of the liberal arts; they were prevented from doing this, as the Holocaust and their immigration to Israel ended their plans.

Nevertheless, even though Devora brings healing to her parents by her very existence, or possibly even because of this, she feels a lack of self-worth, a lack of self-confidence, and a sense of anxiety. Her identity is still blurred and undefined.

In the two examples I brought, of Menahem and Devora, what stands out is that they 'pull the family hearse' by themselves, and their siblings have no part in the task. Menahem's two sisters, like Devora's sister, feel free of their parents' burden. They have married, they have children, and they have established their own homes. But Devora and Menahem, the 'memorial candles' of their families, have not yet succeeded in throwing off the yoke that attaches them to their parents and to the traumatic family histories.

Menahem's sisters and Devora's sister are the physical healers of the family; they are taking care of the physical continuity of the family and the nation. By having children they are reviving the family and the link between the generations that was nearly severed by the Holocaust. This division of labour appears over and over again in the families of many survivors – one of the children, the 'memorial candle', remains emotionally tied to the parents; he is the emotional healer, who liberates his siblings, the physical healers, to establish their own families and thus rebuild the whole family.

This division fits the findings of Ackerman (1967) concerning families in trouble; according to these findings, the family pre-judices are generally irrationally concentrated around special meanings associated with the variance among the family members. Here, in the families of the survivors, the variance stems mainly from the parents' background – the Holocaust – and its effects, more than from any particular trait of one of the children. In Ackerman's view, in troubled families neutralizing forces come up and the siblings trade roles – the scapegoat becomes the healer and vice versa. But in the families of survivors such neutralizing forces or tradeoffs are very rare, because the healing provided by the children who are not 'memorial candles' is purely physical, while the role of 'memorial candle' is generally rigidly maintained and designated for only one of the children, perhaps because the libidinal investment of one or both of the parents is too great for them to agree to a re-investment.

It should not be forgotten that the 'memorial candle' plays the ordinary role of the family scapegoat – that is, he discharges his parents' unresolved unconscious conflicts – while simultaneously serving as a link connecting his survivor parents with their own parents and siblings who perished and their past that was wiped out. But because of the ambivalence of his role, or because of the emotionality mutuality it engenders, the 'memorial candle' does not feel rejected by his family but loved and special. Menahem, Devora and many other 'memorial candles' are confronted with a problem that touches upon physical separation from their parents, but is mainly a problem of emotional separation from them and from their past.

The interaction in the family is considerably affected by the family myth. The most profound influence of the myth is expressed in the ego, which internalizes it and uses it as a guide for the understanding and analysis of human relationships in general and those within the family in particular. When the inner life of each family member and the interpersonal interactions between them are joined together and interwoven within the ego, a synthesis of feelings and internalized representations of the totality of family relationships is created (Gill and Klein 1964). This synthesis may lead to symptoms and pathology, which are expressed in particular character traits and in difficulties in defining one's personal identity. And the 'memorial candles' do indeed unconsciously internalize within their egos the complex emotional system interwoven in the family myth. Bowen (1960) defines the state of families caught in such an emotional thicket as 'a state in which there is an undifferentiated mass of family ego'. In such a situation the indivdual's process of separation from the family and construction of a well-defined ego with a unique identity becomes extremely difficult, and sometimes nearly impossible without the intervention of some therpeutic factor.

Appelfeld (1983a) depicts a situation of enmeshment and undifferentiated ego in a family of survivors in his description of the relationship between Rosa and her two daughters:

> In the course of the years the three of them became one unit. They would eat together and sleep together. And they had their own language. . .After Paula's marriage Brigitte became completely hers. She fed her and dressed her and put jewelry around her neck.
>
> (p. 99)

In Grossman's book (1986) Momik is aware of the situation in his family:

> and a moment later the door opened and there stood Mama and Papa who quietly said hello, and with their coats still on, and their gloves and the boots lined with plastic bags, their eyes devoured him, and even though he could actually feel himself being devoured, he just stood there quietly and let them do it because he knew that was what they needed.
>
> (p. 48)

These two examples demonstrate the place of the 'memorial candle' in the undifferentiated family ego. Brigitte, the younger daughter of Rosa and Bartfuss, is an inseparable part of the family ego and particularly of her mother's ego – she lacks the capacity to separate from her mother and consolidate an independent identity of some sort.

Momik, in contrast, is stronger. His awareness gives him inner strength. He sees his parents' need and cooperates with them, but this ability to see also gives him the possibility of voluntarily choosing between participation and nonparticipation in the enmeshed symbiotic relationship of the family triangle. Nevertheless, avoiding participation in the network of the family relationships, and separating himself from it, constitute a difficult task for him, as for all 'memorial candles'.

The various contradictory tasks imposed on the 'memorial candles', and the chains attaching them to one or both of their parents, may be understood within the complicated system of identifications and internalizations of the parents, who lost their families. Just as, in his internalized identification with his own parents, the survivor parent depicts himself sometimes as the aggressor – the one who abandoned his parents – and sometimes as the victim – the one who was abandoned by them – so in his identification with his child there is interwoven a parallel internalization of the child's image – as aggressor and as victim. In order to free himself from the distress that creates the conflict between rage and guilt, the parent compels the child chosen as the 'memorial candle' to participate in his intrapsychic drama and play the roles of victim and aggressor alternately. Sometimes he pushes the child into the role of 'the bad one' – as he depicts himself in his own eyes because he abandoned his parents – so that he can punish the child and thus, through the child, free himself of the guilt feelings within himself, and also punish himself. But when he forces the child to play the role of 'the bad one' he is also punishing his parents, and thus he achieves a catharsis for the aggression he feels towards them for abandoning him, an aggression that could not be discharged at the time he was abandoned. At other times he casts the child in the role of 'the good one' – in order to placate himself as one who defends him from death, and at the same time to express his forgiveness of his parents.

The survivor parents thus dress the children designated as 'memorial candles' in a 'Holocaust cape' out of their own unconscious needs and internal conflicts (or at least those of one of them). One may ask why the children agree to wear this cape. Behind this question is the assumption that if the child did not cooperate, the parent would not be able to transmit his contradictory feelings to him or project them onto him. This issue is a very complicated one and there are conflicting opinions about it, so I do not intend to discuss it extensively here, but it does touch on two relevant points.

The first point is the continual concern of the 'memorial candles' with topics that may be able to shed light on the psychological background of the Jews during the Holocaust and their participation in the mechanism of extermination – whether passive or active, covert or overt. The second point involves the hidden messages transmitted by the survivor parents to the second generation, messages that often included mixed feelings towards the relatives who perished. The victims were generally perceived as heroes who sacrificed their lives for the sanctification of God. But if they really were heroes, then the survivors, in contrast, are not only morally inferior because they were unwilling to sacrifice their lives, but actually wicked, as in order to survive they had to violate many moral rules; as is well-known, in the kingdom of death the laws of morality either did not exist at all or were fundamentally different.

If this is so, then it seems that the violent separation from their parents and other relatives, and the rift in the sense of belonging and identification that accompanied this separation, caused the survivors irreparable psychic damage. The survivors had almost no opportunity to achieve inner completion of the process of separation and individuation (Mahler and Furer 1972). The cutting-off of this process in childhood, adolescence or young adulthood warped the survivors' personalities and prevented the healing of their self-identity; therefore the task of healing was imposed on the 'memorial candles'.

During the course of therapy the members of the second generation become aware of their role as 'memorial candles'. This topic arises over and over in a discussion held in a 'second-generation' group towards the end of their second year of therapy:

Baruch: 'Since I was a child pictures and stories about the Holo-caust would arouse great sadness and emotion within me, often bringing me to tears. I had only to read or hear the stories, even if they were not directly associated with myself or with my family, and I would become agitated. I never saw such deep feeling in anyone else in my family, and I never understood why I became so agitated. I often felt as though I myself had undergone all these things. I felt a strong identification – beyond the stories I heard from my parents. After all, it wasn't so terrible for them, they were caught only in 1944 and were not sent to an extermination camp, but to a different camp. They got off relatively lightly. But the strange thing is that I identified precisely with the harshest stories I heard about the death camps. I really should have felt relieved that my parents got through it as they did. I never understood this. Only now am I perhaps beginning to understand that I took upon myself, somehow, some kind of role of this sort, I don't know what to call it. Perhaps the role of guardian of darkness. The guardian of the Holocaust and of death and of the crises in the family. I remember when I was a little boy, about five years old, perhaps a little older, lying in bed for hours without falling asleep. Lying half-dozing, unable to fall asleep, and feeling around me all the images of my dead relatives hovering in the space of the room – the whole house was filled with them. Sometimes I was very frightened, and afterwards I would have frightening dreams, nightmares. It's beginning to annoy me that my family gave me this role. This is the first time I'm thinking about it this way. It's probably not conscious for them either.'

Yosef: 'You know, that reminds me that last time I spoke about a feeling of godliness. This is related to what happened before I was born. When I was a little boy I asked my father where all the dead things go, if it's possible to see them again. I was thinking mainly of a dog I had that had disappeared. But I wasn't thinking, as I am today, of all the relatives who had disappeared. My father answered that if one goes to Heaven then one can see them again. . .I was very excited then about the possibility of seeing them all again. I felt as a child that I was their salvation, something that was never said openly. Now I am reminded of something associated with my mother. I'm thinking about the dependence between me and her. She was always everything for me. Without her I would feel lost, but I was also everything for her.'

Therapist: 'To feel like God means many things – it means being protected from ordinary human feelings like sadness and anger, and it also means feeling that you have a calling or a special role. This reminds me a little of what Baruch said before about his role in the family.'

Yosef: 'Yes, when I was very little my parents gave me a copy of the Bible but they didn't say anything. I used to read about Moses, who led the people in the desert, when they were so helpless. To this day I sometimes feel like Moses and I'm not sure if I'm a god or just an ordinary person. I know that I'm not a god, but it still bothers me. Together with this book they gave me some kind of message. It was as though my father gave me the message: you must experience all the things we can't experience here and now. I want you to experience all the suffering I went through there in Europe, in the camps. But what he actually said to me was: "It's impossible to talk about it. Either someone knows what it was like there, or he will never know."'

Baruch: 'Actually, my father told me: "You have no chance of getting close. Maybe you'll learn something from books, but not directly from me."'

Therapist: 'This sounds like a double message that you received from your parents about what happened to them during the Holocaust and how that relates to you. On the one hand, "If you weren't there you'll never know," and on the other hand, "Read this to find out what we went through there."'

Hava: 'I always felt that my mother gave me more than she gave my brothers. I was born when they were still in Germany, right after the war. I was named after my grandmother and one of my mother's sisters, who had remained there as a little girl. I felt a lot of sadness and anger this week, as in all the past months, but I thought about the fact that my mother had no brothers. She had only two little sisters, and I suppose I remind her of everything that happened to them. In the past years, since I've been so preoccupied with the subject of the Holocaust, I'm always going to Yad Vashem and to all the meetings and conferences, and I watch all the programmes on television. This year, on Holocaust Memorial Day, I felt very emotional and I thought a lot about what my parents went through. I felt, perhaps for the first time, that I want to write to my brothers about this and share it with them. I wrote a lot, but I didn't get any answer. Finally I got an answer from my brother Yitzhak. But he didn't discuss this topic at all in his letter, even though it was most of my letter. Instead he asked me all sorts of questions about my new refrigerator. I thought I would explode with rage, and I was also hurt. How could he think about the refrigerator when I'm writing to him about something like this?'

Therapist: 'It seems that your brothers really aren't as concerned with the subject as you are and they had no idea how to respond.'

Menahem: 'My father, where the Holocaust was concerned, took upon himself a kind of historical task of learning a lesson from it, of passing on information about the Holocaust, something sort of intellectual. My mother, when people are talking about the subject, only transmits sadness in her eyes, without words. It's as if she's saying: "What do you know about what happened there?" And my two sisters – I have no idea where they are with this topic. I never asked them and I never shared my feelings or thoughts with them, not like what you did, Hava. I always took care of the family. If there was some kind of crisis, I was always there to deal with it. I ask myself if this doesn't have some other meaning. Even the anger that was in the Holocaust I took in a very extreme way. Also, the feeling of "It won't happen to me" is with me all the time. When I'm here, in the group, or in the army, or in any other group, and there's a situation of conflict or pressure or something's needed, I'm always the first to jump up and hurry to look for a solution. It's as if I said to myself: "I must find a solution, I won't go through what everyone goes through." If there's a situation of danger, whether it's real or imagined, I'm always the first to find a solution.'

Yosef: 'Sometimes I feel something very similar to what you feel. Especially in connection with my family. I've never understood what makes me run around so much. This is the first time I understand it. Now I also realize that I'm like you, functioning very well in emergencies, but in routine situations I don't stop to consider and sometimes I mess things up. If there's an exceptional situation and I'm not called, I get angry, because I'm not being allowed to prove myself in a case where I can really do it.'

Baruch: 'Yes, in my family there's a very clear division between me and my sisters. They deal with the normal routines: husbands, children, daily life, everything I don't have; and I deal with the Holocaust, with the crises and unique situations in the family. I see that this is a way of life I've taken upon myself, and perhaps this is also true of you, Yosef. And I also see that it affects every area of my life.'

Miriam: 'I have a repeated dream that I was reminded of now. In the dream there is a ship and all of my relatives who already perished, as well as my parents and my brother, are on the ship, but on the coast there are SS men who aren't letting people get off the deck of the ship, and their lives are in danger. I jump off the ship and swim and swim all night in order to find a way to rescue them. I manage to fool some of the SS men and reach the coast in danger of my life, and in the end I manage to rescue some of them. This is a repeated dream, but it's quite appropriate to my feeling within my family. My brother is married and lives happily, he has four children and lives quietly in his daily routine, but in the dream on the boat the one who is very pressured and has to do something to rescue the people is me. All the years, my whole life, this was my job at home. When my brother, as a child, would come home late from the beach and my mother would get into a terrible anxiety, I, a little five-year-old girl, would go down to the beach and search and search until I would find him and bring him home. He had a good time on the beach, and I sat at home with my mother and all her anxieties.'

Therapist: 'In all the things you've said today, what stands out is your special position in the family, the feeling of something special that fills you and the role involved with this feeling. You have to solve the difficult problems, to rescue people in crises, to carry the burden of the Holocaust and of your parents' past, perhaps to carry something for them or instead of them, and even to rescue them from death in your dreams. The question is how all this ties in with what happened to your parents during the Holocaust. There's no doubt that there's a connection, and we will have to understand it better later on.'

Roni: 'What you just said reminds me of a dream I had recently. In general, I've been going around lately with this feeling that I belong to a generation that has to pay some sort of price. In my dream I felt my mother's mourning and my father's depression, but all without any words. I am walking around and dragging very heavy packages with my hands. Next to me is walking an older woman that I'm somewhat related to, looking like my mother, but I'm not sure. Because of the packages it's hard for me to go quickly. I'm not sure what I feel for this woman, if I love her or not, but I'm sure that I have to do all sorts of work for her. We are coming near a sort of very pretty private house, with lots of trees and green grass all around, but on the slopes of the grass there's a deep trench, and this woman is calling me to show me her work, and there are rows and rows of models of graves and monuments, made of some white material, I'm not sure if it's cardboard or stone. The jobs I have to do for her are somehow connected with these models.'

In the stories reported here several motifs stand out. The central motif emerging from the stories of Baruch, Menahem and Yosef is the message they receive over and over again from their parents – to preserve the memory of the Holocaust, to preserve the memory of the dead. But sometimes the message transmitted is unconscious and unclear, so that it takes different forms; Yosef, for instance, receives it as a prophetic messianic message. He senses that he has been assigned the task of leading his family into the future and worrying about its continuity, as Moses led the Israelite people in the wilderness. Constant concern with the topics of death and the Holocaust, which is sometimes compulsive, stands out in the stories of Baruch, Yosef and Hava. They are the only members of their families who visit Yad Vashem and take an interest in the Holocaust on both the public and the personal planes. The gap between their role in the family and the roles of their siblings also stands out in their stories. Hava describes this gap as a profound contrast between concern with death and concern with life, with everyday life: 'I am concerned about the Holocaust and my brother is concerned about my new refrigerator.'

Another motif is the rescue of the family, which stands out in the stories of Hava, Miriam and Menahem. This rescue is expressed on two levels, the level of reality and the level of feelings. In the world of reality many 'memorial candles' tend to come to the aid of their families in any situation which seems to them to be a family crisis or conflict, and they attempt to find a solution for it. In the emotional world they tend to pile the entire burden of responsibility for the crisis situations onto their own shoulders, without the will or the realistic capacity to share this responsibility with their siblings.

The motif of 'solving the Holocaust' or 'return to the Holocaust' appears in the group members' stories on an unconscious and almost symbolic level; this is the unconscious message that the survivors transmit to the 'memorial candles'. It is as if they are commanding them: 'Experience the Holocaust and solve it for us.' This can explain the motif of rescuing the family – every crisis situation, even if it is not very serious in objective reality, is perceived subjectively in the minds of the 'memorial candles' as something of tremendous proportions, almost as a Holocaust. This is nothing but an expression of the compulsive need of the survivor parents and the 'memorial candles', who are involved in one symbiotic system, to return to the Holocaust and escape from it alive over and over again. By repeated simulations they try to solve the problem of the Holocaust and expose its hidden mysteries. This is also what Momik does: he returns in fear and trembling to the cellar crawling with fearsome animal life, and repeatedly reconstructs the Holocaust that his parents went through in order to release them from the thicket of the past. However, the compulsive return to and escape from the Holocaust do not have the capacity to release those caught in the thicket.

NOTE

1. The sum of Jewish-law precepts.

Chapter 3

The dialogue between survivor mothers and their infants

> You transmitted to me the smell of the little death, perhaps in the milk, perhaps in the blood, perhaps in the dream, perhaps in your midnight screams. . . Not in vain do I check all my limbs to see if I am hurt. Not in vain does she send samples of her blood to the doctors. The blood will never be cleansed of the memory, of the forgiveness.
>
> (Semel 1985, p. 80)

Most of the survivors became mothers when still young, in the camps of the displaced persons, on the roads, on the Italian beaches or in Eretz Israel, while they were trying to adjust to the new land.

Although each survivor had her own personality, with different emotional growth experiences and psychological developmental levels, and even though the traumas the survivors went through were different in nature and severity, all of them shared the experience of the terror of the Holocaust. The rough uprooting from their familiar surroundings, the loss of their families, the extended exposure to humiliation, hunger, torture and sometimes even sexual abuse of their own bodies or the bodies of their close relatives, the defence of their physical existence in conditions of extended life-and-death anxiety – all of these left scars on their souls. After the Holocaust both the young women and the more mature women felt that they were in an infinite existential vacuum and that a profound isolation filled their inner existence; that is, this experience was characteristic of all the survivors, whatever their age.

Some psychologists, especially Erikson (1959), believe that maternal identity is anchored in a feeling of continuity and similarity between the generations, a feeling shared by the mother herself, her close family and the entire community. Erikson stresses that maternal identity involves the consolidation of previous identifications, which fit (or oppose) the woman's inner drives and needs on the one hand and her social roles on the other.

Benedek (1956) too considers the experience of parenthood a biopsychological experience that arouses and maintains within the parent a developmental process that makes her a link in the chain of the generations. But the intergenerational chain was broken by the Holocaust, and the few links that remained were scattered to the winds. Thus, when the young survivors found themselves without any links to connect them with the intergenerational chain, they lost the inner tie to their past and their roots. It was not only the physical extermination of their families that broke the intergenerational connection. More important was the necessity to forget their loved ones and to repress their feelings of pain about their loss. It was the very forgetting and repression that were the conditions for physical survival which also concealed the mines that eventually destroyed their psychic wholeness.

The mother's ability to revive her feelings of connection and identification with her past, and especially with her mother – which constitute, as we have seen, the basic elements of feminine and maternal identity – is thus an important factor in her ability to construct and consolidate a maternal identity appropriate to her role as a mother. Psychologists distinguish among three principal factors that affect the changes of identity taking place in a woman when she becomes a mother: the nature of the new mother's identification with her own mother; the degree of her success in resolving the identity conflicts of adolescence; and the ease with which she is able to accept the assistance of her mother and other family members as a source of support and comfort in times of difficulty, pain or tension.

In the psychoanalytic literature it is accepted that of all the identifications transmitted from a mother to her daughter, the most significant are those transmitted to her just before she becomes a mother herself. The new mother's identifications with her own mother are not necessarily based on features located in the realm of consciousness, but on features located in the preconscious or even the unconscious; each of these identifications may become loaded with positive or negative feelings, but in either case they will be adapted to the daughter's own ego.

Deutsch (1946) ascribes great importance to the feeling of

being a 'good mother' that the mother bestows on her daughter just before she herself becomes a mother. Empirical studies have shown that the awareness of the nature of the relationship between the new mother and her own mother just before the birth is positively correlated with the degree of the new mother's adjustment to her new role. The identity crisis that sometimes occurs to new mothers at the time of their first childbirth is generally a result of some difficulty or incapacity in establishing a synthesis of identifications between themselves and their mothers. The establishment of such a synthesis depends, on the one hand, on the positive attitude of the new mother to the mother image internalized in her consciousness and, on the other hand, on her ability to solve the conflict of her dependency on her own mother and achieve differentiation without losing the feelings of closeness and continuity.

We do not possess sufficient data to characterize the nature of the identifications of survivor mothers with their own mothers before the Holocaust, but it seems plausible to assume that if we had such data we would find the same variety of identifications that appear among women in general – from the closest and most positive to the most distant and negative. But the Holocaust cut off the natural identification processes of the survivors, and only afterwards did a new identification process begin to taken place in their psyches. This process was undoubtedly nourished by fragments of their memories from the period of their childhood and adolescence, but it was principally stamped with the terror of life in the camps and the trauma of being torn away from their families. Thus, in order to understand the characteristics of the survivors' functioning as mothers after the Holocaust, it is necessary to measure the degree of their success in reconstructing their feminine and maternal identities. This reconstruction was largely dependent on their ability to disconnect themselves from their inner dependence on the image of their mother (who had perished), and on the necessary process of a synthesis of identifications with the image of the mother or some other close woman, in order to attain differentiation and establish a personal identity that could cope with the world on its own.

However, immediately after the Holocaust – and perhaps even during the Holocaust itself – an inner struggle took place within the psyches of the young survivors who were shortly to become mothers. This struggle took place between the parts of the ego, the superego and the id which were in a state of latency and which served as a dam preventing a flood of feelings of anxiety, pain and longing, on the one hand, and another part of the ego, which was struggling for its right to experience the new feelings that were being aroused in the present as well as fragments of feelings from the past, on the other. The traumas of the Holocaust brought about a break in the survivors' identity, or, for those whose identity was not yet established, an arrest of the process of its construction. The regressive situations they were exposed to caused the destruction or the distortion of those components of their identity that they had succeeded in constructing and internalizing before the war.

But not all the survivor mothers preserved the destruction and distortion of these components to the same degree. It seems that immediately after the Holocaust their desire to preserve the defences they had constructed during the war, which had the capacity to prevent an excessively poignant confrontation with the feeling of absolute loss, came into conflict with the desire to rediscover a link with their memories and images of their lost relatives, and thus to rehabilitate their identity and with it the feeling of continuity. It was the survivor mother's degree of success in resolving this conflict, and the way in which she reached this resolution, that eventually determined whether she could feel any security at all in her identity and role as a mother.

The primary internalized identification with the mother, which had been distorted or destroyed, now underwent an internal process of preservation, but this process was often accompanied by an idealization of the mother image. This helped the survivor in her struggle to repress the feelings of mutual abandonment, guilt and rage, and even enabled her to retain the memory of the 'good mother' which is the vital foundation of all maternal identity. An internal struggle of this type is described in Appelfeld's book (1971). Betty, who is vainly trying to fight her physical and emotional sterility, remembers the many years she had spent in Siberia, where the ice and the infinite distance from home and from all that was dear to her gradually caused her to lose her inner contact with herself and her past, especially the elements of maternal identity internalized within herself.

So Betty sat and thought. . .the first year in Siberia: the cold, the longing. But the second year a person loses his memory, he doesn't remember a thing any more. People torture themselves uselessly. They won't remember any more. The third year people stop torturing their memories.

(p. 96)

Within her heart Betty knows that the secret of her sterility is hidden in her emotional blindness, in her inability to see the locked-up parts of her inner existence. She doesn't stop sleeping, and her body blossoms and lives without her, disconnected from her inner existence, which gradually sinks into profound forgetfulness.

Gruzman, Betty's husband, understands that she is searching for a path to her ancestors and trying to reconnect herself to her severed roots. 'One can reach such a degree of forgetfulness only in Siberia. . . He knew that she herself did not know; if she had known, the pain of the knowledge would have eaten her alive' (ibid., p. 65).

Gruzman participates in Betty's intrapsychic struggle, repre- senting the active side of her inner conflict, the side that is struggling against disconnection and forgetfulness, because Gruzman is aware of reality. He is not 'blind' like Betty, and he sees clearly how her defences have become so rigid that there is almost no possibility of penetrating them. 'One innocently believes that one can escape under the thin cover of forgetfulness, curl up in an abandoned room, sleep, and kill one's memories daily until they die' (ibid., p. 30). He sees his Betty so disconnected from herself that she has stopped talking and no longer feels any pain or guilt. Then he attempts to shake her awake: 'You remember, he would try sometimes' (ibid., p. 61), and for a moment it seemed as if Betty was succeeding in waking up from her torpor and grasping her memories once more, but she had only a weak and passing hold on them.

Just as her attempts to become pregnant were doomed to failure, so the buds of her inner emotional life, which flowered in her for a moment, soon died. The fate of her attempts to fight her emotional sterility did not differ from the fate of her struggle against her physical sterility. In essence, Betty was in a state of diffuse chronic depression, 'she was neither happy nor sad. She was slow and heavy, like a river with an unchanging flow. It was as if the seasons did not affect it' (ibid., p. 62). She functioned in the real world like an ordinary woman, she cooked and cleaned the house, she sewed and worked in the garden, but the death of her feelings and the loss of her heart's links with her mother and her family caused her a profound sense of loneliness. In this condition Betty was unable to overcome her sterility and produce a child, and even though she was married and living with her husband, she gave the impression of a lone woman.

The figure of Betty expresses something that is hidden in one way or another, and in varying degrees, in the inner heart of every survivor – that part of her personality that has lost its sense of continuity. This continuity is the intergenerational identity and identification so vital for the existence of an emotional life in the heart of any mother, which she then transmits to the foetus in her womb and to the baby after it is born.

As mentioned, the elements of the identity that had been constructed and internalized in the psyches of the survivors before the Holocaust were not damaged to the same degree for all of them. Three main groups of survivors can be distinguished according to their stage of emotional development when the Holocaust began, the process of consolidation of feminine and maternal identification they were undergoing at that time, and their state immediately after the Holocaust. The first group includes women who were still girls in the latency period or in adolescence at the time of the Holocaust, so that their feminine identity had not yet been formed or had just begun to bud. The second group includes women who had been near the end of adolescence when the Holocaust began, so that their feminine identity was already partly or fully formed. The third group includes women who had become adults before the Holocaust, some of them wives and mothers, so that not only was their feminine identity consolidated, but in some cases their identity as mothers was already formed. Immediately after the Holocaust, in their first encounter with the figure of the mother, the survivors of all three groups were engaged in an internal struggle, but the components of the struggle were different for each of the groups.

The survivors of the first group were separated while only girls from the figures that were close to them and that protected them, and they had to fight for their existence from the start. It is no wonder, then, that they matured before their time, skipping over the ordinary stages of both physical and emotional maturation. They also had to cope with the first signs of their femininity in a state of isolation, anxiety for their lives, and exposure to traumas;

some of them were also exposed to sexual abuse, both of their own bodies and of the bodies of other women around them. Their broken or unformed psyches could not cope with these traumas, and their self-image, especially their body image, was left with scars that never disappeared.

Kestenberg (1982), Krystal (1968), and other psychologists claim that even girls from warm and loving families, who had a positive identification with their mothers, were thrown into such severe regression at the sight of their mothers being humiliated before their eyes in the camps that they lost all trust in them. The natural process of identification was cut off, and many girls were caught in an incessant seesaw between bitter anger against the parents who had not protected them and idealization of the parents' image. In addition to the loss of trust, the idealization and the anger, when the war was finally over they also had to cope with the terrible realization that the vast majority of their relatives, and in some cases all of them, would never return. This realization led not only to feelings of loneliness and terrible emptiness but also to harsh guilt feelings for having survived instead of them, as they saw it.

Immediately after the Holocaust the feelings of anger were repressed, while the feelings of loss and heavy grief expanded to take over the survivors' consciousness completely. As a result of the repression of their anger, the need arose in the girls' minds to rescue and preserve the memory of their mothers. Their idealization was thus the reverse side of their guilt feelings. This idealization served another important purpose: the preservation of the memory of the 'good enough mother', which is a vital component in the maintenance of the feeling of intergenerational continuity, and the prevention of a sense of disintegration and breakdown of the ego. Fragments of the survivor daughter's identification with the mother figure, which had been internalized before the Holocaust but destroyed or distorted during its course, were re-established afterwards in the girl's consciousness. This was the only way she could even partially achieve the synthesis of identifications without which there would be no way for her to ground her maternal identity. But not all the women succeeded in achieving even this much. The establishment of this synthesis of identifications in the face of the traumas of the Holocaust, and the difficult conflicts produced by these traumas, involved many difficulties and was sometimes totally impossible. Not only Betty remained childless – many other survivors did not have the strength to reestablish their identity and so remained childless.

Moreover, when a young woman becomes a mother, her own mother and other female relatives and friends are generally at her side, thus helping her, paradoxically, to separate herself from her dependency on her mother and construct a new and differentiated identity as a young mother in her own right. But these young survivors, whose adolescence was clouded by the Holocaust, generally became mothers in a state of total isolation, without their mother or any other feminine figure at their side. And as if this were not enough, they were engulfed by feelings of loss and guilt on the one hand, and longing and idealization on the other, which added even more difficulties to the process of separation from their dependency on their mothers. In the loneliness and depression most of the survivors suffered after the Holocaust, many of them tried to dam up the feelings flooding their psyches by hasty marriages that were not preceded by a sufficient opportunity to get acquainted and become close. These women simply projected onto the nearest available man their feelings towards their mothers and other relatives, including intense dependency feelings that had not been resolved. It is thus not surprising that the dominant pattern in the marriages of survivor couples who got married immediately after the Holocaust was either mutual or one-sided dependency.

Tzili, the heroine of Appelfeld's book (1983b), was the only one left of her entire family from the age of about eleven, at the heart of the latency period. While wandering alone between farmhouses in a state of terrible life-and-death anxiety, she encountered the first signs of her femininity. When she noticed the first signs of blood emanating from her body, there was not even one familiar figure at her side to comfort her and explain to her that this phenomenon was associated with her femininity. She was engulfed in mortal fear and an animal instinct impelled her to enter a river to wash off her body. In essence, Tzili skipped over all the stages of adolescence. When she was about fifteen she met Mark, who was also wandering alone around Europe. Mark and Tzili immediately clung to one another. For Tzili their sexual relationship was nothing but a temporary substitute for the warmth and security she had lost. When she found herself pregnant she was alone once again, as she had lost Mark as well. At the beginning of her

pregnancy she tried to remember the figure of her mother, perhaps in order to find an end of the thread of continuity that had
still survived within her.

> The night was warm and fine and Tzili remembered the little
> yard at home, where she had spent so many hours. Every now
> and then her mother would call, 'Tzili,' and Tzili would reply,
> 'Here I am.' Of her entire childhood, only this was left. All the
> rest was shrouded in a heavy mist. She was seized by longing for
> the little yard. As if it were the misty edge of the Garden of Eden.
> (p. 158)

Tzili held onto the memory of her childhood with her fingertips,
and immediately the process of idealization began. The house
becomes the entrance to Paradise, and her mother becomes totally
gentle and sympathetic. In actual fact Tzili had been born when
her parents were relatively old, with a sick father and an over-
burdened mother, and she had been left to grow up by herself
among the junk in their yard. But she held on tightly to every scrap
of security and belonging, since without them she would lose all
her sense of identity and even all her capacity for self-connection,
and she would be like a leaf driven by the wind. The small yard
had, after all, been a familiar and safe place where Tzili belonged,
and her sense of belonging had been lost when she was torn away
from her home and her family. In her mother's repeated vague
calls to her Tzili finds evidence of her mother's warm attitude to
her. From this memory, which she tries so hard to preserve, she
draws the capacity to contruct an image of the 'good enough
mother', which Benedek (1956) and Deutsch (1946) consider a
vital element in constructing one's maternal identity.

'Tzili was happy. Not a happiness which had any outward manifestations: the fetus stirring inside her gave her an appetite and a
lust for life. Not so the others: death clung even to their clothes'
(Appelfeld 1983b, p. 156). Her pregnancy and her link with her
past and with her mother enable Tzili to find the will to live and a
little bit of happiness, if only for a short time. But is this partial link
to a past memory and to the 'good mother' enough to provide a
really secure foundation for her feminine and maternal identity?
Not only did Tzili lack the experience of real mothering and
extensive warm parenting, but she went through adolescence without warmth, security or support. Her identity was therefore built
upon rather flimsy and fragile foundations. The repressed feelings

of rage and guilt against her lost family were transformed into feelings of depression and grief that were not sufficiently worked through. At the same time that Tzili draws strength and happiness from the child in her womb, she is attacked by feelings of loss and depression:

> The survivors were not happy. A kind of sadness darkened their daylight hours. Tzili did not stir from her corner. She too was affected by the sadness. Now she understood what she had not understood before: everything was gone, gone forever. She would remain alone, alone forever. Even the fetus inside her, because it was inside her, would be as lonely as she. No one would ever ask again: 'Where were you and what happened to you?' And if someone did ask, she would not reply.
>
> (ibid., p. 140)

H. Klein (1971), like many others, gave some consideration to the frequency of depression and anxiety appearing in one degree or another during pregnancy among survivors in general, and particularly among those women who were still girls in the latency period or in adolescence at the time of the Holocaust. These girls' self-image, and particularly their body image, was severely damaged during the Holocaust, and this damage often resulted in a sense of emotional dissociation from their own body. The source of this sense is the feeling that there is something impure and forbidden about their body. This feeling of stigma was so strong that they were unable to avoid feeling that their foetus, who was part of their body, was absorbing it from them.

Ariela, one of the participants in the therapy sessions, once showed me a birthmark on her arm, and said in confusion, 'I inherited this from my mother,' adding with wonderment, 'All the years, since I was very little, I have known that I inherited this mark from my mother.' When I asked her to explain what she meant, she said that her mother had a deep, ugly scar in the very same place. The scar was formed from cuts that were made over and over again in the same place on her mother's arm, when experiments were performed on her. 'I don't know if my mother told me anything about my birthmark, but when I asked her about her scar, which is in exactly the same place as the birthmark on my arm, I was sure that I had inherited it.'

The hearts of the survivors who became pregnant immediately after the Holocaust were filled with intense expectation for the child, but this feeling was mixed with fear of the damage they were liable, as they felt, to transmit to their offspring – a kind of perpetuation of the stigma. They were also fearful of the disasters the future might hold for their children. Ariela's story indeed shows that she internalized her mother's non-verbal and almost unconscious messages, and held them as part of her inner identity for more than thirty years. The young women survivors suffered from nightmares and from compulsive thoughts – all related, in one way or another, to the health and wholeness of the child about to be born. These anxiety states, and the damaged self-image of the young women survivors, were, in the view of Russel (1974), the main causes of the severe bleeding many of them suffered during their pregnancies, as well as their miscarriages or total sterility.

Krystal (1968) reports on the particularly high rate of miscarriage among those survivors who were girls at the time of the Holocaust, and this also arises from the stories of many of the 'memorial candles', some of them only children, about their mothers' frequent pregnancies, most of which ended in miscarriage. Ahuva, the daughter of a survivor who had been taken to the concentration camp when still a girl in the latency period, related that everyone – and particularly her mother – considered her birth a miracle. Both before and after, Ahuva's mother became pregnant more than a dozen times. Each time the pregnancy ended in stillbirth. 'You were born only by virtue of your own strength,' her mother told her. 'You were strong and you fought for your life and so you succeeded in being born, not like the others.' This sentence expressed Ahuva's mother's own inner conflict as well as her own intense desire for existence, which drove her to become pregnant so many times in spite of her weakness and depression and the guilt feelings that echoed within her and her identification with death.

Many psychologists, among them Verny and Kelly (1981), studied the intrauterine communication between mother and foetus and the foetus's response to the feelings transmitted to it by its mother. They found that the bonding process between mother and infant begins while the infant is still in the womb. Sontag (quoted by Verny and Kelly) investigated somatopsychic phenomena – the effect of basic physiological processes on the individual's personality structure and level of perception and performance. He found that when a pregnant woman is tense, stressed, depressed or anxious, her glands secrete an increased amount of neurohormonal substances, such as adrenaline, nor-adrenaline, and serotonin. Some part of these substances, which are secreted into the blood, eventually reach the placenta and are transmitted to the blood of the foetus. They increase the foetus's biological sensitivity and create a predisposition to psychological disturbances, such as anxiety and depression, in the future. Other studies demonstrated that neurohormonal substances arouse anxi-ety and fear in the infant while still in its mother's womb. It was also found that whenever the mother's heartbeat is accelerated, this occurs in the foetus as well, and that from the sixth month the foetus responds to the emotional messages its mother transmits. These findings provide at least a partial explanation for the many miscarriages and difficult pregnancies of many survivors, especially the youngest ones. At high levels of anxiety and depression of the mother, the neurohormonal substances transmitted to the foetus are liable to cause extremely severe reactions, including death of the foetus.

Rottman (1974) investigated women's emotional attitudes towards their pregnancies – to what degree the pregnancy was desired, consciously or unconsiously. On the basis of the results of psychological tests he administered to them, he divided the women into four groups. The first group included women whose attitude towards their pregnancy was extrememly negative. He found that these women had severe problems during their preg-nancies; there was a high rate of premature births; the infants weighed less than average at birth, and as they grew up they were found to have psychological problems. The second group in-cluded women whose attitude towards their pregnancy was ambi-valent – outwardly they seemed content, but their unconscious feelings were different. Their foetuses received the negative mess-ages as well, and their reaction to these messages was expressed, after their birth, in behavioural problems such as hyperactivity and digestive disorders. The third group included women whose atti-tude towards their pregnancy was also ambivalent, but in reverse: that is, on the surface it seemed as though the pregnancy was interfering with their plans and ambitions, but unconsciously the pregnancy was desired. Their infants were found to suffer from confusion, stemming from the opposing messages they received in the womb. Many of them were apathetic and lethargic. The fourth group included women whose attitude towards their pregnancy was positive, both consciously and unconsciously.

It seems that most of the survivors who gave birth shortly after the Holocaust involuntarily transmitted their complex feelings to their foetuses. Into this convoluted emotional world the post-Holocaust children – the generation of 1946 – were conceived and born.

As mentioned, most of the survivors who gave birth shortly after the Holocaust felt lonely and empty, even if their husbands or partners were with them. This was the case with Tzili, the heroine of Appelfeld's story (1983b), who gave birth in a field hospital in the middle of nowhere, in utter anonymity; and it was also true of Ahuva's mother, who gave birth in Israel with her husband and a few relatives near her, yet nevertheless felt a sense of loneliness:

'When you were born,' she told Ahuva, 'I didn't know where Daddy was. I felt that he was very far away. I don't remember anyone being right at my side, and most importantly my mother was not with me. If she had been there everything would have been different.'

At this time the survivor mother generally still considered her husband a stranger; his presence did not blunt her feeling of loneliness and perhaps even sharpened the sense of emptiness that was created after the loss of her family of origin, and particularly her mother.

At one therapy session Zvia, the daughter of a survivor mother, described the experience of her birth as she heard about it from her mother:

'My mother told me that right after I was born she lay in bed for two weeks and couldn't stop crying. She was totally alone – no mother, no sister, no grandmother – because all of them had remained "there". Even my father's physical presence didn't help her much and didn't change her feeling much. She described to me this feeling of a great emptiness that surrounded her on all sides. Even I didn't fill this emptiness of hers, it was too great.'

The second group of survivors were young women overtaken by the Holocaust when they were both physically and psychologically more mature than those who were only girls at the time. Their emotional identity and development were more consolidated, and gave them some means for coping with being uprooted from their homes and separated from their families, as well as with the severe traumas they underwent in the camps. These young women were often exposed to various types of sexual abuse, and sometimes they themselves used their sexuality as a weapon in their battle for survival. Either way the traumatic experiences left deep scars on their souls and generated severe conflicts and ambivalence towards their sexual identity; these were later expressed in their intimate relationships with their spouses. Nevertheless, the damage done to their self-image and their body image was less severe than that of the first group of survivors. They had already ended their dependency on the mother figure before the Holocaust, and so they were able to cope more successfully with depression and anxiety.

Rosa, another character in Appelfeld's book (1983a), represents the second group of women. Rosa's reaction to her pregnancy and childbirth was totally different from Tzili's, but their situation during the war had been different as well. Rosa also lost her entire family in the Holocaust, and during the war she worked as a maid in farmhouses, but she was already a mature adolescent at that time. Her femininity and her sexuality served as weapons for her survival. It is thus plausible to assume that her mature feminine identity and her synthesis of identities with respect to her mother and sisters, which had already been internalized, helped her preserve the integrity of her personality, despite the deep scars the Holocaust left in her soul. During the course of her pregnancy, as well as during and after childbirth, Rosa was not only able to avoid depression and emotional and physical weakness, but also became progressively stronger. The living foetus in her womb filled the space of her inner existence with a sense of power and confidence that she had not possessed earlier. There was a transformation in her existence, which did not go unnoticed by her husband, Bartfus:

> He would sit and look at her for hours. She was not beautiful, and now that she was pregnant she even looked coarse, but there was some sort of power in her existence, a power that was not understood. . .
> Immediately after Paula's birth there was a change in Rosa's face, muscles sinewed her chin. He thought this was a passing change but he was wrong: Paula's birth increased her confidence.
>
> (p. 97)

And later on:

Rosa had many faces at that time, but she was never alone. Her two cubs clung to her and she poured an abundance of affection on them. Even Brigitte, the lazy, vague one, was at her side. He had to admit to himself that she was a mother. . . Rosa was zealously devoted to her daughters. They resembled her not only in their appearance. When they grew older she got them to like the colour of her dresses as well.

(pp. 99, 103)

The symbiotic enmeshed attachment between the child and his mother frees the survivor mother from her sense of loneliness, and from the necessity of dealing with her complicated inner world and with the problematic intimate relationship between her and her spouse. The emotional disconnection between Rosa and her husband stands out with greater painfulness against the background of the symbiotic dependency relations she constructs between herself and her daughters.

After the birth of their child many survivors tend to sink into a depression (H. Klein 1973; Krystal 1968; and others). Sometimes this depression is overt, and is expressed in apathy, indifference to the infant, and weeping – as was the reaction of Zvia's mother, for example. In other cases the depression is hidden and is expressed indirectly, in weakness and psychosomatic ailments – as, for example, in the case of Tzili, after her stillbirth:

Tzili lay awake. Of all her scattered life it seemed to her that nothing was left. Even her body was no longer hers. A jumble of sounds and shapes flowed into her without touching her. . .

The next day, when she stood up, she realized for the first time that she had lost her sense of balance too. She stood leaning against the wall, and for a moment it seemed to her that she would never again be able to stand upright without support.

(Appelfeld 1983b, pp. 175, 176)

Both the overt and the covert forms of depression keep the mother in bed for a long time and compel her to hand over her infant to the care of others. As we have already seen, however, there are some survivors for whom the birth of a child gives their lives meaning. They draw from their infants physical and psychological powers they did not possess before, and these powers help them deny their feelings of depression and guilt.

Another pattern of behaviour in survivor mothers is characterized by an active life, often to an exaggerated extent. These mothers are not closely attached to their infants; on the contrary, after a short time spent with the infant at home they become restless and rush to go out to work, even if they do not need the additional income. It seems reasonable to suppose that this difficulty in staying home and caring for the baby stems from an inner disquiet arising from unresolved conflicts and from the continual attempt to flee from these conflicts and repress them.

The various patterns of behaviour of the survivor mothers are often reflected in the reports of the second generation, who describe what has been told to them about their mothers's state after their birth and about the primary dialogue that developed between them. (These reports will be introduced later.)

The survivors of the third group had been married and even mothers before the Holocaust. Most of them lost their parents, their sisters and brothers, their husbands, and – most difficult of all – their children. Appelfeld (1983b) describes the feelings of a survivor whose children had been torn away from her during the Holocaust:

> 'I,' said the woman, 'have lost my children. It seems to me that I did everything I could, but they were lost anyway. The older one was nine and the younger one seven. And I am alive, as you see, even eating. Me they didn't harm. I must be made of iron.'
>
> (p. 157)

The loss of one's children damages the most primary and basic instinct of all parents, and especially of mothers. The bereaved mother may survive, but the memory and internal image of her children remain with her for the rest of her life:

> Mother's children are crying, they cling to her body, they try to return to their place in her flesh. She is screaming: 'Don't take them away from me!' She never saw them again. They lie on their back inside Mother's head. A cemetery of memory.
>
> (Semel 1985, pp. 44–5)

The Holocaust broke the natural chain of continuity between the generations in the most terrible and violent way: the mother survived and continued to live, while her children – the essence of her existence and continuity – were lost.

The main conflict that generated the survivor mothers' guilt feelings for having 'abandoned' their children was based on their feeling of having been deceived – their instinct had betrayed them. Every mother has a basic and primary instinct intended to guide her senses to detect danger approaching her offspring so that she can protect and rescue them. This instinct did not work during the Holocaust, and when it did work it was too late, when the mother no longer had the power to save her children. In utter helplessness they were forced to allow their children to be lost. The survivor mothers perceived their lack of awareness and alertness to the danger that was approaching their children as a failure or a disruption of the functioning of their maternal instinct.

> Two golden children at her two sides, tensely facing the camera, the boy wearing a strange kind of hat on his head, the girl in lace-edged sleeves and white knee socks. These are your dead brother and sister. They died before you were born. Daddy, does it hurt when you're burnt? You don't feel it, all the screams are swallowed up in the shower. They tell them they're going on a trip, they believe it because they see Mother carrying a little suitcase. . . That's how she sits, my closed mother, burrowing inside her secrets, inside the end of her shame. I am innocent of all guilt and I didn't know. The children will never come back.
>
> (ibid., pp. 35, 52)

When the mother got on the train, a suitcase in her hand and her two children at her side, she was without any doubt a hopeless victim of the intentional deceit organized by the Nazis. But according to her own feelings she was the only one responsible for the terrible deceit. Her children trusted her and relied on her and she betrayed their trust. This is the feeling of guilt the survivor mother carries in her heart, and such a feeling cannot be overcome.

As mentioned, the maturation process of the survivors of the third group had been completed before the war, and so had the process of separation from their emotional dependency on their mothers; when the war broke out they (like the survivors of the second group) already had a separate and independent identity. They had already experienced pregnancy, childbirth and life with a partner before the Holocaust. They dealt with their maternal identity in a familiar and secure setting, surrounded by their family. The Holocaust's damage to their personalities was not as severe as the damage to the girls in the first and the second groups, but they could never overcome the loss of their children, which became a central emotional void within them, particularly because they had not been allowed the opportunity to mourn for them properly.

> Mother did not tear her clothes in mourning for her children. She was not allowed the relief of ordinary mourning. She tore thirty-nine years of mourning into her flesh. Her sorrow descended within her like an overdue pregnancy. She did not repeat their names even in her dreams. She did not have it in her to long for them. She had been pushed to try to forget, to make hurried copies of the children. But the second time is a difficult reconstruction, and just as she failed in her second marriage, perhaps this was also true of her copied daughter.
>
> (ibid., p. 54)

No mother could forget her former life, and it remained imprinted on her flesh and in her soul. The new marriage and motherhood would always remain a copy of what she had had before. Her previous children, whom she had not mourned or separated from, would not permit her to rest.

And indeed, the new husbands and children of the survivors live with the feeling that something is missing, with the knowledge that they are a faint substitute for what their wives and mothers had before. '"She told me that it had been better then. With him, with her first husband." The faceless primordial man. And perhaps it had been better for her with her first children as well' (ibid., p. 35). The survivor cannot succeed in being really happy with her new family. The images of her first husband and children are always in the background, returning and casting their shadow over her new life.

From the stories in the literature and the many reports I heard from the sons and daughters of survivor mothers of the third group, it appears that these survivors did not succeed in drawing strength from the birth of their new children (unlike some of the survivors of the second group). They were steeped in chronic mourning, and they were therefore unable to establish a strong and clear bonding with their new infants, because such a link might arouse the strong feelings they had experienced before towards their children who had perished and undermine the delicate balance in their psyches. A direct encounter with the feeling of loss would exacerbate the pain, and in order to protect themselves against the flooding of the ego by unbearable feelings they had to maintain an emotional distance and disconnection from the nightmares of the past.

The feeling that they are only substitutes, copies of children, that they do not have a clear and unique place of their own, was expressed by many 'memorial candles'. 'I didn't take anything from you that didn't belong to me' – writes Semel (1985) – 'I asked permission. She was always hesitating. As if behind the little girl there were the shadows of previous children' (p. 36). The child-hood memories of the 'memorial candles' may sound too harsh – perhaps they were painted over the years in harsher colours than was justified by reality – but we should not forget that childhood memories do not reflect the totality of the real experiences we went through. What remains in our sober adulthood are vague feelings, mainly repressed but very significant, that have been with us from earliest infancy. During the course of therapy with the children of survivors these feelings rise to the surface. Sometimes it may be a sense of loneliness and abandonment, sometimes a sense of suffocation – the parents, especially the mothers, clung to them excessively. Among the children of mothers of the third group the feeling is that they did not come into the world for themselves and that they are not living there by rights – that their lives are only a substitute for the lives of their brothers and sisters who perished 'there'.

During pregnancy complex psychological processes take place. Colman (1969) and others show that the main conflicts of preg-nant women are expressed in rejection of the pregnancy, in turn-ing their emotional energy inward, and in an ambivalent attitude towards motherhood. Blitzer and Murray (1964) and Smith (1968) describe narcissistic states accompanied by feelings of despair, hatred, jealousy, anxiety and loneliness, which are greatly exacer-bated in the last months of pregnancy. All these feelings and conflicts clearly existed, and perhaps even more severely, among the survivors who became pregnant immediately after the Holo-caust. But these women suffered from an additional conflict, unique to them, that stemmed from the contrast between the special significance they attributed to the birth of a child and their psychological state. For them having a child constituted an attempt to heal their ruined, empty inner world and to give new meaning to their lives, as well as an attempt to rejoin the broken inter-generational chain, both of their own families and of the entire nation. The immensity of their task increased the degree of their longing. But in contrast to this longing was the reality: the psychological state of the survivors, their existential loneliness, the conditions of their lives in their state of migration and of hasty connection with a partner, and the absence of the support of friends and family. Many psychologists who studied the psychological state of the survivor mothers – including Lipkowitz (1973), Rakoff (1969), and Sigal (1971) – stress the chronic, unworked mourning they were in and their incessant preoccupation with themselves, especially right after the Holocaust. Thus the psychic resources they could give their foetuses during pregnancy, and their infants afterwards, were extremely limited and certainly insufficient.

Semel (1985) refers to this point:

> I thought, it's no coincidence that all these survivors have only two children. This is their entire emotional capacity. They can't take the risk of having only one, as something might happen to him, and two is all they can bear.

> (p. 142)

Naomi, an only child born after the Holocaust, described the atmosphere surrounding her birth:

'Recently my mother told me what happened when I was born. Not that she offered to tell me, but this time I insisted and I must have asked in a different way than usual, as she really told me about it and didn't avoid it as she had in the past. I always knew that in her other pregnancies [all of which had ended in miscarriages or premature stillbirths] she lay in bed for long periods, for months. I thought about this recently, that it must have been very hard for her, because she's like me, full of energy and always running around and doing things. So when I asked her what happened when she was pregnant with me, she told me that when she felt me beginning to move within her, she got right into bed and didn't get out again, in the terrible fear that she would have another miscarriage. Recently, when I was home in bed the whole time [during an extended illness] I thought a lot about that time and how it must actually have been for her and for me, there inside the womb – when she was lying in such anxiety, without moving for months and being alone for months. . . Yes, she told me that during that time my father was almost never home. He always had all sorts of business. He ran around outside and he wasn't free emotionally, and he wasn't capable of being with her, and with me, at such a critical period. Now, while I'm talking about it, I'm also allowing myself for the first time to feel some of my anger against my father, for not really being there. I never knew – perhaps I didn't want to know – how partial and unsatisfying the relationship between my parents was, how little togetherness was really there. True, I knew that my mother used to travel abroad alone from time to time, and that my father also had connections outside the home, but I didn't know that it was to such an extent. This week, when my mother told me the story, I was able for the first time to feel and to identify with her terrible loneliness. She added one very poignant and telling sentence: "If my mother had been here then, at my side, everything would have been different." But I am named after my grandmother, who remained there when they shot her on the death march and my mother continued to march. . . You know, I was born on my grandmother's birthday. . . No, not exactly, actually it was two days later. But my mother told me that during her entire pregnancy she planned and wanted very much to give birth on the day her own mother was born. And when that day arrived she actually had contractions and went to the hospital to give birth, but it was only false labour, and the doctors sent her home, and I was actually born two days later. My mother always says that I and my grandmother were born on the same day. She also told me that the moment I was born she asked to see me, to see if I was perfect. I wasn't missing anything, and she calmed down when she saw I had no defects. She immediately noticed that I have long fingers, and right then she decided that I would play the piano just as she had and just as my grandmother had.'

Thus childbirth aroused in the survivors conscious and unconscious conflicts associated with the loss of close objects, a knotted skein of feeling fragments difficult to unravel. But this skein of feelings, fragmented as it was, contained the only available material for weaving the fabric of their relationship with their children and thus for tying together the threads of continuity with their mothers and their past. Now let's take a look at what the survivor mothers managed to salvage from this skein and at the unique components of the dialogue between them and their children born after the Holocaust.

'My mother breast-fed me for about two months. Then she stopped,' said Hava at one of the group therapy sessions. 'I don't know exactly what happened. Perhaps she ran out of milk. Perhaps she ran out of patience. She immediately went out to work and I was left with a baby-minder. My mother was only twenty years old, and my father tells me she had no idea what to do with me. She was constantly tense and anxious, and when I would cry – and apparently, from what I've heard, I cried a lot – she couldn't hold me in her arms. She would give me to my father to hold me because she had no idea how to calm me down. She would get into a state of such anxiety that she wasn't capable of functioning at all. She wasn't happy with me.'

Henia: 'My mother told me over and over – for years I heard that she actually nearly died when I was born. The birth lasted three days, and there were very many difficulties along the way, so that it wasn't certain if either she or I would come out of it unharmed. After the birth she was so weak and depressed that she was forced, or chose, to lie in bed for several months, and she was almost unable to function. I apparently cried quite a lot and didn't want to eat. When I was about nine months old they decided to put me in a WIZO [Women's Zionist Organization] institution, and there, according to the stories, I started to eat a little, but I stopped crying completely. My father told me once that he came to visit me there and saw me standing in the crib for hours and rocking, with a frozen expression on my face – I almost stopped reacting altogether. I was there more than half a year, and then my mother recovered and they brought me home.'

Mordechai: 'My mother told me that she breast-fed me there in the hotel [where they were living four families to a room for several months before immigrating to Israel]. I don't know how it really was. She was always so restless. Even now she can't sit quietly, just relaxed, and enjoy something. She always doing something, always running around, always going from here to there. When I try to imagine the situation there, in a quarter of a room in a hotel, with only a blanket separating the families from one another, I think it must have been very uncomfortable. I can imagine my mother sitting and holding me and nursing me, but she's not looking at me, her glance is travelling from place to place. The tension and anxiety she still feels today must surely have been even stronger then. Every moment someone was coming in, either of her own family or one of the others. Everyone was tense, because no one knew exactly what would happen. They had indeed succeeded in escaping from Hell, but they had left so much there. They also didn't know what awaited them in the future, in the new country, which they wanted but which was so strange. There wasn't a moment of silence for this baby, which was me, and I certainly didn't have my own crib. There was no chance for intimacy at any time. To this day it's hard for me to get really close to my mother, it's hard for me to really talk to her, and especially when I try, I feel a lot of tension. If I do talk, it's more with my father, or when the whole family is there – it's very hard to talk to my mother alone.'

Ahuva: 'My mother told me that when I was born she stopped working and stayed home, to be only with me. She tried to nurse me but she didn't have enough milk. She tried so hard, sitting for hours and squeezing the milk from her breasts drop by drop, and holding me on her lap and feeding me these drops with a spoon.'

Malka: 'You know, it seems very strange that she fed you that way, with a spoon, on her lap. When I was nursing my son, even when I didn't have enough milk and I gave him a bottle, I always held him close to me, this was the most important thing for me, and I think for him too, to feel him close.'

Ahuva: 'Yes, but she tried so hard. . .and she would sit for hours and squeeze her breasts. Perhaps it's connected with the fact that her first baby died of hunger in her arms, there in the ghetto. . . She once told me that there wasn't any food at all, and she had no milk to give her and so she died. . . I don't know exactly what happened there.'

Shimon: 'I don't know. This story of Ahuva's doesn't sound so strange to me. My mother told me a story a little bit like that. She said that when I was nursing she had problems. It hurt her to nurse me because she had sores around her nipples.' With an embarrassed smile he went on, 'Perhaps I bit her so hard that she got sore. Then she took a kind of tube that the milk from her breasts would be pumped into, and I sucked on this long tube. Now it actually does seem very terrible to be connected to my mother through this tube and not directly.'

Zippora: 'I can't even imagine nursing from my mother, or even sitting quietly on her lap and enjoying it. Even picturing it makes me tense. I have pictures of myself as a baby, and I look terribly fat, with such a round, full doll-face. The only thing my mother gave me was food. More and more food. But my face in the picture seems empty, totally expressionless.'

Itzhak: 'The feeling or memory I have inside me, in my innermost feelings – and I don't know exactly where this feeling comes from, after all it's impossible to remember from such an early age – anyway, my feeling as a baby was that my mother was around, nearby, but she didn't hold me really close to her. I wanted so much all those years – this I remember from a later age – to feel held, to feel her body. All in all I've always felt very lonely.'

Arye: 'I remember that when I was very little, my mother would often sit in a closed, dim room, with the shutter half-closed, and chain-smoke. Or sometimes she would sit on a chair and hold my sister on her lap, when she was a baby, and rock her for hours and hours. Even when she hadn't been crying. My mother would hold her close to her breast and murmur all sorts of vague things, something between speech and crying, or a kind of repeated, incessant groaning. When I would come in, I would stand in the corner and stare at her quietly, and she wouldn't even notice that I was there. Finally, when she would pick up her eyes, she would look at me with this strange sort of look. Her expression seemed to be frozen, and her eyes frightened me, she had such a glassy and empty look, as if she didn't recognize me, as if she were somewhere else, far away, scary. Of course I didn't know then what this was doing to me. Now, when I see my mother with this look sometimes, it makes me angry. It makes me want to shake her. Now I realize that it arouses quite strong anxiety in me, or some kind of disquiet, heart-pounding such as I feel sometimes here too, and sometimes in various situations in my life. And then I cut myself off, I run away from this anxiety, I don't know what I'm afraid of at these moments. Now, for the first time, I can connect this somehow with my mother, with her frozen glassy look. She doesn't respond to me, she doesn't sense herself or me. Her loneliness became mixed with my loneliness.'

Hava: 'As a baby, they tell me, I screamed and cried. I cried for days on end, and my mother didn't know what to do. She couldn't cope with my crying. To this day I'm not sure why. Perhaps I also had a feeling of loneliness like what Itzhak describes.'

Ahuva, very pale and agitated, now rejoined the conversation: 'I, on the other hand – this is what my mother says – I was a terribly good baby. I didn't cry at all. My mother says that when I was a few weeks old she taught me and got me used to not crying, and I learned quickly and stopped crying. Actually, until this very day, my whole life, I almost never cry. Even when I want to very much I feel that I can't really cry. I can count on the fingers of one hand the number of times I've shed tears in my life. Even in therapy.'

I responded that we had indeed sensed that even here, in therapy, she doesn't allow herself to cry, and I commented that crying is a means of expression, a way of expressing strong feelings, and for a baby who doesn't have any language to express herself with, crying is one of the only ways she has to express her discomfort and ask for what she needs.

Malka supported me: 'If my baby didn't cry, I wouldn't know what he wanted or needed. I wouldn't be able to respond to him in all sorts of situations. How do you understand this, Ahuva, that your mother didn't want you to cry, how did she manage to communicate with you?'

I commented that perhaps Ahuva's crying caused her mother intense pain because it reminded her of her first baby, who cried and cried and died of hunger before her eyes, and she couldn't save her.

Ahuva began to sob quietly. The other members of the group were very moved, and some of them began to cry with her. Then Ahuva began to murmur through her tears: 'Perhaps that was why she couldn't hold me close to her. It was like holding that other baby once again.'

Indeed, it's almost certain that Ahuva's mother had to defend herself against the feelings that would have flooded her psyche if she had held Ahuva when she was crying: if she had done this she too would have begun to cry. Not only for her dead baby, but also for her parents and her sisters, for her young husband and her grandfathers and grandmothers. If she had begun to cry, she might not have been able to stop at all.

The first dialogue between mother and baby after the birth generally takes place during nursing. M. Klein (1948) considers nursing from the mother's breast the crucial factor in the infant's psychological development, as during nursing a real interaction takes place between mother and baby, leading to the internalization of the object relations in the infant's psyche.

From the reports of 'memorial candles', drawn from the world of dreams, fantasies and inner feelings, an apparently surprising fact arises: despite their poor physical and psychological condition, most of the survivor mothers nursed their children. Some nursed them only for a short time, two or three months, and when they stopped a few of them began working outside the home. Others had various difficulties in nursing, but nevertheless did not give up and put up a stubborn fight to continue nursing. It seems that their struggle to nurse was an inherent part of the emotional polarity that characterized the stages of their pregnancy and childbirth. On the one hand the survivor mother longed for the birth of a live child, whose very existence was supposed to serve as a compensation for what she had lost, but on the other hand she was given to depression, anxiety and continuing grief. With the birth of the infant – miraculously alive and whole in all its limbs – the mother felt that she must nourish it no matter what, so that it could grow up strong and immune, as it, and only it, had the task of maintaining life and rehabilitating the chain of the generations, for her sake and for the sake of her dear ones who had perished.

The milk of her breasts, even if it was scanty, or had to be squeezed from them drop by drop, symbolized the essence of her psyche and the little vitality that remained in her. She felt that it would help her maintain the natural continuity of her family. Her grandmother had nursed her mother, and her mother had nursed her, and now she must nurse her own baby.

This 'nevertheless' nursing, in spite of its difficulties and its draining of her strength, demonstrates the vitality of the survivor, arising from the primary instinct of every mammal, which continues feeding its young even when it is itself in danger, or sick, or hungry. This vitality is nothing but the physical translation of the drive to continue the species and the will of the survivor to overcome amputation and loss.

The mothers of Ahuva and Shimon stubbornly dripped their milk into their infants' mouths, yet were unable to hold them close to their heart; the connection with them by means of spoons or tubes tells us of an attachment between them and their infants which could not be immediate. The survivor mothers feel a very strong sense of belonging towards their children. They are emotionally attached to the infants, they need them and are dependent upon them, upon their presence, and especially upon their very physical existence at their side; but at the same time they are full of anxieties and conflicts and are not free to sense their children's true needs. Their attachment to their children therefore includes some dependence, anxiety and worry about their children's existence, but it generally does not include the settled feeling of security and calmness that is vital for the infant's normal development (Bowlby 1951).

Many survivor mothers have difficulty 'holding' their infant emotionally. Benedek (1956) calls the capacity for holding 'motherliness', in contrast to 'motherhood'. According to Winnicott (1965) and other psychologists, this holding includes more than just the physical holding of the infant next to the mother's body – although this too is difficult for the survivor mother. It also includes the ability to look at the infant with joy and pleasure stemming from the experience of sensing his physical and emotional needs and responding to them. But when the mother is sunk into a depression she is not emotionally available, and her face does not express joy and pleasure – it remains expressionless, as some of the 'memorial candles' have described it. The mother's face, which is supposed to reflect the infant's moods like a mirror, becomes opaque and unable to reflect anything. From his mother's empty face the infant cannot receive a sense of his meaning and value and internalize it, and without such a sense how can he know that he truly exists? How can he develop an independent and secure ego? Zippora's expressionless face reflects nothing but her mother's face.

An infant can be fed even without love, says Winnicott (1965), but neutral caretaking, without love and joy, cannot raise an autonomous child. Indeed, Zippora, like many other 'memorial candles', describes just such a situation: neutral feeding on the one hand, and a child without autonomy on the other. Bowlby (1951) explains that it's possible for a mother to be physically present but emotionally absent. Many psychologists have found that those survivor mothers who were in a state of chronic depression and unresolved mourning found their infant a heavy emotional burden. Zippora's expressionless face, Ahuva's mother training her not to cry, and Itzhak's oppressive sense of loneliness are all faithful testimony that the survivor mother took care of her child physically, but a large part of her inner existence was involved with her own pain and distress, and so she was not capable of holding her child emotionally.

The infant's primary perception of his mother's image – the experience of the object – serves as a foundation for constructing the capacity to form interpersonal relationships throughtout the child's life. The object experience has two dimensions: 'being' and 'doing' (Ehrlich 1987). The central experience of being is the constant presence of the object (generally the mother), and it includes physical sensations and the primary awareness of the self and the other. This experience is supposed to be accompanied by a feeling of pleasure, but its essence is the presence itself. In contrast, the experience of doing is associated with some activity or sequence of activities. This is the experience of the self with others through interaction. Being and doing are two dimensions along which the self and the object (the other) are experienced in early life, and sometimes these two modes of experience are interwoven.

After many years of therapy Dalia described her primary relationship with her mother, who had been a young girl at the time of the Holocaust:

'This is the oppressive feeling that I have to this day: a sweet baby girl was born and her mother was incapable of giving her anything more than food and clothing. I also feel angry and upset about this. Is it possible? It seems that it must be, but how? How can one treat a baby like a doll? Like a china doll? Doesn't a baby have feelings? Doesn't she need warmth and love and attention? To be perceived and understood? I feel the anger inside me but it's mixed with emptiness. And then the pressure in my head comes back, the pressure of absence, of lack, of what I never had and I never will have from my mother. For years I was a china doll. Always nice, neat, pretty, well-dressed and well-tended. Eating and eating whatever they gave me. Not loving, not angry, not feeling. All those years everything was buried. Just like with my mother, with me too everything is buried. It was impossible to get it out. Just as I was a china doll for her, so I was a china doll afterwards for myself. I didn't feel anything all the years. Everything was only in my head. The doll belonged to her and she held on to it with both hands. So everyone knew that I was hers and she wasn't alone. I was her cute baby, without which she couldn't exist, she couldn't continue her life, which had stopped then, during the Holocaust, and she wanted so much to start it again after all that death. Now I think about what kind of mother I really had, not hugging, not wanting to love, only knowing how to cook, to buy things, to help physically and only to pretend to be there. That's my mother. My mother now and forever. The mother who always dressed her little baby so nicely, all ironed and buttoned. But she never really saw me and sensed me. She could never understand my feelings and my problems. That's how it was then, and that's how it is now.'

Dalia's story expresses the terrible lack of the experience of being in her childhood, and how much she feels its absence to this very day.

The Holocaust stamped the psyches of the survivor mothers with a constant fear of catastrophe that might occur at any moment; this fear was reflected in their attitude towards their children, in keeping them as close as possible to themselves and to the house (as may be seen in the stories of many 'memorial candles' who remained in their parents' home at a relatively advanced age), and in the tendency to overprotect and over-control the children.

But Dalia's story describes another behavioural pattern – the mother's inability to feel her daughter's emotions. In order to understand what caused the formation of this pattern we must discuss the concept of cumulative psychic trauma. Khan (1963) used this concept to explain the failure of some mothers to provide their children with a sufficiently protective environment in their primary relationship with them. One of the most important elements the mother contributes to the interaction between the infant and herself is the regulation of the level of internal and external stimulation the infant receives from his immediate environment and from the world in general. The infant does try to regulate this stimulation himself (he avoids initiating interactions or reacts negatively to various stimuli), but this is not enough. It seems that when the mother's psychic state is not strong enough (due to insufficient emotional resources, depression or ego impoverishment), her sensitivity is lowered and she is incapable of receiving the infant's responses and interpreting the signs he sends her of too high a level of stimulation. She is therefore unable to react appropriately and to help him by lowering the level of the stimulus or stopping it for a while if necessary. In such a situation the mother is likely to set up intrusive patterns of control that necessarily constitute an exaggerated stimulus, and to fail in what Khan (1963) calls the 'setting up the protective shield'; the lack of this protective shield has negative effects on the infant's normal psychic development.

The survivor mothers' psychic strength was so impoverished that not only were they unable to serve as a protective shield for their infants and regulate their level of stimulation, but they also clung to their live and healthy infants to ease their own pain and anxiety. Rosa, the heroine of Appelfeld's book (1983a), clings with all her strength to her daughters from the day of their birth, and fights like a tiger for her existence. Like other survivor mothers, she draws from her daughters the sense of liveliness and self-esteem that were destroyed in her during the Holocaust.

The traumatic memory of absolute helplessness is still alive in the innermost hearts of the survivors, and they are afraid of being trapped again in a situation that resembles – if only in the slightest degree – the one they experienced then. The best way of avoiding such situations is by reversal – by exercising complete and exclusive control over the children's lives. Thus Rosa clings to her daughters and controls every inch of their lives, so that Brigitte, who doesn't know how to cope with her mother's totalitarian control, is not even able to construct a differentiated and independent ego.

According to Ehrlich (1987), when a child's experience of being is denied, this lack is noticeable mainly in a sense of failure in the perception of the self. But actually the opposite often occurs as well: the ego of the children of mothers who were in a state of overanxiety or overprotection while raising their children is sometimes found, on the contrary, to be strengthened in many areas, and the children become adults with a good capacity for functioning and adaptation. This outcome is attributed to a process of compensation, with overemphasis and expansion of the area of doing, with which the ego confronts the partially denied or degenerated experience of being. Many members of the second generation, especially the 'memorial candles', have attained outstanding achievements. Dalia and Itzhak, for example, always excelled in all their activities: from kindergarten, through school, army and academic studies, to their adult occupations. I have often been astounded by the deep chasm between the high level of functioning of some of the 'memorial candles', their talents and achievements on the intellectual, social and public levels, on the one hand, and their fundamental difficulties on the interpersonal level, which brought them into therapy, on the other. The most frequent reason for the children of survivors to seek therapy is their difficulty in forming intimate relationships with partners and with people in general, and in maintaining these relationships over the long term. It is true that some of them have formed intimate relationships and have even married and had children, but they still suffer from difficulties and crises in their married lives, caused by sexual or emotional problems or both.

It thus seems that the two hypotheses we have suggested – the unregulated stimulation the 'memorial candles' absorbed during their infancy and the experience of doing that has dominated their lives – are able to explain the gap in their personalities. On the one hand, the unregulated stimulation they absorbed in infancy and the limited emotional presence of their mothers led to an imbalance in their experience of being, whose effects can be seen in the deep disturbances in their sense of self; on the other hand, the mother's overprotection and massive physical presence in their lives strengthened their ego in other areas, thus enabling them to function well and even to excel in certain areas. The achievements of the survivors' children have another explanation: from their earliest childhood their parents instilled in them a sense of uniqueness and pinned great hopes on them. The supreme significance of their very existence and the great expectations of their success also served as a strengthening element in their personality structure. There is no doubt that the centrality of the 'memorial candles' in their parents' lives gave them the incentive – in spite of the emotional deprivation they suffered – to do their best to succeed and fulfil their parents' expectations on the one hand, and not to cause them any worry or disappointment on the other. They, and they alone, bore the obligation to compensate their mothers and fathers for their enormous losses, and they could not allow themselves to cause their parents any additional pain.

But we must not forget that behind these impressive achievements there is a defective, frustrated and conflictful experience of being. Kernberg (1975), Masterson and Rinsley (1975), and other psychologists who dealt with the topic of narcissism found that children develop a false self to justify defensive and regressive behaviour and to prevent, come what may, feelings of depression and anxiety. This self reacts to the mother's actions and non-actions with apparent submission and acquiescence, but at the same time develops a system of pathological defences. This intra-psychic system is later internalized and projected onto the environment when the need arises. In the end, the false self relates to the environment and to external reality from the same standpoint it attributes to the mother: avoidance of any response involving the expression of feeling or of true needs. That is, a mother suffering from depression, apathy or a feeling of emptiness – and these were frequently occurring states among the survivor mothers in the years after the war – ignores her infant's most basic needs and thus causes the development of a false self.

Another central and vital need in the child's development that causes difficulties for the survivor mother concerns differentiation and separation. As mentioned, the process of separation is of crucial importance in the stages of the infant's and child's psychological development (Mahler and Furer 1972). But for the survivors every separation means a renewed experience of the trauma of the loss of their families. The intense emotional load inherent in separation cannot avoid being reflected in the relationships between the survivor mother and her children, and it is thus not surprising that in every life situation involving separation from her children she feels threatened and anxious. This difficulty in accepting separations necessarily has some effect on the developmental processes of the 'memorial candles' and on their ability to consolidate a separate and independent identity.

It seems plausible to assume that the survivor mother often reacted to the signs of separation and individuation of her child by either ignoring them or trying to dominate the child. A mother who is unable to respond to her child's developmental needs clings to him and prevents any sort of behaviour that might attest to a tendency toward separation. In fact, she is encouraging regressive behaviour in the child. On the other hand, there are times when she cannot bear the child's expressions of dependency, and so she encourages expressions of individuation instead – but inappropriately and at a time when the child is not yet ready for this.

The main behaviour patterns of survivor mothers towards their children, especially those who were born immediately after the Holocaust, are thus compulsive clinging on the one hand and encouragement of independence and individuation on the other. The stories of Dalia, Hava, Itzhak and Ahuva exemplified these patterns, which sometimes occur together.

The child interprets each of these patterns as a failure on his mother's part to decode the signs he is sending her and respond to them. He reacts to this lack of response as to abandonment, as if she was intentionally ignoring his most vital needs. He internalizes his response as part of the retreating maternal object. Later he will internalize this experience of self–object (or self–other) relations as a part of himself, but meanwhile it makes him feel depressed because of the feeling that he has been abandoned. In reaction he constructs a defence system – a combination of primary defence mechanisms such as splitting, denial, repression, and compartmentalization – which helps him avoid anxiety and depression. It is to this that Dalia was referring when she said: 'I didn't feel anything all those years. Everything was only in my head.' Indeed, Dalia's defence system served her very efficiently for many years.

The motif of abandonment generally does not arise in the first stage of therapy. The 'memorial candles' first learn to construct a sense of self-confidence and of basic trust in the therapeutic setting and in the therapist. Generally the motif of abandonment first appears in dreams or fantasies. Less frequently it also appears in memories, but in a rather detached and unemotional way. The struggle of the 'memorial candles' to defend themselves against emotional attachment to feelings of depression and the fear of abandonment is generally very intense and stubborn.

Ahuva: 'I have a dream I want to tell. In the dream there was a house of abandoned children. I am in this house and there are many boys and girls there. They say that some boy and girl have run away from the institution. The institution is in an isolated area, on a little hill, and there are white buildings there that look a little bit like a closed prison, and there is only one train that goes there and back all the time. I am there in the institution, very worried about these children. And there's one little girl who's crying all the time and saying that her parents left her and they never come to visit her. I go away from there and I see other children. And there's also a pond there, and I'm afraid they'll fall into the water. Then I go to meet this mother in her house, and I'm very angry with her because she doesn't go to visit her daughter. She sort of explains and apologizes, but it seems to me that she doesn't care.'

It's plausible that the two little girls in Ahuva's dream – the girl who was crying, who felt abandoned, and the girl who ran away – together represent the two sides of her personality. I asked Ahuva who the boys and girls in her dream were. Ahuva answered with a smile that perhaps they were the members of the group; she has lately been feeling close to them and has even begun to identify with them. I told her that perhaps she was identifying mainly with the feelings that the group members had recently begun to express openly, about various situations in which they did not get what they expected or what they needed from their parents.

Ahuva answered: 'Yes, it is still somewhat difficult for me to communicate directly with my parents. But I know it's connected to what I said at the last meeting. What I said about the relationship between my mother and me remained with me very strongly – how she stubbornly insisted on feeding me the little milk she had with a spoon, and how she taught me not to cry. I noticed that I was dreaming a lot about children and food. The part of the dream with the white buildings and the train seems to me now to be connected with the Holocaust. A closed place that you can't leave, and the train. Maybe it's the ghetto where my mother. . . where my mother's first baby died of starvation. And I always felt that the fact that the baby stayed there, and my mother nevertheless remained alive and came to Israel, and the baby died of starvation and was left – that it was as if my mother abandoned her there. And you know, food in our family is a big thing. Even now I can't go out of my parents' house without them giving me pots full of food. There was always enough food in the house, even when I was a 'latch-key' child, coming home from school and roaming around alone until the evening, when my parents came back from work – even then there was always food. My mother would take care to cook and to leave the food with the neighbour where I would eat, because they weren't home all day. When I think about this nowadays, I think that maybe I felt abandoned. I remember that I was never afraid and I never cried, I actually felt that it was fun that I was free to roam around. Perhaps the girl in the dream who was crying, and I was angry with her mother, was really me. Finally I am allowing myself to feel, at least in my dreams, but really not only in my dreams – both to cry and to be angry. I am also beginning to feel more alive. . .'

The motif of abandonment appears in Ahuva's story at various levels of consciousness, and the images are interwoven with one another, as they were internalized in her inner self. Ahuva's mother's parents, her five sisters, her husband and the rest of her family abandoned her in the Holocaust. The mother herself abandoned her baby daughter there. And now Ahuva's parents abandoned her for hours every day. But Ahvua's real feeling of abandonment is mixed up with the fact that her mother never gave her the experience of good enough mothering, which could have held her and all her infant needs, especially the intense need to express herself by crying. Thus since infancy Ahuva had been repressing and denying all her feelings, especially those of sadness and anger.

Nurit, who was born on a kibbutz, responded to Ahuva's dream with deep feeling: 'From the time of my childhood I don't remember myself with my mother at all. My parents never refused me anything. They never set limits or said no. Because of this I can't ask them for anything. I always had to set my own limits. This put great responsibility and pressure on me.'

Therapist: 'And how did you feel about this pressure?'

Nurit: 'Now that I'm talking about it, this is the first time I clearly feel the pressure in my stomach, but even now it stops around the area of my chest. I don't allow myself to feel completely. But I remember that for years I didn't feel anything. I would talk about everything from my head, without any problems, completely cut off. Now it's less. . . When I was a little girl, there were many times when I would go to the collective dining hall in the evening to eat with the family of one of the children in my group. My adoptive family, that is, the family I adopted for myself. And then it was very difficult for me to decide if this was fair to my parents or not. They never said anything of their own initiative.'

Malka: 'How did it happen that you went with an adoptive family?'

Nurit: 'Well, I had already spent the whole afternoon with them, so I just went along with them to supper as well, but it weighed on my conscience. . . I can't remember as well as Ahuva. In my own house, with my mother, I hardly remember anything, except that I would come home and it would be dark and they would be sleeping. At five in the afternoon, when all the parents are on the lawn with their children. My mother slept in the dark and I was not permitted to bother her, God forbid. I only remember one thing, that sometimes I would play on the porch. This was when I was four–five years old, and I would play with the toys in my doll corner. I would arrange the cupboards and the tables and the chairs, but I didn't play with the dolls themselves. I almost never played with the dolls themselves. I would prepare food for the dolls in the doll pots and pans. With cigarette ashes.'

Therapist: 'With cigarette ashes?'

Nurit: 'Yes. You know, my parents smoked a lot. There were always a lot of ashes in all sorts of ashtrays. There wasn't any food in the house, so I made food out of this. I'm not just talking about cakes that my mother never baked. I would look for a carrot, for a piece of bread, and even this wasn't there. The house was just empty. My adoptive mother always had chocolate cake and they would save a piece for me.'

Therapist: 'And did you ever say anything to your mother about this?'

Nurit: 'No. Never. She never reacted to anything and I didn't either. She always had this suffocating kind of silence. Because of this I never wanted to be in the house and very often I would stay with another child in the children's house the whole afternoon. I thought it was great that no one told me what to do. I thought I was free. Now I'm not absolutely sure it was so great. . . I don't know.'

Unlike Ahuva's mother and many other survivor mothers, Nurit's mother didn't cling to her daughter. Not even for the most basic physical needs. There was no food in the house nor any real life, because the mother was entirely enveloped in her work or her depression, and she actually perpetuated, in a paradoxical way, the hunger that had reigned 'there'. Nurit's difficulties with object relations were already apparent at a young age: she didn't play with her dolls at all but only with their furniture and things. It seems that in her play, especially in the food she prepared for her dolls out of ashes, she was reconstructing her experience of the primary relationship with her mother as it was internalized in her psyche.

Many 'memorial candles' have considerable difficulty establishing continuing intimate relationships with their partners and their children. It seems that they use their relationships with close objects to reconstruct the behaviour of the false self they internalized in their early childhood in their primary relationship with their mother. This self is so accustomed to avoiding any reactions and any expressions of feeling that an important and intimate relationship is an unfamiliar experience to it, and since it is unfamiliar it also becomes threatening.

The images and representations belonging to object relations that arise in the minds of the 'memorial candles' tend to arouse, among other emotions, feelings of emptiness, of abandonment, and even of hostility. These images are absorbed into their psyches and become an integral part of their self-image. Until they reach the stage of therapy in which they succeed in facing the harsh and painful feelings and contents that were repressed, every attempt to feel anger, frustration or hostility is doomed to failure. The 'memorial candles' have a double difficulty in their relationships with their parents: the parents were unable to define the boundaries between themselves and their children, while the children are incapable of dealing with any sort of aggression.

Arye described his primary interaction with his mother in a stage of therapy in which he was attempting to break through his defensive armour, which had been preventing him from truly feeling the depression stemming from his abandonment.

'There's still a part of me that's connected to my mother, that I'm not yet quite ready to give up. This is a kind of imaginary hug, and if I give it up, I will be giving up a place to rest. In my depression I can be with her. It's enough that I can lie curled up next to her. She doesn't even have to touch me. I lie bent over at her side, sort of curled up, there's something warm and enveloping about it.'

Therapist: 'Do you mean that this sadness envelops you like a hug?'

Arye: 'Yes, that's it. I lie curled up like a foetus. I feel as if I am in the womb. You know, hugging with great feeling and joy – I never had that with anyone. Not with my mother, not with my father, and certainly not with my sister. But to be like this [he lies back in a foetal position] also makes me tense. As if the womb will swallow me up. I want to get out of there. As if my mother actually wants me like that – passive, inside the womb. When I was there, she didn't have to make any efforts, or to feel, or to think. I came naturally to her.'

Therapist: 'But actually, when you are inside her womb she has something alive inside of her.'

Arye: 'Yes, that's true, I never thought about it that way before.'

Therapist: 'Try to think that when you were there inside of her you gave her some life, for a few months at least, and when you came out she remained alone with herself once again, with her loneliness and with death.'

Arye: 'I came out so soon. But on the other hand, sometimes it seems to me that perhaps I haven't come out completely yet. She's so miserable. I felt her misery in all sorts of situations – both when I was fighting with her and when I was trying to make her happy or to make her laugh.'

Therapist: 'You seem to have felt the need to continue to bring her to life, to give her some joy from yourself.'

Arye: 'You know, there were years when she was somewhat more alive. After that, for about twenty years she wasn't living at all – depressions, long hospitalizations in mental hospitals, and many drugs. Now, thank God, she's a little better. I am sad now because of her, but not too much. Now I feel that I can sit, or even lie down, a little more quietly and with less tension than before, but I need an external anchor that can assure me that I'll get out of it.'

Therapist: 'It seems that therapy serves as an anchor for you. You still don't feel self-confident enough, so you need to look for an anchor outside yourself.'

Arye: 'The best place for me was there, inside my mother, but from the moment I came out into the world I lost this. Now I feel good sometimes with Edna, my girlfriend, when she's close to me and caresses me. Then I manage to feel relaxed, quiet and not tense, and outwardly even somewhat happy. But inside there's this tension that comes very soon and takes control of me. Even the happiness is not enough. How can I give up this part of me?'

Therapist: 'Do you mean the part that includes sadness, death, longing and passivity?'

Arye: 'Yes, there's a lot of passivity in it. My mother made me very angry when she gave in to her depression and passivity. This drove me crazy. I never let her defeat me with this. I would get angry and defend myself, even though on the other hand it attracted me very much. The active and the passive parts within me have not yet made peace with each other.'

Therapist: 'Your mother gave in to depression and passivity. She allowed herself this privilege, because after everything she went through "there", after everything she lost, she didn't have any other choice, but you weren't actually, really "there".'

Arye: 'Yes, that was her privilege. I, like my sister, couldn't get along with it, because her quiet, slow and relaxed side was always connected with such frightening, such terrifying pictures, that I couldn't accept it. Perhaps I'm trying to grasp that I can also be quiet, and not so nervous and aggressive and outstanding in everything, without this quietness being accompanied by pictures from "there", that were always so frightening.'

Therapist: 'Do you know anything about your mother when she was a girl, before the Holocaust?'

Arye: 'She actually told many stories from that time, stories about a nice life, walks in the forest, swimming in the river. I think that my mother was happy as a girl. She also felt that she belonged. She described many games with others, with her brothers and sister and her friends. She was a good friend. Friendship was very important to her. I don't think it was the same with my father. I think he had problems with relationships even before. But not my mother. The way she describes her relationship with her sister, it seems that there was closeness and love between them.'

Therapist: 'You missed all this part, you didn't have the chance to learn from her about the side of her that was alive.'

Arye: 'Yes. Perhaps the problem is not just the activity and passivity inside me, but also the question of how to feel happiness and closeness and excitement. Perhaps some of this remained with her, deep inside, but it was always very hard to feel and live it together with her.'

Arye is imprisoned by anxiety from which he cannot free himself even in moments of peacefulness with his girlfriend. Sandler (1960b) sees 'a background feeling within the ego, a feeling which can be referred to as one of safety or perhaps of security,' the polar opposite of anxiety. 'It is,' he says, 'a feeling of well-being, a sort of ego-tone. . . [Its] safety-signals are related to such things as the awareness of being protected; for example by the reassuring presence of the mother' (pp. 353–4).

Many 'memorial candles' aspire to reach, through therapy, this feeling of ease which generally exists only when the experience of 'being' with the mother-object takes place normatively and positively in infancy and childhood. In the primary relationships of many 'memorial candles' with their survivor mothers, this experience either did not exist at all or was defective and insufficient. When this experience is absent or defective a feeling of non-existence arises, stemming from the defect in the ego's feeling of wholeness and from the absence of the feeling of the continuity of the self. These two feelings are vital for existence and for development over the years. To feel real, says Winnicott (1965), is much more than just to exist. It involves finding a way to exist within a self that is independent and meaningful. Only then can the child have a self into which he can retreat in order to relax and find ease. Arye fought his feeling of non-existence for many years through the use of defence mechanisms such as splitting, repression, aggressiveness and control. At an advanced stage of therapy he began to make use of significant figures – the therapist, the members of his therapy group, his girlfriend – as anchors for security and calm.

Chapter 4

Identification with death

At the end of the war death still reigned everywhere. Many survivors died of disease, of exhaustion, or of overeating, and the sense of death, of depression that had not been worked through, of anger and of guilt filled everyone's hearts. It is no wonder then that the children born right after the war, or even somewhat later, absorbed and were affected by the sense of death that enveloped their parents, and sometimes the identification with death became a central element in their personality.

In this chapter I deal with the importance of the identification with death in the intergenerational transmission of the trauma, and I attempt to show how the attitude of the 'memorial candles' to the motif of death, and its centrality in their personality, is related to their parents' traumatic experiences.

Lifton (1980) emphasizes that the stamp of death is impressed on the personality of Holocaust survivors – the smoke and odour of the furnaces, the gas chambers, the cruel murders, the tearing apart of families and friends, all remain with them and occupy them throughout their lives. For many survivors death, in its most terrible form, became a sort of prism through which they experienced their lives after the Holocaust. Although the death images might have served the survivors as an important source of energy, in most cases they had a paralysing effect and caused the survivors to feel fixed in time.

Many psychologists, including H. Klein (1987), have shown that the death images engraved on the consciousness of the survivors were associated with harsh guilt feelings – feelings of 'death guilt'. There is no doubt that some of the survivors remained immured in the world of their images, partly because of their feeling of obligation and responsibility to those who had perished. The guilt feelings are associated mainly with the death of relatives and friends, but they are also laden with the memory of the thousands of anonymous people who died before the eyes of the survivors. These guilt feelings are especially salient among the survivors of the extermination camps, but they also appear among the survivors who hid in various hiding-places and felt that they had survived at the cost of the lives of others. The source of this 'death guilt' is the gap between the physical and emotional helplessness of the Holocaust victims in the face of its terrors and the survivors' perception of their own and their society's expectations from them under these circumstances.

Appelfeld (1983b) describes the severe guilt feeling attached to the abandonment of relatives:

Suddenly the man rose to his feet and said: 'What am I doing here?'

'What do you mean, what are you doing here?' they said. 'You're playing cards.'

'I'm a murderer,' he said, not in anger, but with a kind of quiet deliberation, as if the scream in his throat had turned, within a short space of time, to a clear admission of guilt.

'Don't talk like that,' they berated him.

'You know it better than I do,' he said. 'You'll be my witnesses when the time comes.' . . .

'You'll say that Zigi Baum is a murderer.' . . .

'A man abandons his wife and children, his father and his mother. What is he if not a murderer?' He raised his head and a smile broke out on his face. Now he looked like a man who had done what had to be done.

(pp. 150–1)

Death images arise in the conscious and subconscious of the many survivors, both while awake and in dreams and nightmares. Such strong guilt feelings that had become fossilized within the ego could not but control the survivor's existence, so that he was entirely immersed in the world of the dead. He was generally unable to find within himself the power to cope with this situation, and he developed a pattern of avoidance leading to psychic closing-off; this closing-off is combined with feelings of discomfort and depression and the inability to control the anger that arises and spreads within him.

We will now see how these death feelings are reflected in the consciousness of the survivors' children and what death images were transmitted to them by their parents.

Ariela told me about a dream she had:

> 'A large hall. A smell of smoke. Darkness, torches burning. In the middle of the hall there's a black coffin with blood pouring out of it. The coffin is in the middle of the room and on the coffin there's a little bird. I am very afraid of the bird. Suddenly the bird comes down from the coffin and approaches me, and then a deathly fear attacks me.'

At the end of the recital of the dream Ariela was silent and immersed within herself. After a while she began speaking again, with her head down, in a whispery and monotonous voice:

> 'It's really strange, I can cope with the coffin pouring blood, but not with the live bird. I'm so scared and helpless. In general, in all sorts of areas it's hard for me to cope with life. With the dead it's easier.'

Many years have passed since Ariela related this dream to me and it is still etched sharply in my memory. At that time I had not yet become closely acquainted with the motif of the encounter with death in the personalities of the survivors' children, and the dream interested me greatly but also made me wonder. However, in the many therapy sessions I have had since then, I have come to realize that Ariela's dream was not exceptional. The dualism of life and death together is a central motif in the personalities of many members of the second generation. At the same session Ariela also told me that the coffin in her dream reminded her somewhat of the chest of drawers in the therapy room, and that her fear of the bird was associated with her fear of animals in general and of dogs in particular – a fear that still dominates her. When I asked her for her associations to dogs, Ariela became confused and murmured something vague about her mother, who is also afraid of dogs and doesn't like animals in general, and that maybe this is associated with something she experienced 'there'. In the early stage of therapy Ariela was not able to bring up any additional associations or memories.

The vision Ariela saw in her dream was very graphic: an old, dark hall lit by torches, apparently drawn from stories she had heard about the lives of knights in the Middle Ages. The symbolism and ceremony in the dream create a division between Ariela's experiences in her dream and their origin with her parents. Death and the Holocaust are hinted to her paradoxically in the associations aroused in her by the bird – the dogs that frighten her just as they frighten her mother.

The little bird on the coffin, against the background of the dark hall, may represent life, the aspiration for freedom and movement, a kind of instinctual or sexual expression. But it is small in comparison with the darkness and death reigning in the dream. The fear of the bird – of life – is still very great in Ariela's heart, as can be seen from the restraint and the emotional closedness in her whispery murmurings when she answered my questions.

The association aroused in her by the coffin – the chest of drawers in the therapy room – exemplifies the anxiety and suspicions that are always aroused at the beginning of the therapy process. Here, in the therapy room, it is necessary to open the 'coffin' and confront by daylight what is hidden in it. The coffin thus also represents the thick armour that Ariela had already constructed around herself during her childhood, while the blood pouring out of the coffin may represent a narrow crack that has appeared in her armour, through which her pain may be glimpsed.

In my opinion the coffin also represents the womb. After the Holocaust Ariela's mother tried to have more children, but, like many other survivors, she miscarried with all of them. To Ariela the womb therefore represents death. The anxiety appearing in Ariela's dream is not exceptional in itself; what are exceptional are the intensity of the fear and the motif of death reigning in it. Many children of survivors, especially 'memorial candles', are filled with anxiety and suspicions interwoven with death motifs, to the extent of hostility. This is a combination unique to the children of survivors and it is expressed at the beginning of the therapy process.

Ruth, twenty-eight, the daughter of two survivors, related a recurrent dream:

'My father and I are on a tour of the Weizmann Institute. The place is very beautiful and full of greenery. Grass, trees and flowers everywhere. We reach Weizmann's grave, and there, in the middle of the grass, under a tree growing near the grave, we take a picnic table and chairs out of the car and we start eating in the middle of nature. We eat lentil soup, like the kind my

mother usually cooks at home. But suddenly, while we're eating,
I sense a strange odour and taste in the soup. There's something sticking to the lentils, and suddenly I know that they are
made of ground-up human bones. I stop eating and feel very
nauseous. I look at my father, but it seems that he doesn't notice
anything, and he continues eating with enjoyment.'

Ruth told this story in a distant, expressionless voice, and every so
often she smiled an incomprehensible smile that had nothing to
do with the content of the dream. When I asked her opinion about
the meaning of the dream, she had trouble giving a clear answer.
She said that she had recently visited the Weizmann Institute
because of her work, and perhaps that's why she dreamed about
the place. She didn't even mention her special relationship with
her father, which she had told me about during previous sessions,
even though both she and I knew very well that her father was
deeply immersed in the loss of his parents, his sister and the rest of
his family, and that the relationship between him and Ruth was
based on feelings of death and loss.

In Ruth's dream as well, the surrealistic contrast between life
and death stands out – the contrast between the beauty of the
greenery, the grass and flowers at the Weizmann Institute, which
symbolizes progress, and the gravesite on which they held their
picnic. The family celebration in the midst of nature is that of Ruth
and her father alone. The mother is absent, but it is she who
cooked the lentil soup made of ground-up human bones. There is
no celebration that is not penetrated by death. Anyone familiar
with psychoanalysis cannot help but identify an oedipal relationship here. This relationship necessarily arouses feelings of guilt
and anxiety in the daughter. And she is indeed immediately
punished: The 'poisoned' soup was prepared by the mother. Based
on M. Klein's (1948) hypotheses, the soup made of the bones of
dead people belongs to Ruth's archaic world, to the fragmentary
world of the infant, full of fantasies and hallucinations, in which all
anxieties and aggressive feelings are projected onto the mother's
breasts, which represent all the good and all the bad in the infant's
life. It seems that for Ruth the soup made of human bones symbolizes the milk she nursed from her mother's breasts. This is milk full
of bitterness into which death has been 'cooked'. Death is thus a
central element connecting Ruth to both her parents.

Eliyahu, thirty-five, the son of two survivor parents, related this dream that he had in the beginning stage of therapy:

'I'm in Europe, wandering around a cemetery, perhaps like the British Military Cemetery from World War I. It's a nice sunny day, everything all around is green and full of trees. There are many tourists wandering around among the graves. I am also there as a tourist, with a camera on my shoulder. I see a priest there and people praying around him, as if they were holding a memorial ceremony for fallen soldiers. I am looking on from a distance. I don't feel that I belong to them. Suddenly I see a Jew dressed in black, with a long beard, a kind of rabbi, who is also praying there. He calls to me, and I approach him. He tells me that we have to dig some graves here, and he hands me a spade. I start digging small holes, but the rabbi says they aren't deep enough. I dig new holes, but now he says they aren't in the right place. Finally we are approaching some sort of round cave that's there, and we go into it, and I start to dig in the cave. Then he says: "Yes, this is the place." '

When I asked Eliyahu what thoughts the dream aroused in him, he responded that he didn't know, and in a matter-of-fact and almost joyous tone he added: 'It was actually fun to wander around there as a tourist, not belonging and not obligated to anyone or to anything.' He didn't understand the meaning of the graves at all, but when I commented that the small graves aroused in me the association of children's graves, he seemed surprised and whispered: 'I didn't think of that. I don't think it's related to my father, who had a wife and three little girls who perished in the Holocaust.' I was surprised, as during the therapy Eliyahu had not mentioned these half-sisters even once, and I said that we would have to discuss this later; he became confused and murmured in an emotionless tone: 'There were three big, dim pictures in the house that my father talked about all the time. I don't have the strength or the wish to discuss it. I had enough of them then. . .'

Later in therapy we tried to interpret his dream again. The rabbi apparently represented an authoritative figure, father or therapist, who showed him the place where he had to start 'digging'; that is, to look for the burial place of the dead parts of his psyche, which are the conflicts that were repressed during his childhood. This place was a cave; that is, the intricacies of his ego or even perhaps his mother's womb, as she had become pregnant with him in Europe, immediately after the Holocaust.

There is much similarity between the digging of graves in Eliyahu's dream and the opening of the coffin in Ariela's dream. Both of them knew that in the course of therapy they would have to scratch around in the intricacies of their psyches and dredge out of it images from their parents' past, images that the parents had buried within the children. But we must not forget the other aspect of the guilt feelings and the death images: the fact that they were the link connecting the Holocaust survivors with themselves and with their past. That is, the guilt feelings and the unresolved grief for the dead objects, which were internalized in the survivors' psyches, are, paradoxically, their living core.

The primary, biocultural, drive for continuity still bubbled in the hidden psyches of the survivors. They transmitted to the 'memorial candles' the task of building and maintaining a bridge of continuity over the chasm that had been created. The internalization of and identification with the death images was thus vital and necessary for the survivors' children, because the living seed was buried within them. The encounter with death, however dismal and painful it might be, gradually turned into a dialogue with figures possessing forms and faces, and with a past dipped in colour and surrounded by odours of life. In the encounter with death was thus hidden the only real chance for renewing the intergenerational continuity.

Kestenberg (1972, 1982), Grubrich-Simits (1979) and other psychologists claim that not only are many of the survivors' children 'memorial candles' for the Holocaust in general, but they also serve as living memorials for the dead, generally family members who perished. They became an inseparable part of the mourning ritual that was frozen in the hearts of the survivors at the time that they were prevented from resolving their grief and working through it in the normal way. Many survivors therefore preserve the memory of family members in their children and name them after dead relatives. They thus decree for their children a double sense of identity and emotional life; the children must live simultaneously as themselves and as the relatives they were named after. This is not a mere identification with those who perished, but a more complex mechanism – a transposition of the world of the past; during the course of which a divided ego is created in which two or more identities exist simultaneously, side by side.

According to Gampel (1982), the dreams or fantasies shared by the survivor parents and their children create the illusion that these children, who were born after the Holocaust, had always been with their parents – even before they were born. The purpose of this shared illusion is apparently to deny the parents' loneliness, since if the children had actually been with them in the camps then they had never been left totally alone and, conversely, they had never abandoned their families.

According to Epstein (1979), sometimes this shared illusion led to an understanding of the parents' feelings by their children, and even caused them to agree to join the magic circle of the nightmarish reality in which they and their parents were immersed with a common fate and shared guilt feelings. In this magic circle the child might take the place of a father or mother, of a brother or sister, of a previous son or daughter or some other dear relative who had disappeared. If this is so, then the 'memorial candle' served to strengthen the denial of the loss that the parents had been unable to mourn at the proper time, and at the same time to preserve its memory. But not only double identity is involved here. Often the survivors' children had several identities, when one or both of the parents, by using projective identification mechanisms, projected onto the child not only one figure but several figures from among the lost loved ones.

Semel (1985) describes the desperate struggle of a daughter named after her father's sister to go on a three-day trip with her class and to free herself to some extent from the chains tying her to her father:

'But Daddy. . .you never let me do anything. Just this once! Please?'

She remembers how she pleaded, she almost went down on her knees.

'We never went on any trips. Your aunt stayed home until she got married. She only took one trip. A very long trip. . .'

'Which aunt?' she thought, 'I don't know any aunt, maybe she never existed,' and aloud she said: 'That was a different time', her voice gradually dying down.

'There isn't any other time,' he defied her.

Then she spoke to him as one revealing a terrible discovery. 'Your sister is dead.'
. . . 'She's dead! Dead! And I'm alive!'

(p. 110)

'You're all I have left. If something bad happens I won't be able to continue living.' It was as though he was pleading for his life in front of the hangman. . . He put a heavy responsibility on her. Her life was a guarantee for his life. He buried his head in his hands and said: 'I touch a switch in my head and I return to my previous life. My sister is putting the baby to sleep before the decrees, she's playing with him on her lap.' Then he said to her: 'Come!' and took her to a dark back room. There, on the walls, he had brought his lost loved ones back to life with a paint-brush, and hung them like a royal dynasty, with her aunt and the baby in the middle. He climbed the walls of memory but found nothing to grasp. He forced her to stand in front of each of the strangers in the pictures and say: 'I beg forgiveness.' She gave in, but her heart was filled with resentment. Who wants to mourn belatedly now?

(p. 113)

The transposition mechanism is very clear in this case: the father transmits to his daughter the burden of his dear objects, from which he cannot separate. The daughter is frozen in the father's internal world in the fear of death and loss, and she represents his sister and the other images engraved on his heart. The father cannot distinguish between the past and the present, between there and here, between his lost sister and his daughter who only wants, after all, to go on a three-day trip. The daughter is chained and helpless. She feels resentment and tries to fight for her right to an independent identity of her own, but the attempt fails and she gives in.

Momik, the hero of Grossman's book (1986), had been given several names. Momik describes how the representations of the family figures were transmitted to him – both those he was actually named after and many others that were transmitted to him openly and consciously by his grandmother or in a conspiracy of silence by his parents.

His full name, it should be mentioned, was Shlomo Efraim
Neuman, in So-and-so's and So-and-so's memory. They'd have
liked to give him a hundred names. Grandma Henny did it all
the time. She would call him Mordechai Leibele, and Shepsele
and Mendel and Anshel and Shulem and Chumak, and Shlomo
Haim, and that's how Momik got to know who they all
were. . . Little Anshel, the frail one, they wondered how he
would ever get through the winter. . . there he sits in his sailor
suit with his hair parted in the middle looking so serious with his
big eyeglasses; Goodness me, Grandma clapped her hands, you
look just like him. She told him all about them long long ago,
in the days when she could still remember, and they thought he
was too young to understand, but once when his Mama saw that
his eyes weren't staring blankly any more, she told Grandma
Henny to stop right away, and she also hid the book with the
amazing pictures. . . And now Momik is trying as hard as he can
to remember what was in the pictures and the stories.

(p. 27)

Gampel (1987) writes:

A child does not choose his name, nor his parents, nor his body.
When he enters the world he finds a place of love or of hate, he
is a result of longing or a mistake, he is given space to live or he
fills a vacuum.

Our given name accompanies us. It constitutes our human
essence. It is enough to utter a few phonemes, to say a few
syllables, almost without meaning, and their mere utterance
arouses love or hate, happy or sad memories, confusion or
clarity – all related to the person bearing this name.

(p. 28)

Naming a child after an ancestor is a kind of attribution ceremony,
establishing the individual's place in a long chain of images from
the past. The name becomes a means of control over time's de-
structiveness. By repeating the names of the relatives who died, the
family organizes historic time and creates continuity between the
past and the future. In the families of survivors what takes place is
not the internalization of the images of the dead relatives but the
resurrection of the dead themselves.

Naming children after dead relatives is not, of course, unique to the families of survivors, but it is especially prevalent among them because of the unconscious attempt and desire to resurrect those who perished by giving their names to the children.

Many 'memorial candles' grow up from birth with a sense of deep semantic confusion and absolute fragmentation of their identity. The many names they bear represent the identities of different figures, various segments of their personalities. It is thus no wonder that it is so difficult for them to consolidate a clear, well-defined, and independent self-identity.

At a recent extended session the members of the therapy group were asked to create an image of themselves out of plasticine. Hanna did not succeed in shaping a human image with a clear identity. Hanna is the eldest daughter of two survivor parents. Her father, who was a child at the time of the Holocaust, was saved in some mysterious way; her mother lost her entire family. Hanna modelled a kind of complicated skein, with intertwined ropes extending from it. At first the meaning of the ropes was totally obscure to me, but after a while I understood from Hanna's words that the ropes symbolized, above all, the objects in her parents' lives that had been lost in the Holocaust. They were projected onto and transmitted to Hanna, and she carries them in her psyche as if they were part of her own identity and personality.

At the group therapy sessions Hanna often seemed to be only partially present. She was aware of this and said the following about herself:

'Sometimes I'm sitting with a friend and having a very intimate discussion with him, but part of me isn't there. I don't know where that part of me has gone or what I'm involved with, but the feeling that part of me is immersed in something else and is not free for reality is with me almost all the time.'

At the same group session Ruth modelled two plasticine figures intertwined with each other like Siamese twins – two legs, two arms, two chests, and two heads – with each figure in a different colour. One was the figure of a woman and the other was the figure of a girl. Ruth said:

'There are several identities here in one figure. The adult woman is my mother and the girl is me – sometimes I feel these two parts within myself. Actually, the adult woman may also be my grandmother who remained there, whose picture hangs on a wall in our house. My mother was a girl when she was separated from her and she never saw her again. . .'

In the ego of the 'memorial candles' there is thus a complex synthesis of identifications with the figures of the dead. This synthesis is constructed from a simultaneous adaptation to present reality and to the world of the Holocaust. Although this adaptation is the element keeping their personality together, it also leads to the multiplicity of contradictions in their identity. A true, complete integration of their personality can take place only at the completion of a long, complex process in which the parts of their ego are revealed, and the patient gradually faces the many identities running about within himself. In the first stages of therapy, as in the course of their lives until this point, the survivors' children are wandering between the hidden, unknown past of their parents and families and the uncomprehended vagueness in their psyches. The coffin in Ariela's dream and the cave in Eliyahu's dream represent these two elements – their parents' past and their own internal world.

A distinction must be made between identification with the parents' past and transposition, through which the 'memorial candles' derive the images of the dead themselves. In the pattern of transposition there is an attempt to construct a bridge over two chapters of history in order to adapt to the present. Perhaps this pattern serves the survivors' children as a substitute for the mourning for lost, loved relatives, with whose deaths the parents themselves have not yet come to terms. As long as the 'memorial candle' accepts the task of immersing himself in the past and playing both the parents' role and the role of the lost family, the parents do not have to confront the loss of their dear ones and truly come to terms with it (H. Klein 1973).

Mitscherlich (1979) and others stress the survivors' inability to achieve true mourning. This is also the case with the 'memorial candles' – they seem immersed in mourning, but it is not a real mourning; rather, it is a depressive state resembling mourning only in its external manifestations.

The normal mourning process leads to identification with the lost object along with increasing emotional liberation from it, restoring the equilibrium in the mourner's psyche. Thus in order to come to terms with the loss of their families the 'memorial candles' must transform the objects that were unconsciously transmitted to them, through transposition, into clear and living objects, with a form and an identity, that they can truly mourn on the one hand, and join up with, as a source of identity and continuity, on the other. The break in the family and in the community is mended during the emotional encounter of the 'memorial candles' with their parents' and families' past, an encounter which involves the ability to come to terms with the pain of the loss and to mourn. The therapy setting is intended to help them cope with this encounter.

Roni, like many survivors' children, borrowed her father's world with its objects, and took upon herself the task of reviving them instead of giving them up. Roni was thus undoubtedly expressing her need to become acquainted with her parents' past and to mourn the relatives she had never met; she accepted the task of transforming them into real images, but it was nearly impossible for her to do this, because Roni's father, like many other survivors, refused to talk about the past.

Roni's psyche was torn between the desire to know and to cry and the prohibition on knowing or expressing feelings. In one of the group sessions she related the following:

'Not far from my parents' house they recently set up a memorial engraved with the names of all the people from my father's town who perished in the Holocaust. I very much wanted to go with him to see the memorial. I was very excited and I thought that this was my chance, that I would finally be able to ask him questions and talk to him about all the relatives whose names I don't even know. My father's father, his brothers and sisters. I only know his mother's name, because it's my name. I hoped that my father would allow himself to tell me about it this time, and perhaps he would even cry.' Here she was silent for a while, and then she continued: 'I have never yet seen him cry, not for this or for anything else. Perhaps I even wished that we could finally cry together. When I asked him if he was willing to come with me to see the memorial, he agreed gladly, and I was happy. But when we got there he stood like a lump of wood and I could hardly express anything of what I wanted and what I had felt before. My father stood there and spoke about the aesthetic aspect of the memorial and the amount of money it probably cost to build it. I was stunned, paralysed, frozen inside. The only thing I managed to ask him was to tell me the names of all our relatives in the list on the memorial, and what his place was in the family tree. This he did without any emotionality. All the way home and all the following week I kept repeating and muttering the names, which I won't forget any more, I hope.'

The repetition of the names of the lost relatives is the way Roni tries to hold onto the end of a real thread of the past, perhaps the first one she was given. This is a thread that may lead her to an emotional encounter with the dead and the revival of her father's past.

Yoel is about forty, the son of two survivor parents. His mother lost her husband and her two daughters and her entire extended family in the Holocaust. In most of the group sessions Yoel sat silent and closed. In one session he related the following in a flat, choked voice:

'In the picture album we had in our house since I was a child there were pictures of two little girls, about eight and ten years old. I think they were my mother's children. I never asked her explicitly and she never told me anything. Forty years. . . Even now I'm not sure that I want to, or can, really talk to her about it. . . I don't know anything, not their names or what happened to them. She never mentions them at all. . .'

As mentioned, the emotional encounter with the children who perished in the Holocaust is perhaps the most difficult for the survivor parent and the most fraught with emotion. The parent is trapped between his inability to truly mourn and the chronic mourning from which he cannot free himself. The 'memorial candle' is well aware of his unique position: a substitute for the dead in general and for the dead children in particular. He senses the shadow of his predecessors and absorbs from his parents the burden of the emotional load.

Where could her mother find the strength to become pregnant again? With her, the third daughter. How she had deceived her! She said to her at every birthday: 'You are the eldest, you are my only one,' when actually she was a substitute for the earlier ones. Why didn't she tell me, 'You're the only one I have left. I gave birth to you so that I should not, God forbid, forget the earlier ones'?

(Semel 1985, p. 48)

And in another part of the book:

> People try to tear the threads connecting them with a previous
> life history they didn't choose, with a burden they didn't want
> to bear, but they can't do it.
>   The hidden thread was woven into her. Now she knew, her
> mother's first children were also gathered into her. . .
>
> (p. 56)

The 'memorial candle' senses that the shadows of the dead children are standing behind him, and he does not have the natural
right to demand and receive the devotion that every child expects
from his parents. '"I didn't take anything from you that didn't
belong to me – I asked permission." She is always wavering, as if the
shadow of a multitude of earlier children were lingering behind
her' (Semel, 1985, p. 36). But the awareness of this is generally
achieved only when the 'memorial candle' has grown up, after he
has experienced the years of his childhood and youth without
feeling that he has this natural right. The loss of his children is an
open wound in the soul of the survivor parent, and he transmits
the burden of this pain to the 'memorial candle', who cannot rid
himself of it. Therapy enables the 'memorial candle' to become
aware of his heavy burden and thus to deal with it.

The therapy process

Just as survivor parents close up before their children, so the
children are unable to speak about their feelings or express them
openly in some other way. Their reticence stands out at the beginning of therapy (whether individual or group); during many
sessions they are silent for long periods of time and take an
extremely passive stand. Their silence is generally broken only at
the initiative of the therapists or other members of the group, who
turn to them with questions. In the first stage they consistently
refrain from beginning a dialogue, not to speak of initiating an
interaction that might lead to exposure. Their facial expressions
and bodily postures express frozenness and impenetrability. The
group matrix is saturated with tension, hostility and suspicion. In
general, their few remarks to the therapists express the expectation that the therapists will accept the full responsibility for what
takes place in the group.

But these are only external behavioural expressions. One may ask how the children of survivors feel in the group at this stage. A common expression of theirs at the beginning of therapy contains an appropriate answer to this question: 'I feel as though I am made of glass,' meaning: 'Don't handle me too roughly because I might shatter.' The unfamiliar setting – the group members and the therapists – arouses great anxiety in all patients, but with the children of survivors the degree of anxiety is extreme and sometimes goes as far as apathy and paralysis. Their few utterances make massive and almost compulsive use of defence mechanisms such as denial, rationalization, isolation and projective identification, which eventually lead to emotional dissociation.

Another characteristic of the first group therapy sessions of the children of survivors is the discussion of the topic of death. These people tell many stories about various sorts of accidents and about funeral and memorial services they attended. Death arises immediately at the beginning of therapy, and this stands in contradiction to their need for denial and their inability and unwillingness to discuss this stage in their parents' traumatic past; at most they mention the subject as a mere biographical fact of no particular importance, and with total lack of feeling.

At one therapy session the conversation was opened by Zvia, about thirty-five, married and the mother of two daughters, herself the daughter of a survivor mother. She related that she had arrived straight from the cemetery, from the funeral of a friend. When she had exhausted this topic she began speaking about a cousin who had been killed in the Yom Kippur War.

In another group, in which most of the participants were psychologists and the children of survivors, the first session began with an extended silence, which was broken by the dramatic announcement of one of the participants (the daughter of two survivor parents), who seemed very pale and tense, that she would have to leave the session before the end because she had to hurry to the funeral of a work associate.

These two examples, like many others not reported here, show us that the first topic raised for discussion at the first sessions of the children of survivors is death, even though, as mentioned, at this stage the topic of the Holocaust is not yet touched upon.

In the first stage of therapy the group members are very confused and they often mix up the levels of internal and external feelings, reality and fantasy, and past and present. Perhaps raising the topic of death serves as a defence against coping with the anxieties arising at the beginning of therapy.

The atmosphere in the group and the interaction among the members are characterized by an inability to truly express oneself or to truly listen to one another. The survivors' children project onto the group the frozen atmosphere and the difficulties of communication dominating their families. From the first session the group interaction becomes a matrix of fragmented attempts at communication – some conscious, but most unconscious – in which each member transfers to and projects upon the group the images of his dead family members or internalized parts of his ego (Foulkes 1984; Bion 1961). Gradually the group becomes a matrix representing both the nuclear family of the survivors at present and the extended family, many of whom have perished and exist in the family's consciousness as the blurred images of dead people or ghosts.

'In our house there is no free flow,' said one group member, the daughter of survivor parents. 'When we all sit together, each of us is immersed within himself, and if we do talk, each of us speaks on a different plane.'

Another daughter of survivors added:

'I feel as though everything is buried deep inside me, and so it is difficult for me to express myself. This is part of my upbringing, part of the fixed vocabulary in our family, which does not include expressions like "I love," "I'm angry," or "I'm afraid." We never translated our feelings into words.'

Only after many months of group therapy can the survivors' children begin to share their hidden feelings with one another – the death images that have been concealed in their hearts for years as a secret they do not dare and are not able to share with anyone else, especially not their parents or siblings. And yet, as paradoxical as it may seem, the first topic with which the group members manage to communicate with one another is precisely the topic of identification with death.

The following took place at a group session in which most of the members were the 'memorial candles' of their families. Death was the principal topic of communication among the members.

After a heavy silence lasting for fifteen minutes, Arye began to speak in a whisper:

'You know, I thought a lot this week about how I got to the group. Last week, when I was still on reserve duty in the south, I had to wait a long time to hitch a ride, and no car would stop for me. When I had begun to despair and to think that I would not manage to get to the group on time, suddenly a funerary van came by. Without any hesitation I waved to it and when it stopped I got in at the back.'

Arye stopped talking and I asked him how he had felt there, in the funerary van. 'Quite strange,' he answered, 'as I was riding for hours and hours in this black car of the dead. But you know, I felt really good, simply comfortable. I was sitting there quite depressed and sad, as that's what I've been feeling recently in general, but I also had this kind of quiet. It seemed like my natural place.'

Therapist: 'You are actually saying that the ride in the funerary van fitted your inner feelings.'

Hava: 'You know, I thought of that. On the one hand it's quite strange that you rode in a funerary van. Most people would consider it quite frightening to sit there, in the place where the dead lie. But on the other hand I really understood you, since I've recently been feeling that I'm the memorial candle of my whole family. . . When I visited my uncle's grave last week, I related to him as if he were alive. I asked him, "How are you doing there inside? How is it to rest there, far from this world? How is it to look at living people running around and doing things all the time – and to be far away?" I live among the dead rather than among the living. I can sit comfortably next to my uncle's grave. With the living I'm really afraid. I always see everything as black. I don't feel that I'm really alive, and I actually don't get along very well with the people around me. Part of me wants to live, but another part doesn't.'

Therapist: 'I am reminded that last week you said that you feel calm only when you're immersed in nature. In the cemetery, among the dead, you feel comfortable. You're describing some kind of death feeling you have that you're comfortable with, just as Arye felt comfortable in the funerary van.'

Hava: 'I feel comfortable among the dead. They don't demand anything of me. I don't have to be really involved. I remember that as a child I would lie in bed for hours and I wouldn't be able to fall asleep, and I would actually see every empty space in the room and in the entire house as filled with images of ghosts and skeletons. I didn't understand what they were, but it didn't bother me. I wasn't really afraid of them, since I would hear my parents shouting and fighting in the next room, and this frightened me more. Actually, everything living is bad. I laugh on the outside, but inside I cry most of the time.'

Baruch: 'As a child I too always saw and imagined all sorts of images that seemed to me like ghosts without definite faces. Sometimes, when I was very lonely, I felt that they were my only friends. And now I ask myself how you feel here with us, what we are here – are we alive or dead? I, for instance, have been feeling very dead lately.'

Therapist: 'At today's session, as in all the last few sessions, there's been a heavy feeling here. It seems to me that this unpleasant feeling is paradoxically also protective in some way.'

Menahem: 'I've been feeling lately that everything is buried deep inside me. I've often told myself that I'm living in my own burial cave. It's very quiet there, you don't hear any noise, any humming sounds, and I lie there inside and I feel good, kind of quiet. . . Actually, it's also quite protected there. . . I remember that I had a strange dream this week. I'd like to tell it to you. I'm in Europe, in Switzerland, which is where I was born. There's something white and square there, like a wooden board, but it's not exactly wooden. There are some letters written on the board. These are the letters of my name, but mixed up, and in two parts, half straight and half upside down, as if there were two names, as if there were two Menahems. On the writing there's a bunch of flowers in red and blue. That's what my parents prepared for my birth and forgot to give me.'

Here Hanna interrupted and asked: 'What do you think this white thing is? The board reminds me of a grave, or a monument, like my uncle's.'

Menahem: 'Yes, it reminds me a little of a monument. It reminds me of the sensation of white cold that I feel when I'm lying in my tomb. I remember that here, in the group, I once spoke about the fact that I felt such a sensation of cold. But then it was very unpleasant.'

Therapist: 'Menahem, what exactly happened with your name in the dream? Something wasn't very clear – the name was divided in two with one half upside down. Perhaps the cutting of your name reminds you of what you've been experiencing lately, when we worked together on many topics: part of your name and identity is already clear while another part is still misty or upside down.'

Menahem: 'Yes, I think that maybe later I'll be able to change what they prepared for me – to fix my name. . .'

Hanna: 'It's interesting that I, for instance, have recently noticed that many of the things I spend time on are connected with death. I don't miss any memorial service or monument un- veiling or funeral or attendance at all sorts of accidents, both in the kibbutz and among my friends in town. I'm always very emotional at these events and very often I also cry. In other situations this doesn't happen to me so easily. Perhaps these are the only places where I can really feel anything.'

Yoram: 'It seems to me that my wife reacts differently from me in all sorts of situations of separation and death. My attitude is different. I don't know exactly why. When we were touring abroad and we sometimes came to a cemetery, I felt that I wanted to go in and look around. It interested me. I would go in there as if it were nothing. For me the dead are part of life, and to go into a cemetery isn't anything special, while my wife was always afraid and it was very hard for her. Each time she was somewhat upset and trembling. But I – nothing. I've also noticed that I've been dreaming recently about my father and my first wife, and they both appear in the dreams as completely alive, and it's not at all clear that they've died.'

Therapist: 'Perhaps this is saying that part of you has actually not come to terms with their death, as perhaps you didn't have the chance, or you couldn't allow yourself the chance, to really mourn them, giving yourself completely to the pain and grief involved in separation.'

Yoram: 'Yes. No. I don't know exactly. It seems that something like that happened. Even when I remember my father's death – I was with him in the hospital room when he died – I remember that the only feeling I had was one of relief. I was relieved that his suffering was over. I didn't feel particularly sad, and I didn't cry at all. I'm one who doesn't cry. I can't even remember the last time I cried.'

'And what happened when your wife died?' burst out Hava.

Yoram: 'Even then the only thing I was concerned with was to continue to exist with the baby that was left with me. How to manage and what to do. Even then I didn't cry at all.'

Hava: 'It's strange, I'm like you, always in cemeteries, but I find myself crying a lot. Just like that, about all sorts of things. Not about the death of someone in particular, a relative of mine who died. Besides the uncle I told you about, I haven't yet encountered death close up. And you, when your father and your wife both died on you, you never cry.'

Hava was silent, thinking, and after a while she continued: 'But perhaps it's not so strange. I've never seen my parents actually crying either, and so many relatives of theirs have died. And you too were born there, right after the war.'

Yoram: 'Yes, there in Poland, in Warsaw, on every other street there's a sign: "Here such a number of people were killed" or "Here such a number of guerrillas were shot to death" – wherever you look everything is full of death. We played there as children in the middle of this death. It was an ordinary and natural part of life.'

Baruch: 'It's strange, I too dream about death, funerals, again and again, yet I remember that when I was a child I was very much afraid to see a real dead person or to come close to one, not like you, that it doesn't do anything to you.'

It's difficult not to be impressed by the centrality of the topic of death in the contributions of all the participants in the session. Indeed, death appears again and again in the world of the survivors' children. They are attracted to places and events with the odour of death – cemeteries, the Yad Vashem memorial, funerals, memorial services, and even the funerary van. They don't consider their presence at these places and events as something extraordinary; they feel comfortable, calm and secure there, while life arouses avoidance and anxiety in them.

The 'memorial candles' are thus living in a double reality – in the present, as young adults building their lives and their families, and in the past of their parents. In essence, a large and important part of their emotional world is in the past, when death was the central axis of life. However, the identification with their parents takes place in a misty sphere in which feelings of guilt and death are mixed together in their consciousness, as they are in their parents' consciousness. Under the layer of attraction to death there are guilt feelings, and it is these feelings that continue to disturb both the parents and the children and do not leave any room for even a tiny bit of pleasure or joy (Epstein 1979).

The emotional and instinctual world of many 'memorial candles' is repressed and depressed. Life is frightening and threatening, like the little bird in Ariela's dream, and it is better to avoid all contact with it. Death, in contrast, is a calming presence inducing a sense of security. That is, the psychic closing-off of the Holocaust victims, which served as the principal psychological defence for many of them, eventually led to a tendency to apathy, depression and surrender to feelings of despair, or, alternatively, to hyperactivity due to restlessness; it also compelled the survivors to distance themselves emotionally from people in general and from their relatives in particular. The sons and daughters of the survivors were exposed throughout their childhood to these moods of their parents, and they absorbed and assimilated the principal emotional message the parents transmitted to them: always beware of any emotional outburst, as it holds the danger of death. The chronic ambivalence in the psyches of the survivors' children has its source in this message, which led them to a 'redemptive' psychic closing-off – due to their need to identify with their parents and their lost families and to become 'memorial candles', as was expected of them.

Nahum, the 'memorial candle' of his family, described a dream in which these characteristics appeared:

'There's a funeral. A long line of people progressing slowly toward the grave. At first I'm at the end of the line, but suddenly I find myself in the first row, right next to the open grave. I'm not sure who exactly has died but it's a little boy. The scene shifts and now I'm in a cold cellar with many doors. I'm very cold and I'm scared. I want to go out and I try the doors one after the other. I stop next to one of them, and there, behind the door, I know somehow that that's where they wash the dead. I hear a voice calling me. I open the door a little and I see a man with a beard holding a dead boy and washing him. "Come help me," he says to me and looks at me strangely. Blood is dripping from the child. This frightens me, but I have to stay and help him. I think he looks somewhat like my father.'

The son Nahum assists his father, the 'undertaker', in washing the dead. The allegory in the dream is clear: the son must share his father's mourning, with which he was not helped 'there'. But it's not so simple. Hanna wanted very much for her father 'to be able finally to cry and to tell and to talk'; but when she and her father arrived at the memorial – a substitute for a real grave and monument – her heart was frozen and all her feelings were closed off. Neither she nor her father are capable of beginning to truly mourn, as Hanna colludes with her father's denial of grief and mourning. The attempt to be liberated from death is exhausted in the murmuring of the family names, which are almost anonymous for her. Only after extensive therapy is Hanna able to return to that scene and perceive its full significance.

The same is true of Nahum. He too, in the task of assistant to the undertaker, comes and goes in cemeteries as if they were his private property. His task is to assist in the burial of the dead in the ground, to say *kaddish*[1] and to help the family at the beginning of its separation from a dear one. As a 'memorial candle' Nahum had indeed unconsciously taken on this difficult task, but he cannot respond to his emotional parts. He is unable to cry, to hurt and to share the mourning process with his father, and he actually did not succeed – as was the case with many other 'memorial candles' as well – in performing his task properly. That is, this situation leads to ambivalence, to a conflict between the compulsive involvement with death, on the one hand, and the inability to cope with it emotionally, on the other.

To demonstrate the changes occurring in the personalities of the survivors' children during the course of therapy, I will cite some passages from what Hava said at one therapy session. At this session I made use of the technique of directed fantasy, and by this means Hava directly confronted the representations of dead objects in her inner world, which was nothing but a projection of the inner world of her mother, who had been left alone, the sole survivor of her entire family, at the age of nine.

Hava: 'I see a figure. I'm not sure if it's my mother or myself. Two voices are roaming around my head. . .' Hava burst into silent tears, but continued talking: 'One voice tells me, "You're not allowed to live," and the other voice says, "No, no, I want to live." And I can't manage to combine them. I shout, "I want to live. I don't want to live among the dead. I don't belong there. It's hard for me." Now finally the other voice is quiet.'

Therapist: 'Who is the other voice? Who is the other figure? Can you identify it?'

Hava: 'The figure says to me, "How can you live in this ruin?" I see her family, my mother's family, the grandmothers and the sisters, and they tell her, "You're not allowed to live."'

Therapist: 'Is it to you or to your mother that they say this?'

Hava: 'I don't know, perhaps they're actually saying it to me and not to her.'

Therapist: 'You are undoubtedly confusing yourself and your mother. Perhaps you feel that it is even more forbidden for you to live than it is for your mother.'

Hava: 'I see all the family figures. Two pictures: in one my father, mother and brothers, and in the second my mother and her whole family. I see two things that are actually one. I combined the voices of the dead with my living family, and I am on the other side, apart from them, and I don't want to be with them.'

Therapist: 'Actually, all the years, your whole life, you've carried all their pain inside you.'

Hava: 'But now I feel that I'm coming closer to the voices of the dead, or joining their voices, but at the same time I'm separating from my family and looking at them from the outside.'

Therapist: 'And what do you see when you look that way at your family?'

Hava: 'They seem to me like wax figures. They seem to be alive but they aren't.'

Therapist: 'Let's try to make some order here. It's not clear who's dead here and who's alive. You are with the dead, who actually, before they died, were very much alive, and you're looking at the living people who are emotionally dead.'

Hava: 'Yes, I'm still staring with my mouth open and asking myself where I am.'

Therapist: 'Actually, on the one hand there are the dead – the aunts, the grandmothers, your mother's sisters and parents, who remained in her heart as if they were still alive – and on the other hand are the living – your father, your mother and your brothers, who are emotionally dead – and you have to choose between them or join them together.'

Hava sat all cramped up and caressed herself gently. 'It's very cold here,' she murmured. 'It's like a scary movie. It's crazy, I can't stop looking, I shout, it's horrible, but I can't stop.'

Therapist: 'There's something in you that apparently wants to go on. It's attracted to death and is still unable to cut itself off and separate itself from there.'

Hava: 'I want to turn my head and go.'

Therapist: 'Now that you've looked at the dead, and you've really met them, you don't have to keep on looking at all the horrors, all these scary things, you can stop!'

Hava: 'I'm dressed in black, everything around me is black. I turn my body and my head.' Hava looked at the floor and started crying again. 'I don't know what to do, I don't know what to do. . . Everything around me is black. I don't know what will be. I just keep crying. Walking around seems attractive to me, but I don't want to do it. I don't want. I'll go on.'

Therapist: 'You know, you can tell them you're leaving them, separating, going away from them.'

Hava said in a very weak and hesitant voice: 'I'm going away from them, I'm going away from them, I'm going away from them.' Her voice became stronger. 'I can't do anything. I go around with the pain. I just glanced back and suddenly I heard a voice telling me, "Go, it will be all right."' She looked up from the floor and a smile broke out on her face.

Therapist: 'Who smiled at you? And why are you smiling?'

Hava: 'Everyone is smiling. They want me to go.'

Therapist: 'Do you believe that they are really happy and are giving you permission to go?'

Hava: 'Yes, they're laughing with me now, and not at me. It will be easier for me to start going.'

In the discussion reported here we see clearly two levels in Hava's life: the levels of the present and of the past, of life and of death. The dead objects appear alive in her psyche as well as in her mother's. It is easy to distinguish the transposition mentioned above, which leads Hava to confuse herself with her mother. Other sessions revealed a two-fold confusion within Hava's identity. Not only did she confuse herself with her mother, but various figures from her mother's family were also entangled within her, including her grandmother and her aunts. Each of these figures appears clearly, even though they are not completely separate from one another.

In an advanced stage of therapy Hava was able to begin to identify, one by one, each of the figures internalized in her personality, and to play all the roles in the dramas in her mother's and father's lives.

The complex synthesis, full of contradictions, that was formed in Hava's ego is composed, as mentioned, of two levels, the

Holocaust of her parents, especially her mother, and present reality, which is represented by the nuclear family in which Hava is actually living. Through the use of directed fantasy Hava confronted for the first time the emotional death hidden in her parents' inner existence.

In the last part of the session one can discern the feeling of relief and liberation that Hava began to sense. This feeling stems from her ability to encounter, within her complex inner world, contents and figures relating to death and representations of dead objects. The encounter and dialogue between the various voices, between the living and dead in both families (hers and her mother's), which represent different parts of her identity, open the door to a new and more real integration within Hava's identity.

And in fact, after this session Hava really 'took off'. Of course there were many setbacks, but this was the beginning of a new path after a long and difficult period which she went through in silence and psychic closing-off.

NOTE

1. A prayer for the dead, usually said by a relation of the deceased – preferably the son – at the burial.

Chapter 5

The aggressor and the victim

Healthy Nazis dressed in uniforms, with polished boots and weapons, helmets on their heads; opposite them, skeletal barefoot Jews in striped clothing, piles and piles of formless bodies; controlling aggressors on the one hand and controlled victims on the other – this is the picture that is generally formed in our imagination when we think about the Holocaust.

In the extermination camps in Europe Jung's (1946, 1952) theory about the aggressor–victim archetype was actualized in terrifying proportions that Western culture, and perhaps even the entire world, had never known before. The archetype, says Jung, finds its expression in everyday images, symbols and behaviour patterns. In our everyday life the two facets of the aggressor–victim archetype exhibit characteristic behaviour patterns: the aggressor is strong, controlling and violent, while the victim is weak, subservient and vulnerable.

However, aggressor and victim are nothing but the double face of one archetype existing in a single person. The active aspect of the personality wears the mask of the aggressor, while the passive aspect wears the mask of the persecuted victim. In each of us there is thus both persecutor and victim, and both together are nothing but the two opposing facets of the same archetype. That is, if one sees the archetype as an intrapsychic phenomenon, then the aggressor is simultaneously also the victim, and vice versa. Jung says that in psychotic states the collective unconscious populates conscious thought with archetypal figures. Was the Holocaust such a state, not in the psyche of an individual but in that of an entire society? According to Jung, archetypal images influence all human behaviour, and so every antisemitic Gentile carries within himself 'his own' image of the Jew, which embodies everything that is intolerable to him in his own personality (Dreyfus 1984).

The psychic process beginning with the projection of the image of the 'inner Jew' onto the actual Jew eventually leads to the formation of a stereotype including all the despicable character traits in the image. From here it is only a short way to what we call 'prejudices'. Shoham (1985) and many other scholars are convinced that it was the outbreak of prejudices against the Jews at the beginning of the Nazi regime that turned the Jews into the scapegoats of the German people during the entire time that the Nazis were in power in Germany. Through the projection of all 'evil' onto the image of the 'inner Jew', the actual Jew was turned into an outstanding object of antisemitic hatred. The antisemite cannot deal with the image of the 'inner Jew' in his psyche and accept it as a part of himself, and so he feels hatred for the actual Jew outside himself, and sometimes he goes and kills him.

According to Shoham, many Nazis simply and truly believed that the 'Elders of Zion' had taken control of the world, and it was they who had brought upon Germany the knockout blow at the end of World War I. The SS General von dem Bach Zalewski, for example, attested at the Nuremburg trials that it was only when he saw helpless Jews being slaughtered en masse, without anyone running to save them, that he stopped believing in the omnipotence of the Elders of Zion. The prejudice gave birth to the scapegoat.

On the other hand, due to a long history of suffering, the Jew has been caught for centuries in the emotional conceptual system of the 'eternal victim'. The Jew is Isaac who was led like a lamb to be sacrificed, and like him he identifies with the victim he represents. Conscious identification with the victim is a vital component of the archetype of sacrifice, since there cannot be a victim if an aggressor for his victimization cannot be found. This identification generally also leads to cooperation. There are those who believe that during the Holocaust there was often unconscious cooperation between the victim and the aggressor, and that the Jews' resistance to the slaughter could have been greater, and the Nazis' goal more difficult to carry out, if the Jews had not had this shared subconscious tendency to self-sacrifice. The Jews' disposition to become victims strengthened, in their opinion, their national uniqueness and moral force. The motif of 'sanctifying God's name' – sacrificing one's life so as not to relinquish one's moral principles – runs like a thread through human culture in general and Jewish culture in particular, as, for example, in the story of the binding of Isaac, the crucifixion of Jesus, and the death of Janos Korczak in the Holocaust.

But not everyone agrees with the view that the Jews have a subconscious tendency to self-sacrifice. In a totally different context Rotenberg (1987) gives the story of the binding of Isaac a completely opposite interpretation to that of Shoham (1985). Shoham considers this story a manifestation of the myth of the intergenerational life-and-death struggle whose essence is the preparation of the sacrifice, while he considers Isaac's rescue an addition of marginal significance. Rotenberg, in contrast, considers the miraculous rescue to be of essential importance. In his view, the appearance of the ram and the nullification of the sacrifice created a total transformation of the situation: the victim was rescued and the two generations stood side by side. The antithetical relation between the generations was cancelled and was replaced by a relationship of dialogue between them. The dialogue between parents and children, thanks to which the children become the continuers of their parents' ways, is, in Rotenberg's view, the unique characteristic of the relationship between the generations in the Jewish world-view. This interpretation negates the inference from Shoham's interpretation concerning the Jews' subconscious tendency to self-sacrifice.

But even if we accept the image of the 'eternal victim' in the Jew's soul, we must not ignore the fact that each rule always includes its opposite (as it appears in the Jungian archetype). This implies that inherent in the Jew's psyche is also the feeling of the aggressive warrior, filled with enmity and battle-lust. He cathexes this feeling onto his alter ego, the 'Gentile' in his heart. But the Jew is not always conscious of the existence of this alter ego in his psyche, and if we are unconscious of the aggressive drives within ourselves, one day they may be projected onto others, or perhaps even onto ourselves, and we will eventually be controlled by them (Dreyfus 1984).

The victims and the fighters

Danieli (1980) divides the families of the survivors into four main categories – the 'fighters', 'those who made it', the 'victims' and the 'numb' families (in the sense of psychic closing-off) –

according to the experiences of the survivors during the Holocaust. In her research she found that the survivors' experience during the Holocaust affected the behaviour patterns they adopted afterwards. The fighters and the successful ones had active experiences during World War II – whether fighting with the partisans in the forests or with the rebels in the ghettos, or participating in escapes or the smuggling and rescue of others, or taking a stand of responsibility in the ghettos and concentration camps. In contrast, the victims and the closed-off ones had passive experiences at this time – in ghettos, in hiding-places, and in forced-labour or extermination camps.

The atmosphere pervading the families of the victims is characterized by depression, anxiety and worry (Epstein 1979; Zwerling 1982). The members of the family often cling to one another symbiotically, while they relate to their nearby surroundings, not to speak of their more distant surroundings, with distrust, suspicion and fear.

Sara, the daughter of two survivor parents who established a typical 'victim' family, was born and grew up on a kibbutz. She described the atmosphere within her family thus:

'There was always this really obsessive need to be in my parents' room all day. Even in high school, when the others rebelled and quarrelled with their parents, I could never do this. I had the need to share everything with my mother and to tell her everything that happened to me. My mother knew all my friends as if she were my best friend, although sometimes I wonder how real the closeness between us really was. Our house – that is, my parents' room – was the only stable thing I could rely on. The only thing that was secure. In contrast to the bad feeling outside, in the kibbutz and actually everywhere, with my parents I felt protected and secure. Sometimes I became close to children of my own age on the kibbutz, but it was always a passing thing, like comets that disappear. When I would fight with the other children, or when I felt bad, I would sit alone afterwards for hours in my mother's room. Then I would take my mother with me to fix things outside. I was always false, like my mother. Outwardly always nice to everyone, 'because maybe you'll need them', but keeping one's true feelings inside. My mother – it's very important for her that everything should be private – just us, the family – and that no one else should have any foothold, not even my aunts and uncles who live outside the kibbutz. We have no real relationship with them, only something formal.'

Sara's description accords with the findings of H. Klein (1971), who studied families of survivors in kibbutzim in Israel. Klein mentions the intense feelings of the survivors' children towards their parents, as expressed in their close link to their home. His findings show that the children of survivors actually do visit and stay at their parents' homes more than the other children.

Zwerling's (1982) research on survivors' children in the United States supports the assumptions of his colleagues (H. Klein 1971; Lipkowitz 1973; Sigal 1973). He also notes that after they have left their parents' home the survivors' children visit their parents more often and express more homesickness than members of a control group. He also found that the survivors' children feel obligated to protect their families, especially their mothers, from illness or emotional difficulties, to a much greater extent than the members of the control group.

Nira, about thirty years old, an only child in a 'victim' family, related that until the present time she had spent most of her vacations with her parents alone, and whenever she goes through any sort of difficult experience, whether physical or psychological, she finds shelter in her parents' home. Her parents still go with her when she goes to the doctor. When she feels bad she cannot share her pain with anyone close to her – friends or colleagues – she always rushes to her mother and father, as she did in her childhood.

In the opinion of other psychologists, including Russel (1974), the parents in 'victim' families, especially the mothers, tend to feel exaggerated fears concerning their children and to overprotect them. The source of these fears is undoubtedly their memories of the Holocaust, which raised the pain threshold of the survivors, and their reactions are based on a catastrophic view of the future. Their fears of the physical harm that outside forces might bring upon their children cause the survivor parents to warn their children again and again about hidden dangers lying in wait for them, so to speak, outside of the home. The survivors try in every possible way to prevent their children from experiencing pain and suffering. In the end, their compulsive anxiety tends to change joyous occasions into times of grief and mourning.

Semel (1985) describes the difficulty of feeling and arranging a truly joyous occasion in a survivor family:

Mother contorts her face and a sneer is stretched on her lips. How do people dare to be happy? A family is a kind of hump attached to one's shoulders. Mother continues to carry the burden of her dead life almost with pleasure. She doles out her love like a charity donation in thin slices that she grinds to a powder.

(p. 36)

I have occasionally been present at the weddings of survivors' children who had been in therapy with me. I particularly remember David's wedding. He was about thirty-two years old, the son of two survivor parents in the 'victim' group. From the beginning there was an atmosphere of restrained joy among the many guests. When the mother of the groom entered and stood under the canopy beside the bride, it was impossible not to sense the sharp contrast: the bride dressed in white, and the mother of the groom dressed completely in black from head to toe; even the fancy lace kerchief on her head was black. Deep sadness was frozen on her face, as if she were saying to herself: 'How can I be happy when I know that they, all of them, were left there, and cannot participate in our joy?'

At the wedding of Zippora, who was also from a 'victim' family, the mother appeared in colourful holiday dress rather than in black, but she was very confused and restless, and throughout the wedding she circulated among the guests radiating anxiety and tension to her surroundings. Every so often she would go over to her daughter, and in an incoherent murmur mixing Polish, Yiddish, English and Hebrew she would scold her angrily and criticize her wedding dress, her hairdo, the guests and anything else that entered her mind. Her daughter answered her with restraint and attempted to calm her, but she wasn't free to speak to her guests and to be happy and excited on her wedding day. She considered it her duty to take care of her mother. Anxiety, anger, guilt and depression, mixed together with blurred memories, cancelled the joy.

Semel (1985) describes the preparations for Veronica and Uriah's wedding, where Uriah is the son of survivor parents. Veronica is sewing her wedding dress:

I went to the fabric shop and chose a thin white fabric. Perhaps it's the material that is used to make shrouds, in which one places the purified dead. . . Under the face-covering, that is, the bridal veil, I will hide. And I will not appear before the eyes of your father and mother, Uriah, as I don't want to discern the pain.

(p. 173)

Veronica absorbs the pain and sadness mixed with the joy of the wedding. Life and death are mixed together: Veronica sews her wedding dress out of fabric meant for shrouds.

Another characteristic of 'victim' families is their almost compulsive occupation with physical survival. Food especially occupies them intensely. Such phenomena as the hoarding of food and overfeeding children or putting pressure on them to eat excessive amounts of food are very common among these families. These phenomena are sometimes expressed among the children in a confused attitude to food or in various symptoms connected with food, such as compulsive overeating on the one hand and anorexia on the other.

Semel (1985) describes the anxiety and compulsivity surrounding food-hoarding and feeding in a survivor family:

> She stood stunned facing the sight of tins of food piled up one next to the other in exemplary order, sorted according to the food they contained, and reaching the top of the cupboard. And not only that. Among them were jammed little packets of sugar and tall bottles of oil, and bread in plastic bags one on top of the other, like a display in a scientific shop-window.
>
> 'Mother,' she whispered, daring to touch her sagging shoulder, 'are you preparing for a siege?'. . .
>
> 'Don't touch it, Naomi,' she said with estranged eyes, 'I've already told you there will be a famine.'. . .
>
> Then she saw that the fork in her mother's hand was like a little magic wand, which moved the food up the high walls, leaving in the middle an empty, concave opening, surrounded by a closed circle. Or she would answer her question: 'I've already eaten, just before you came,' and she would push her: 'Eat! Eat!', standing guard at her side, tense as a wire, until the plate was completely empty. Then she would look sadly at the necessary remains of the food, and once she pleaded: 'We must gather strength for the coming days.'

(pp. 117–18)

'I was very tense this week,' Mira related. 'It seems I have some anger inside. Once again I found myself eating and eating. Yesterday I remembered that in pictures of me as a child of four I look like an inflated balloon. When I went to nursery school at this age the children actually called me 'Balloon', and they would laugh and make fun of me. I was really fat. Mother fattened me more and more. . . For four years I stayed home with her. I don't remember that we did anything together, I would sit in a corner of the house in total passivity, not doing anything, only my mother would feed me once in a while.'

Another syndrome of 'victim' families is extreme anxiety about the safety of property and people – the fear lest they vanish. Sometimes this anxiety leads to compulsive behaviour with respect to the opening and closing of doors.

'The outer door of our house,' related Zvia, 'was always locked with several locks. When someone rang the doorbell, my father would first look for a long time through the peephole, and until he was completely sure who was behind the door he would not open it. Sometimes we had the feeling that our house was a kind of locked fortress, very secure but also suffocating. Inside the house, on the other hand, the doors were always left open. I don't remember what it's like to close a door. My parents slept in a bedroom with an open door, and so did I and my brother. When I went to the bathroom my mother would complain if I closed the door. Often she would come in there with me, even after I grew up. There were no boundaries and there was no privacy. At night, when I lay in bed and pretended to be asleep, my parents would come to check on me to see if I was still breathing; actually I also do this to my daughters now sometimes. I know it's crazy, but I can't control it, it's stronger than I.'

Semel (1985) also describes the closedness and insecurity in many survivor families:

Her father purposely chose to live on a mountain, where it's easy to disappear and easy to ignore things. She asked him, 'Why don't we live in a big house with an elevator? Where you can push the buttons, stop on all the storeys, and if an open door gapes out of the dimness, you can find out how the houses of strange people look?' Her father said, 'I despise those who walk down

below. Be careful of anything that infiltrates. However tightly
you close the shutters, there will still remain a malevolent ray.

(p. 106)

For the second generation of the survivors, and – as can be seen
from Ziva's story, for the third generation as well – a message of
total distrust of the other is transmitted, a message that one must
not rely on anyone outside the circle of the immediate family.
Danieli (1980) has an explanation for the desperate struggle of the
parents against the closing of doors within the home: in 'victim'
families the parents see their children's attempts at establishing
natural boundaries and partitions among themselves as a threat to
the family's unity and wholeness; to be separated from one
another means to disappear and to be lost for ever.

The studies of Russel (1974) and Trossman (1968) quote the
stories of survivors' children who relate that during their childhood their parents never encouraged them to be independent, to
stand up for their rights and to rebel in a healthy way, and never
respected their privacy. Whenever they expressed the slightest
degree of autonomy they were scolded, whether openly or covertly.
Their parents always saw this as a gesture of infidelity, of treachery
and abandonment.

Survivor parents in general, and those in the 'victim' category in
particular, tend to disparage feelings of happiness because of their
continuous anxiety. Security is the only goal that has any meaning
and that must be striven for; happiness, aspirations for self-
expression and creativity are nothing but valueless luxuries.

Miriam described the relationships prevailing in her home:

'She [the mother] was like a bird sitting and protecting her fledg-
lings and nothing else. When my brother had to go to the army
and he had a fight with his commander, my mother went to talk
to the commander. She was compelled to watch over us. When
it was my turn to be drafted she wrote letters to the army not to
send me far away from home.' After a short silence she continued: 'I should have been angry but I couldn't be. How could
I? What right did I have to be angry with her after everything she
went through? After all, she's alive, she functions, she cares.
Every trip involved terrible worry. Whenever I went to the beach
– a thousand worries. Even as a little girl I understood that my
mother worries, that she's allowed to worry. Now I can connect
her fear that we would disappear with the disappearance of her

whole family, just as her mother disappeared, when they took her and put her on the truck, and she ran and pleaded with the Germans to substitute her for her mother. But they didn't agree and she never saw her again. . .' Miriam began to sob. 'This is the first time I can connect her worrying with the disappearance of her family. I am beginning to sense the pain she felt. I wonder how, after all she went through, she could continue to live, to establish a family, as if nothing had happened. I want to get angry and then the thought immediately arises: "How is she to blame?" I have to continue defending her even now, here, I feel this. This is actually what I have always done, in all sorts of ways, as long as I can remember: My mother suffered enough in life. This is what's always in my head. Silently, but in my head, only in my head, only in my head, without entering into the feelings themselves. . . Today I allowed myself a little bit, and it hurts.'

Miriam's anger brings us to the reactions of the survivors' children to the atmosphere of worry pervading their parents' home. H. Klein (1971) describes at length the conflicts generated in the children's psyches in relation to their parents and their tendency to deny these conflicts as far as they can. After two years of therapy Miriam succeeded in confronting these difficult conflicts head on, but immediately guilt feelings were aroused in her which stood in the way of the feelings demanding an outlet. And indeed, whenever the survivors' children feel the least bit of aggression toward their parents, this immediately arouses harsh guilt feelings within them (Sigal et al. 1973).

Russel (1974) confirms the findings of Sigal et al., showing that although some children of survivors sometimes try to rebel, their guilt feelings generally prevent them from going very far and their rebellion is nipped in the bud.

Her father never touches her, he never even pats her head. She finds his angry eyes staring at her. He is enraged because she has taken the place of the other one. At night she dreams how she will rebel against him, but by day she is covered with shame.

(Semel 1985, p. 109)

Coping with feelings of aggression and rage was one of the most difficult problems of the 'victims' at the time of the Holocaust. Any expression of anger against the Nazis was almost impossible and always involved a reaction that threatened one's very life. Even the feeling of anger alone constituted too great a threat, as it endangered what was left of the victims' psychic balance, which had already been undermined almost to its foundations. The victims therefore had no choice but to repress every speck of rage and aggression. Even after the Holocaust, however, they did not find the appropriate occasions for unloading the burden of anger that had been accumulated over the years. A deep conflict was thus necessarily generated in their psyches, distorting their attitude towards their aggressiveness. This conflict was expressed both in their inability to express their feelings of anger and aggression in a clear and balanced way in their daily life, and in sudden outbursts of uncontrollable rage at their children, using language and images stemming from the Holocaust, where the children's 'sin' was only normal childish behaviour: 'You are acting like Hitler,' 'You are worse than the Nazis,' 'Eichmann is better than you' – these are the sentences that were often heard in the families of survivors, especially of the 'victim' and the 'closed-off' groups.

On rare occasions the outburst of anger went beyond verbal violence and reached physical violence. Arye described a violent outburst of his father's:

'When I was about six years old they took me to school for the first time. My father went with me. All the children and teachers were standing in the yard until it was time to go into the classrooms. Then I was afraid, I didn't want to go up to the classroom and I broke out crying. Father became terribly angry. He screamed at me to stop crying immediately. In general Father couldn't bear crying. When I didn't stop, he took off his belt and started whipping me with the belt in the middle of the yard, in front of everyone.'

And Hava: 'My mother used to hit me for every little thing from the earliest age – actually, as far back as I can remember. Every time she touched me it was to hit me. I don't remember any hugs, any kisses, only being hit. I was happy to go to nursery school at the earliest age – at least there they didn't hit me.'

I don't know how frequent these violent outbursts of the survivor parents were, but they certainly contrasted sharply with the parents's extreme concern for their children and their 'wrapping them in cotton wool'. Both Arye and Haya were the 'memorial candles' in their families, and it was to them that the overflowing emotional burdens were transmitted – hopes and concern on the one hand, and disappointment and anger on the other.

As if to complicate the children's psyches even further, often after these harsh outbursts the parents were attacked by intense feelings of guilt and remorse. Many psychologists believe that the parents' unresolved conflict with their aggression caused their children severe difficulty in identifying with them and treating them as authoritative figures. And as if this were not enough, since the parents have difficulty on the one hand in directing their latent aggression towards constructive purposes, and on the other hand in setting clear boundaries between themselves and their children, the children also have difficulty in feeling and expressing anger, and are almost incapable of acting authoritatively and decisively.

This inability or unwillingness of the survivors and their children to stand up for themselves often influences their choice of career. They tend to avoid positions requiring initiative or authority, or positions with elements of competition or struggle. Unexpectedly, it seems that this avoidance does not stem merely from lack of self-confidence, but primarily from the fear that they might go beyond what is permissible and make excessive use of their authority, or that they might act inappropriately in a situation of competition; the victim is afraid of becoming the aggressor. This avoidance is especially frequent among the survivors themselves, but it also appears in the second generation. One must recall that during the Holocaust the boundaries between the permitted and the forbidden were blurred, or even destroyed, and the survivors never set clear limits for their children – the limits that give children their sense of security.

There is another factor affecting the choice of occupation in the families of the victims. Hazan (1977) shows that survivors who identify themselves as victim generally tend to choose jobs that are considered inferior and involve physical labour, even when they are not at all suited to their intellectual abilities or their socio-economic status, and do not give them any sort of satisfaction. Moreover, any improvement in their work conditions or their social status often leads to severe psychological crises for the survivors, accompanied by depression (Niederland 1964). Perhaps the lowly work reminds them of their life in the forced-labour camps, a life they had grown accustomed to and whose replacement by another type of life arouses latent anxiety in them: they are still living by the motto of the camp prisoners, 'Never stand out!' On the other hand, it's also possible that the survivors' choice of lowly occupations involves a wish to atone for their 'sins', to allay the harsh guilt feelings that are still hidden in their hearts. It's also possible, of course, that both of these explanations are correct.

As mentioned, these syndromes were absorbed into the psyches of the victims' children. Only a few of them chose 'prestigious' occupations, as the honour they would receive might emphasize the gap between them and their parents and humiliate them in their own eyes. Even within the occupation they chose they generally 'keep a low profile' and are careful not to excel. 'Don't stand out,' the camp prisoners warned themselves, and their children continue to obey the survival commandment they inherited from their parents.

As we have seen, the children of many of the 'victim' families feel a high degree of identification with and empathy for their parents' pain and suffering. They are ultimately more sensitive both towards individuals and towards society in general. Their sense of justice with respect to individual and minority rights is especially strong; thus many of them choose occupations involving helping or protecting other people, such as social work, medicine or psychology. The children of the victims are thus able to take on challenges, but not on their own behalf.

The 'fighter' families

According to the present definition, 'fighters' are not only those who fought in the underground or in a partisan group, or those who succeeded in escaping from a camp, but also, and perhaps primarily, those who accepted responsibility for their fate and the fate of others in the ghettos and concentration camps. At the core of the identity of the 'fighters' and the 'successful ones' is their active conception of themselves, of others, and of society. This conception helped many people to survive the Holocaust, but it must not be forgotten that chance and luck played a large role in determining the fate of Jews in the Holocaust, and sometimes it was precisely the active attempts to escape and to fight that increased the danger of death.

For some of the survivors in this group the identity of 'fighter' serves as a cover-up for feelings of anxiety, helplessness, loss and humiliation. Therefore many 'fighters' have very little tolerance for situations and feelings that they see as expressions of weakness

– the very feelings upon which the identity of the 'victims' is based.

In contrast to the 'victim' families, the 'fighter' families are characterized by a very strong – sometimes almost compulsive – drive for doing, creating, and achieving. The 'fighters', like the other survivors, were uprooted from their families and surroundings, yet after the war many of them succeeded in studying and acquiring a profession providing honoured social status. Many of them invested the majority of their psychic resources in the struggle to realize their vocations, and some of them actually attained significant achievements in the academic world, in the business world, in government, in the army and in the arts. But there's a fly in the ointment: this active way of life does indeed function as a defence against depression for the 'fighters', but it cannot erase the terrors of the Holocaust from their psyche. Addiction to work and backbreaking pursuit of achievement have thus become for them, especially for the men, an intoxicating drug, a means of hypomanic defence, without which their defence system would collapse. But since a perfect defence is impossible, the cracks in their armour reveal severe physical symptoms that often imposed limitations on their ability to work. Niederland (1964) shows that 82% of the survivors who were addicted to work suffered from such symptoms. Hazan (1977) found that 10% of the 'workaholics' suffered breakdowns from time to time and were reduced to exhaustion.

As mentioned, the atmosphere in the 'fighter' families was totally different from that in the 'victim' families. Here hospitality and smiles were the rule. Everything had to be 'okay'. Everyone always had to be in a good mood. Depression, sadness and weakness, or any behaviour that might be interpreted as weakness, were considered intolerable and useless – and crying was especially intolerable. Crying was perceived as 'hysterical', and the 'fighter' parents were unable to accept it. When their children expressed their pain by crying, as all children do, they generally got reactions lacking all understanding or empathy, until they had no choice but to adapt to a life without crying. They internalized the overt and the covert message they received from their parents and they learned to cope with their feelings by themselves, generally through denial, repression and avoidance.

Ariela, the only child of two 'fighter' parents, described the atmosphere prevailing in her family:

'Everything was always okay. Both Father and Mother worked. They were both very active and ambitious. Father achieved a very important public position. Many people would come to him to ask for advice or support. But I really don't remember any expressions of feeling in our house. No one shouted, no one got angry, no one cried, we did not kiss or hug each other, everything was simply okay. I can't remember crying in front of my parents or at all. Even when we came home after my father's funeral, the first thing my mother said was, "The last thing I need is that you should start crying now." So obviously I didn't cry. She didn't cry, and neither did I.'

'In school I was always very active, always on committees, always responsible and organizing. When I was seven I was chosen to recite something at an Independence Day ceremony in front of the whole school. I remember that I felt very excited and afraid inside, but no one saw this. I didn't say anything to my mother or father, as they would not have understood. They took it for granted that I had to stand there on the platform, in front of everyone, and do what I had been asked in the best possible way. I realize now that I also took it for granted.'

'All those years I was always outstanding. In class I always had to be the best pupil. In the officers' course [in the army] I felt under pressure to reach first place, to be the outstanding cadet. At the university – a brilliant student, and now responsible public work. Again I'm in the limelight. I never let myself stop and examine what I am doing to see if it's really what I want, or to find out what I really feel about all sorts of choices I made all my life. As if my path was permanently fixed from the day I was born. There was always some sort of pressure driving me, or some sort of drive, that decided everything for me. But I'm not at all sure if this power is my own. I never felt that I really had the opportunity to choose or to consider different courses of action.'

This is thus the appointed path for the children of the 'fighters': the parents' high expectations and pressure to attain intellectual and social achievements, which are internalized in the children's psyches and do not allow them any opportunity for deliberation or doubt about the correctness of their path. Deviation from this path means not fulfilling the parents' expectations, which creates guilt feelings and a lack of self-esteem in the children.

In the 'fighter' families problems are intolerable, and they must therefore be solved as quickly and practically as possible. There is very little tolerance for deliberations, unsolved conflicts, or vague situations, as everyone must always have complete and absolute control over their lives, including the ability to foresee events that might cancel this control. Honour is the most important value: 'They won't humiliate me or step on me, no matter what.' Most of the 'fighter' families experience very little joy or happiness, or moments of calmly sitting together without doing anything; these are all superfluous and unwanted.

The 'fighter' parent's own image of himself – as the hero who saved himself and his friends from certain death – places him very far away from his children. The children don't always know what really happened 'there' and what exactly their father and mother did in order to be saved. Thus the figures of the parents and their experiences are perceived by the children as a kind of myth that cannot be compared in any way with ordinary daily experiences. The child of 'fighters' might want to be like his father and mother and somehow acquire their wonderful, almost superhuman ability, but he knows that he stands no chance: 'I would never have got through it. I would not have been able to stand it even for a month. And to save others besides?' I have often heard this utterance, which expresses the sense of inferiority and weakness that the children of survivors, especially of the 'fighters', feel when they compare themselves with their parents. According to Dor-Shav (1978), the second generation suffers from a lower ego strength than that of their parents, and some of them are more sensitive, dependent, defensive and delicate than their parents. Actually, this personality pattern is characteristic of all the survivors' children in the various groups listed, and it constitutes an insecure, anxious and nervous personality.

Apparently, but only apparently, these characteristics are less in evidence among the children of the 'fighters' than among the children of the 'victims'. On the outside the children of the 'fighters' are stronger and function better than those of the 'victims', they don't cry easily and they don't express weakness, depression, insecurity or fear. This is because the 'fighter' parents transmit a clear message to their children while they are still very young: 'We must be prepared,' they repeat over and over, 'another Holocaust won't catch us unprepared.' Often the children interpret this message as encouragement for expressions of aggression toward others (whoever is not like them) and for refusal to comply with external authority.

However, the feelings of weakness we found among the children of the 'victims' also exist beneath the surface among the children of the 'fighters' as well, as their strength is generally a defence mechanism they inherited from their parents. Only in a relatively late stage of therapy do they begin to allow their feelings to rise to the surface and to express them openly. (I will discuss this extensively later.) At any rate, one thing is certain: most of the children of 'fighters' are less afraid of expressing feelings of aggression than are children of 'victims'. Sometimes they even look for or create opportunities to express their aggression in everyday life, for instance in fights and violent quarrels; this drains away the aggression that has accumulated in their psyches within the family, but which they are unable to express directly towards their parents. This distinction between the children of 'victims' and of 'fighters' is expressed in Baruch's story.

Baruch is the son of a father who considers himself a victim, and who is seen that way to some extent by his son as well, and of a 'fighter' mother who struggled for her life during the war, who was saved and saved others as well. Baruch was thus raised by parents with contrasting identities, and his story shows that this contrast between his parents caused him a severe internal conflict and a rift in his identity.

Baruch: 'Yesterday I had a dream. In the dream my father is dead. I am walking along. I don't know if I am happy or sad. The whole time I have a feeling that says, "Great. Finally he went away. It's over." His existence bothers me. But something inside comes, rises, and right away I want to get rid of him. I am reminded about the war. My mother, you know, was only seventeen. She was very active. She dyed her hair blonde and anyway she looked sort of Aryan. She wasn't afraid. She went out, she did things, she organized things, she smuggled groups of Jews into Switzerland. Once, she told me, on one of her trips with a girlfriend who also passed for Aryan, they even dared to hitch a ride on a truck full of SS soldiers. They laughed and joked with them. She spoke German, so there wasn't any problem, and she wasn't afraid at all. In the end, just when she was transporting her parents with another group of Jews, some farmer reported them. They were caught, of course, and sent to Auschwitz. And from that time on she never saw them again. But she survived. She became, you realize, responsible for her parents' death. This is what haunts her – that's what I think, even though she never talks about it. She doesn't talk, she doesn't cry, nothing. She told me that the moment she got out of Auschwitz she immediately went to Switzerland, and the first thing she did there was to go to a plastic surgeon to have the number on her arm taken off. She was really one of the guys.'

'My father, on the other hand, didn't do anything. Not a thing. When he went back to the village he came from, and they told him that they had slaughtered all the Jews, including his entire family, he didn't react. When I was only eleven I asked him about this once, and he said indifferently, "What could I have done?" He is still always indifferent and apathetic and my mother is always active and I am torn between them. On the one hand I have a very special mission, that's what I sense from my mother. A kind of mission that you not only have to know about but also to actualize. But on the other hand the only thing my father says is, "The main thing is that you should make a living, you don't need much in life." And I'm torn between the two of them: half of me is my mother and half of me is my father. I start doing something, and the other half says, "Leave it." And then I leave and I don't do any more.'

When he stopped talking I asked him to tell me in more detail what his father had done during the war, and then he went on: 'They walked two and a half miles every day, back and forth to the munitions factory. There they ate a little more than in other workplaces. He was responsible for his team, that they should produce their quota every day. In the end there were some people who got together, and my father was one of them, and they performed some sabotage so the bombs and shells wouldn't explode. They accused him of intentional sabotage and whipped him severely.'

Therapist: 'That doesn't sound so passive. It seems that you still have some need to see him only the way he is with you. It's hard for you and you're still not willing to feel what your father really went through there.'

Baruch: 'Yes, that's true. Part of me wants, for instance, to go to Yad Vashem and the other part doesn't want to, it wants to run away. The two parts can't join together and I can't come to terms with either one of the parts. I'm afraid. I don't want to get into it. I know it will hurt so much that I won't be able to stand it. My father went through a lot of pain, but now he doesn't show any pain. And my mother doesn't show any pain either. Only the inner voice of each one of them separately screams inside me: "Be like me." I also have a responsibility towards them, that is, towards those who would see me hurting, and so when I get near anything very emotional I immediately close myself off. This makes me sad, you realize, all feelings have been making me sad recently.' Tears came into Baruch's eyes, and he continued, 'Now I can feel a little bit because I see that it matters to you so much, but I will close up again right away.'

The victim and the fighter in Baruch's psyche are trying to unite, but it hurts and it's not easy.

Let us return now to Jung's (1952) archetype theory and examine the victim type and the fighter type in the light of this theory. As mentioned, Jung considers the victim and the aggressor as opposites which are simultaneously two parts of one whole. The two sorts of survivors – victims and fighters – seem at first to be unbridgeable opposites. But, as we have seen, internalized in the victim there is a repressed aggressive element that bursts out on occasion in rage attacks. This subconscious element, which expresses identification with the aggressor, is an organic part of his personality. (Identification with the aggressor can also be explained according to the object-relation theory; this, however, would require a thorough analysis, too long to be dealt with here.) The 'victim' parent's generally submissive behaviour, coupled with his sudden outbursts of rage, the result of his latent and generally repressed aggression, create the double identity in his psyche. But the survivor of the fighter type also has a double identity in his psyche. Although his daily functioning demonstrates his identification with the aggressor, in his innermost heart there are repressed memories of suffering, helplessness and humiliation which he is not willing to identify with; he feels disgust at the weak part of himself. A child growing up with a 'fighter' parent cannot help sensing the existence of this other identity in his parent's psyche. Thus even though the parent consciously and intentionally transmits to the child his identification with the strong, fighting figure, he unconsciously transmits his identification with the victim figure as well. The survivors' children generally adopt the dominant, overt identity of their parents, and only upon close examination can one find in them the repressed identity with which they are in conflict.

One aspect, the identification with the aggressor, cannot be transmitted directly to the second generation because they did not experience the Holocaust themselves (and this is true of both types of survivors): in the reality of the death camps identification with the aggressor had enormous survival value (Eitinger 1961, 1962). The idea of identification with the aggressor cannot be processed either intellectually or emotionally, and so the survivors transmitted these feelings of identification to their children through their daily behaviour towards the children themselves or towards authority figures in their world. This occurred without the parents themselves being capable of dealing with the feeling of identification with the aggressor lying within them, as the aggressors had such a monstrous image in the survivor's psyche that no force on earth could bring him to conscious identification with them. In the reality of camp life there were no limits to the aggression: it went far beyond the concept of aggression generally accepted in psychology. It is thus clear that it is impossible to experience such aggression and at the same time identify with it consciously. Moreover, the survivor, who had gone through the seven circles of hell in the Holocaust and remained alive, acquired a feeling of omnipotence: with his magic power he had overcome the aggressor and won out over death. This feeling is only another aspect of his latent aggression; the only difference between it and aggression in the accepted sense of the term is the lack of the element of choice and will. Someone who behaves aggressively does so out of choice and will, whereas the magic power granted to the survivor is not under the control of the will. If the element of will is added to the experience of the magic power, the survivor becomes an active aggressor and the boundary between the will and its realization becomes blurred. Thus the survivor has no choice but to act with total repression. Any attempt to raise the feelings of aggression into consciousness arouses such intense guilt feelings that there is no escape from self-punishment, which is expressed in turning the aggression toward oneself and internalizing it.

I have often found that only through slow and painful exposure of the repressed inner part – the 'victim' part of the children of the 'fighters', the 'fighter' part of the children of the 'victims' – can the 'memorial candles' succeed in attaining inner integration between the two parts of the ego and come to terms with the range of their feelings.

I now examine how these elements in the personalities of the 'memorial candles' are expressed in therapy. In the second stage of therapy the topic of the Holocaust often arises more frequently during therapy sessions, both individual and group, although generally not yet in the direct context of the personal traumas of their parents and families. Some of the second-generation patients are prepared to discuss topics related to the Holocaust, while others refuse to do so and deny any connection between the topic and themselves. The latter, who are mainly from 'fighter' families, try to avoid the contents of the Holocaust in general; they avoid reading books or watching television programmes or films dealing with this topic, they do not visit Yad Vashem ('I've never been to Yad Vashem and I have no intention of going there, because I have nothing to look for there'). The conscious suppression of the topic of the Holocaust generally attests to the avoidance of an encounter with the unconscious personal contents that are still perceived as threatening. The 'memorial candles' of 'victim' families are more willing – on various levels of consciousness – to approach and deal with the topic. They do this through dreams, fantasies, and visits to places and participation in events associated with the Holocaust. Sometimes they raise the topic as if casually, unintentionally, as can be seen in Binyamin's story.

'You know, it's strange, I've noticed recently that when I run every morning, at the end of the run I find myself at Yad Vashem. I don't plan this in advance. I never know exactly where I'll run that day, and suddenly, in the last few days, again and again my feet have been taking me there. . .'

Subconsciously, or at the threshold of consciousness, Binyamin was attracted precisely to Yad Vashem without being capable of understanding or explaining to himself why he was attracted there or why the Holocaust was occupying his inner world to such an extent.

The contents appearing in the dreams and fantasies of the survivors' children, like their everyday behaviour, may be classified into two categories – the 'victim' and the 'fighter' – although frequently the two motifs are interwoven at different levels of consciousness. Identification with the victim, with the humiliated and tortured part of the parent as internalized in the children's psyches, arouses anxiety, shame and deep humiliation in them – so much so as to threaten them with loss of identity. This is the most severe threat, and it arouses strong internal opposition that gives rise to repression and denial.

As I explained in the previous chapter, in the process of trans-position taking place between the survivor generation and the second generation, the children internalize representations of the objects that perished in the Holocaust, and the traumas their parents underwent there, as part of their ego and superego. Since the Holocaust included persecutors and persecuted ones, aggressors and victims, torturers and tortured ones, the inner world of the second generation, which is mostly unconscious, is populated with figures of humiliated and tortured people on the one hand, and oppressors and torturers on the other. Both types arise again and again in the dreams, nightmares and fantasies of the survivors' children, which are full of motifs of persecution, torture and murder, and feelings of terror and anxiety, as if some-thing terrible is about to happen at any moment. At times it is clear even at this stage of therapy that it is the fear of death and extermination that encompasses their inner world.

Penina, about thirty-three years old, the daughter of a survivor mother, described a dream she had:

'There's some figure dressed in rags. It's going among the houses of the ghetto and looking for addresses. Addresses of some relatives. All sorts of figures from the Holocaust, grey, with shaven heads, and thin, thin, are moving slowly among the ruins. They're all going in the same direction. A delegation of fat women, very colourful, suddenly appears, I'm not sure from where, and walk around the ghetto in the opposite direction. There are tears in their eyes and I say to myself, "It's only lip service, they're demon-strating because it's expected of them." I cry a little and I'm not sure who I belong to. Everything changes. There's a chase. People are walking in the streets of an ordinary town. I'm still a citizen like everyone else, but there's already a threat of kidnapping in the air. Sudden kidnapping, from the middle of ordinary reality straight into hell. I'm walking with my friend and we see soldiers. I know right away: it's dangerous. "Let's go the other way," I say to her. We go into some store and pretend we're looking at the merchandise. But the storekeepers are already suspicious. We go out and my

friend says to me, "I'm sure one of us will be caught in the end."
As if this whole story has already been written somewhere and
the end is already known. Then I say to her, "Yes, but it won't be
me." '

It's not hard to identify the Nazis in this dream, where they appear
as aggressive and threatening figures. The dream expresses
Penina's identity conflict clearly: she herself does not know with
whom to identify – whether with those who perished or with those
who survived, and whether she's a victim or a fighter who will
survive. The danger of being caught is very concrete, but part of
Penina's psyche refuses to accept such a fate and identify herself,
and perhaps even her mother and grandmother, with the victims.
Penina's dream, like that of other children of survivors, shows her
identification tendencies clearly.

Miriam's dreams reflect her identification with the victim:

'In this dream I was in a closed camp. We had to go through
various torture posts. It was a closed camp, and in each building
there was a post. The earth was red, as in a desert. I was the only
one who survived and remained alive after all the posts. The first
one was a completely closed room, without windows, made of
concrete, very square, small, with a very high ceiling. There was
an exhibition on the walls, black-and-white pictures of German
soldiers beating to death women and men who were standing in
line naked. Me they didn't hit, or I didn't feel the blows. I was
the only one who survived. In the room there were also all sorts
of torture instruments. I was terribly afraid but I waited in line.
Next to me was a women dressed in rags holding a baby. I
thought that this woman had no chance of surviving. There was
another young woman with her hair pinned up. She was dressed
in a German uniform and held a kind of stick or whip in her
hand, and her eyes were frightening, like those of a wild animal
looking for prey.'

Here the dream ended; nothing happened, Miriam survived. In
another dream she had, which sounds like a continuation of this
dream, there is more movement:

'I'm in a concentration camp, in a huge hall that looks like a
storage room. The ceiling is very high and near the top there
are these tiny windows. Along the walls, lower down, there are
bookcases piled with books. We were there, in this room, a few

people, all of us very thin, complete skeletons. Everyone was spread out on the floor like a sack, because no one had the strength to move. I was about twelve years old [the age at which Miriam's mother was taken to the camp]. All my bones stuck out of my body. We heard that the Germans were approaching the yard and we started hiding each other among the books. We simply folded the people in such a way that from afar it would be impossible to tell that they were human beings. I didn't manage to hide among the books and so I decided to lie on the floor and pretend I was dead. One soldier looked at me, then kicked me with his boots and finally turned me over. I rolled over as if I were dead, and he really believed that I was dead and left me. Finally they left the storage room and then we decided to run away from there, and then I ran and ran like in the history books, without stopping again.'

In her two dreams Miriam actually moved into the world of the extermination camps, and we can feel the threat in the air from the beginning to the end of the dreams: the Nazi soldiers in boots and uniforms, torturing, beating, kicking and humiliating. The only way to survive was to pretend to be dead. Miriam described the psychic closing-off – that tried and true remedy for survival – that surrounded many of the camp prisoners. The prisoners lost their human form. They became walking skeletons that could be folded and hidden in bookcases – perhaps a hint at the bunks in which the camp prisoners slept folded up. In their dreams, Miriam and Penina are the only ones who retained any hope of survival. And indeed, Miriam's mother and Penina's mother were saved from death, but the emotional price of this survival is being paid by them and their daughters until this very day. In Miriam's dreams her total identification with the victims stands out: she herself experiences the tortures. And similarly Haya, another member of the therapy group, says over and over to the rest of the group, 'I am a survivor. Even if in my head I know that I wasn't there, in my heart I feel that I am actually a survivor.'

The dreams reported here are 'survival exercises'. Part of Miriam's psyche lives in the present, but another, hidden, part spends all its time living the lives of her relatives, who did not return from the valley of death, and the life of her mother, the only one who survived.

Hedva, another member of the group, described how she identifies with the victims in everyday life, experiences the Holocaust and survives – practising survival exercises again and again:

'Yesterday I was waiting in line for the bus and it was very hot. I was thirsty, I wanted very much to drink and to sit on the pavement, but I said to myself, "No, you're not allowed to sit or to drink, you have to hang on and not give up. You have to be prepared for the next Holocaust, and what if you will have to go through it tomorrow, like them, there, to stand terribly crowded in trains, without food or water for hours. You also have to be able to do it." Every year I measure my children's height and I think, "Good, another year has passed, and they're a year older. How will they go through it there? Perhaps it will be a little easier." I measure them with a Holocaust ruler.'

The world of the Holocaust, with its victims, aggressors and fighters, seeps into the world of group therapy. At the early stages of therapy there is always an intense fear of the undermining of the internal defence system and the exposure of repressed feelings. Everyone tries to defend their parents as best they can and to deny the least bit of anger and criticism of them, or disappointment with the way they functioned as parents. The therapists and the thera-peutic setting encourage the group members, through indirect pressure, to begin dealing with these repressed feelings. It is thus no wonder that the therapy setting and the figures of the therapist soon acquire the form of oppressive and threatening aggressors in the eyes of the group members.

Nevertheless, the therapeutic setting, especially in the case of group therapy, is generally the setting in which the 'memorial candles' begin, for the first time in their lives, to feel security; they are finally permitted to expose to themselves and to others their repressed and tangled inner world, and to share it with the therap-ist and the other members of the group. This inner world, with its dreams and fantasies that speak to them all the time in the lan-guage of vague Holocaust symbols, starts becoming clearer and slowly revealing itself to them during the course of therapy. The traumas their parents went through begin to emerge from the abyss of oblivion and to weave themselves into their everyday life as into a complicated fabric. But to live in the valley of death is not so simple, and so their defence mechanisms are called upon at this stage to suppress the terrors of the Holocaust back into the dark-ness of the subconscious.

The 'director' of this drama is the therapist, and so there is great resistance to him at this stage. Generally, however, the members of the group do not confront the therapist with direct demands or with anger, but they express extreme suspicion, helplessness and absolute dependency. They picture the therapist as an omnipotent, aggressive and threatening figure. It is true that such feelings are familiar and characteristic of the beginning stages of every course of therapy, whether individual or group, but here they are unusually strong and are expressed in the language of the Holocaust. Expressions of suspicion and anxiety generally arise indirectly at this stage, in the language of dreams, and only rarely are expressed directly and clearly.

Ariela, whose mother was a victim of experiments performed by Dr Mengele and his associates, related the following dream to the group in the second year of therapy:

'I see various figures from the group. We're in some kind of guest house that actually seems more like a concentration camp. They make us lie down on beds. There's an unpleasant feeling of stress. Then the therapists come in. They're wearing white coats and they look like doctors. They are going to do some things to us. Perhaps they will put us to sleep. I'm not sure how we'll wake up from this.'

Ariela related this dream in a monotonous and expressionless voice, but one could feel the great tension and psychic stress that streamed from her to the group. Her dream was permeated with an intense feeling of anxiety and threat, and was dominated by the helplessness in her absolute identification with the victim, who was totally controlled by the aggressive figures of the doctor-therapists in the white coats. The doctor-therapists appear here with polar duality – healers on the one hand and killers on the other. 'They will put us to sleep' – this is how Ariela expresses her feeling of lack of control over the therapeutic setting and total dependence on the therapists. This sentence also expresses the difficulty that Ariela has, in common with many other children of Holocaust survivors, in expressing feelings of anger and opposition, feelings that are natural and taken for granted in any psychotherapeutic process. But the unconscious prohibition on expressing feelings of anger, aggression or opposition, which permeates the relationships in most survivor families, is transferred in its entirety to the therapy situation. Anger and aggression are generally not expressed directly, not only towards the therapists, but even towards the other members of the group, whether as individuals or as a unit. As mentioned, the place of anger is taken by suspicion, anxiety and helplessness, which are expressed indirectly through the use of contents and symbols drawn from the Holocaust.

These feelings also stand out in a dream reported by Raphael, the son of two survivor parents:

'I'm on my way to the group and I see that some other members of the group are walking along with me. I feel terribly afraid. My whole body is trembling. Finally, when I arrive, I realize why: there, in the group, is the SS headquarters. I know that no one is actually forcing me to go, but I still have to go on and I do go on.'

The group is identified with the SS command, and Raphael is placed in an ambivalent position: no one is forcing him to go, he is anxious, yet he goes anyway. The outstanding elements of the dream are the victim's cooperation with and dependency upon the aggressor, which are analogous to the sense of ambivalence the patient feels towards the therapist at the beginning of every course of therapy. Raphael too uses the symbols and contents of the Holocaust to express the conflicts arising from the patients' feelings of dependency, anxiety and helplessness, and from the omnipotence they attribute to the therapists. But in his dream there's something interesting: Raphael is not alone, he has friends sharing his fate. He perceives the other group members as sharing a group victimhood – they all have a common identity as victims.

At one of the group therapy sessions there was a very long, oppressive silence. Finally Haim broke the tension and said in a strangled voice:

'I feel as if this group is a train. We're all riding on it but none of us knows where it's going.' Immediately someone burst in and responded: 'I'm afraid that this train will end up at Auschwitz.' The ice was broken. Several more such remarks were made – perhaps humorously, perhaps seriously – and afterwards things started to become clearer and for the first time suspicions and doubts were raised concerning the therapists' competence; one member even related that he had gathered information about the therapists before the beginning of therapy and described how he had been examining them very closely since the first session. The group's suspicion stemmed mainly from the lack of trust they felt in the therapists' ability to control events in the group well enough to be able to eventually pilot it to a safe landing.

Anxiety of this sort – that the therapists may not be able to contain the group members, to stay with them and help them while remaining alive and in control of the therapeutic process – is very common at the first stage of therapy. As mentioned, it is a result of the undermining of the group members' system of intrapsychic defences. In comparison with the members of other groups, the children of survivors find it difficult to express their anxiety freely, because such feelings acquire extreme and sometimes even magic proportions in their inner world. The more intense the anxiety-dependence and the aggression, the greater the difficulty of dealing with and expressing these feelings, and this generates a complex cycle of projection and projective identification. The inner aggressiveness resulting from the feeling of helplessness is transferred and projected onto the therapist, who then turns into a threatening figure – an SS officer, for instance – who holds life and death in his hands.

So far we have seen how the 'memorial candles' identify with the victim in their dreams, and how, at this stage of therapy, this identification is projected onto the group's attitude towards the therapists. The examples brought here demonstrate that the victim aspect and the aggressor aspect are interwoven; the distinction between them is rather artificial, and is made for the purpose of a clearer understanding of the psychic world of the 'memorial candles'.

Ariela, also at the first stage of group therapy, related the following dream to the group:

'The dream takes place in a house with many storeys. A large house, unfinished, with many empty spaces in it.' Here she paused to explain that the word she used for 'empty spaces', *halalim*, can also mean 'people killed in war or accident'. 'On every storey there are many people. A rumour is going around that some people are planning to capture the building. Not bad people, just ordinary people. I usually dream about bad people with weapons, and bad faces of robbers and such, but this time they are people from a different world. They aren't bad but they have so much power that they cancel everything that I really am. It seems to me that they're wearing white coats. We mustn't accept what they say, because it's dangerous, we must answer the opposite to everything. The test here is individual – either you pass it or you don't. It's not permitted to read numbers. If you look and see numbers, you're done for. People who saw the numbers started hovering. There were many people around who encouraged me and said, "Keep fighting." There was a part where I saw one number after another anyway, but I developed a technique for ignoring the numbers: singing.'

Ariela's dream is replete with associations, but I can't discuss all of them here. I'll concentrate mainly on the interpretations given by Ariela herself. She considered the dream to be connected with therapy and with the fear that due to therapy she might lose the feeling that she is in control of her life. The number test is a difficult internal struggle expressing her resistance to encountering and accepting inner contents that are still very threatening. Later the numbers in the dream aroused an association with the numbers tattooed on the arms of the prisoners in the camps. Ariela, like her parents, has the identity of a 'fighter', and this active identity is expressed in her dream. The support and encouragement she received from the group – to be strong and not to stop fighting – show that she feels that the group supports her in her refusal to lose control, to open up what is hidden in her heart and to begin feeling and expressing the feelings of weakness and pain pent up in her psyche. Ariela already knows that in the 'house' of her family there are many *halalim* – both 'empty spaces' and 'dead bodies' – but she still feels an intense need to defend the unity of her family and her images of her parents. Indeed, the 'fighter' parents are portrayed by their children as good parents who established a happy family and always cared for their children.

'All these years I kept the idyllic picture of the house I grew up in with my parents and two brothers,' related Zvia, also a daughter of 'fighters'. 'A white house in a village, with a red roof and a pretty garden around it. This is the happiest house there is, a truly perfect home.'

Both groups – the children of the 'victims' as well as the children of the 'fighters' – put up an intense resistance at this stage to any feeling of direct involvement in the traumatic experiences undergone by their parents. There is a conflict in their psyches between the need to identify with the humiliated parent and their feelings of anger and hostility towards him. This conflict was internalized in early childhood, and now it arouses feelings of shame and anxiety as well, so that they consider it preferable to continue denying and repressing their feelings. They have not yet developed the ability to see the connection between the significance and the effects of the traumas undergone by their parents in the Holocaust and the feelings and images they transferred to them in their childhood, which had a crucial influence on their psychic development.

At a more advanced stage of therapy Zvia said:

'All these years I didn't realize what it means that my mother experienced the Holocaust – Auschwitz – personally. And besides, one must pity her, consider her feelings, and afterwards, much later, really really identify with her, since this might possibly make it easier for her. I never saw any connection between her and me, between the Holocaust and the fact that she gave birth to me and raised me. Everything she wanted to give me and couldn't.'

The latent internal conflict, which begins to arise at this stage, generates a danger of loss of identity and deep internal confusion and fragmentation, and so it arouses in the patients intense resistance and the need for defences separating them from these feelings. One of the ways this resistance expresses itself is in their attempts at controlling themselves and others in the therapy group. These attempts at control are noticeable in their avoidance of handing over intimate information, expressing feelings verbally, or feeling any sort of closeness with the other members of the group. Over the years in which I have treated the children of survivors I have discovered that their need to maintain control over themselves and others at this stage of therapy is a fixed and unchanging pattern. Thus a great deal of the group members' internal resources are invested in the struggle for control over the other members of the group, over the therapists, and over their own threatening and destructive internal feelings. The need to have complete control over every situation is connected with the survival exercises and the preparations for the next Holocaust, which many members of the second generation compulsively engage in. These survival exercises are extremely varied – from physical training for strengthening the body and preparing it to be at its highest capacity to searching for 'safe' seats in public places.

Yaakov, the son of two 'fighter' parents, related the following:

'When I sit in the cinema or on a bus, I always sit in a place that I've thought out, either next to the door or in the middle of the last row of seats. I'm never in such a situation without imagining a terrorist attack or something like it. With me everything is thought out and planned. I know exactly how I'll fight and how I'll escape.'

Another way to prepare for the Holocaust is to hoard food; as mentioned, food hoarding is typical of many survivors and was transmitted to their children. Semel (1985) describes this in one of her stories:

> From the angle at which he was now standing he could see the kitchen very well. The pantry door was open. Naomi was standing on a low chair and arranging piles of tinned food on the cupboard shelves. They rose up to the top of the cupboard like tall towers. And squeezed between them were bags of various sizes and colours. Gideon Adar read the labels: sugar, flour, rice. For the loaves of bread she had a special place. Wrapped in plastic, clinging to one another, with each loaf protecting its neighbour.
>
> Naomi didn't skip over any of them. One by one she caressed them and a whisper of song rose from her lips. Then she got off the chair, holding in her bosom one loaf of bread that was not wrapped. She held it close to her chest, and still did not notice him.
>
> (p. 144)

Some of the survivors still do not believe that they have really remained alive. Survival is not something they can take for granted, but something that has to be fought for again and again, every day, throughout one's life. The survivors who live with this feeling also transmit it to their children, and thus many of these children do not take their lives for granted, and they feel somewhat special and exceptional. This feeling also pervades their therapy. Therapy gives patients the feeling that survival – or at least psychic survival – is not so certain. The threat to the integrity of their personality seems so frightening that they consider it worthwhile to go to battle for it stubbornly and without compromises. In the eyes of the patients the loss of control is a loss of psychic integrity, and so the battle for control turns into a battle for survival.

One means used by the children of survivors to defend themselves from the danger of psychic disintegration is psychic closing-

off. Kestenberg (1982) describes mechanical behaviour in survivors'
children that he has often noticed; their behaviour is quite similar to
their parents' behaviour during the Holocaust: 'Feelings were dangerous because they made her vulnerable to attack. Being inanimate
or dead, she could not be hurt or killed' (p. 144).

At an advanced stage of therapy, in which the threshold of consciousness had been lowered to a great extent, Hava said to us:

> 'I won't show you what I feel, because if they notice me they may
> perhaps still hurt me. I hear what I'm saying; it's for myself and
> also for my mother. I see her again as a young girl in the camp.
> I don't want them to hurt her, she has to be strong. She won't
> show them what she feels inside, because she has to live.'

As mentioned, physical survival was often largely dependent upon
the survivor's ability to attain psychic closing-off, at least partially.
Many years have passed since the Holocaust, but in her world of
feeling and fantasy Hava is still living the dangers that threatened
her mother's life, and she uses the same defence tactics her
mother used; she is still unable to distinguish between herself and
her mother in her consciousness. She sees emotional survival as
dependent upon the preservation of a rigid defence system like the
one that saved her mother.

In therapy groups with many children of survivors it's often
possible to discern the formation of a sort of secret alliance among
them, based on the similar feelings they identify in one another.
This alliance serves as a group defence system that prevents the
expression of any type of strong feeling. On the level of the group
interaction it protects the participants from the exposure of their
repressed feelings, which they still perceive as a threat, whether to
themselves as individuals or to the group as a whole. At the first
stage of therapy the group is still unable to contain too high an
emotional level.

A few psychologists (Aleksandrowicz 1973; Kestenberg 1972;
Trossman 1968) interpret the identification with the aggressor
found among some of the children of survivors as a type of defence
in the face of weakness, anxiety and helplessness. A hint of this may
be seen in Zev's words: 'I always have to be strong. Firm and strong
at any price. I never showed them what I really feel, I always
pretended that everything was all right.'

Identification with the aggressor serves not only as a defence
against emotional disintegration, but also as a means of protecting

the survivor parent. Raphael adopted a rigid and harsh sort of behaviour that can be seen as identification with the aggressor. This behaviour served as a solution for situations in which he felt helpless, confused, embarrassed or anxious. He probably copied this behaviour from his mother, who had been a member of an underground group and had participated in many rescue operations and even in attacks on German installations. Perhaps the mother, within herself, identified not only with the fighting but also with the aggressor. Indeed, she greatly encouraged in her son behaviour expressing strength, firmness and achievement, and she reacted intolerantly to expressions of pain and insecurity.

In the group therapy sessions Raphael tended to demonstrate arrogance and noticeable emotional distance from the other members of the group. At one of the sessions he went too far, and one of the members told him off. Raphael's reaction was as arrogant and harsh as always. At this point I intervened and gave him an example of how he spoke – not only the content of what he said but also his tone of voice and his facial and bodily expressions. At first Raphael did not understand what I was driving at and seemed amazed. Then I decided to use a psychodramatic technique, and I asked him to exaggerate his usual behaviour. At first he was somewhat hesitant, but he gradually entered into the role and soon he was giving out orders right and left, scolding the other members derisively and insulting them grossly. When the group told him that he was actually imitating the behaviour of an SS officer he seemed satisified with this, and continued the game with unconcealed pleasure. Without any inhibitions he dealt out 'compliments' like 'You're a worm' or 'You're just a Jewish whore'. The tension in the group continued to grow. Finally one of the women broke out in bitter tears, and in her pain began speaking to him aggressively. The group members were divided in their reactions: some of them identified with the woman's pain and crying, others identified with Raphael, and a few said nothing. When the tension reached its climax Raphael broke out crying. He groaned in a choked voice that sounded like the cry of a newborn baby. After he quieted down Baruch began reporting a recurrent dream: he is riding on a large black motorcycle, dressed in a uniform and wearing a helmet. Near him other people are riding on similar motorcycles. They are making a terrible noise, but they are actually riding this way, from place to place, without any clear destination. Wherever they go, everyone looks at them with great fear and runs every which way. 'I never understood this dream,' Baruch said. 'This is the first time I can connect it with the SS, who used to ride on their motorcycles and raid one village after another.' Baruch stopped, thought, and continued: 'It still seems terrible to me, how can I be like one of them after everything that happened to my parents there?'

When Baruch had finished, Zippora started speaking. She seemed somewhat confused as she reported her dream. The dream took place at home, which was, apparently, her parents' home during her childhood. She is with a governess [the Hebrew word also means 'therapist'], who is telling her to hurry up and go; Zippora says, 'Okay, but I want to take a shower first.' She goes into the shower and stays there a long time. She feels a sense of threat the whole time, because the SS are approaching and she is afraid that they will catch her. At first it's not clear exactly who these SS men are, but at a certain point the door opens and her cousin Mordechai appears, dressed in an SS uniform and with a large gun in his belt:

'He looked so big and fat with a pot-belly, which he doesn't have in reality. From far away there appear smaller and vaguer figures. Maybe they are my parents, and they too are Nazis in uniform. They ask me questions, investigating, but they don't do anything bad to me. I'm very surprised, but mainly I feel anxiety. Finally I manage to get away in time together with the governess.'

It seems that the legitimization the therapists gave to Raphael's behaviour, and the security all the group members began to feel within the therapeutic setting, allowed Raphael, Baruch and Zippora to expose a bit of the aggression within them. This aggression, like the aggression and bossiness of their parents, was expressed in its full intensity by symbols and images drawn from the Holocaust. The feeling that this aggression is unbounded, which was actually the case during the Holocaust, is as dominant in the psyches of the survivors' children as in those of their parents, and this is the source of their difficulty in coming face to face with it and exposing it to others.

Raphael's outburst and the dream descriptions that followed it were the group's first encounter with the aggressive part of their psyche. The exposure of their aggressive feelings served as emotional ventilation for them. It allowed a catharsis to take place in

Raphael's psyche, and this gave him the ability to face, for the first time in his life, the pain, weakness and vulnerability that had been repressed until this point in the depths of his psyche and had been covered by rigid defences. Raphael ventilated these feelings with great intensity, with pain and tears, and thus granted himself and the other members of the group the right to express feelings of this sort, feelings that they had never dared to express and that the group had been unable to handle.

Hopper and Kreeger (1980) describe a workshop of professional people on the topic of the Holocaust and survival. Only some of the 140 participants in the workshop were Holocaust survivors or the children of survivors, but the reactions of all the participants were interesting and supported what was described above. The moods of the group were crystallized mainly around the motifs of victim and aggressor. The emotional division was projected onto the group members and/or the facilitators, using the mechanism of projective identification. In the workshop as well the emotional division created subgroups and a distinct separation between the facilitators and the members, the controllers and the controlled (Fogelman and Savran 1970), and the use of language of Holocaust symbols and images was evident there too. Hopper and Kreeger (1980) relate that the workshop participants were immersed in a 'death culture' – in a collective sense of anxiety stemming from the terror of annihilation. A few of the participants experienced certain aspects of the group as if they were analogous to the experiences of the Jews taken to Auschwitz; they perceived their participation in this large group as a seductive but evil invitation to participate in a reconstruction of the thing itself. Most of the group agreed that it would be better to avoid any imaginative experience that might lead to the uncovering of the anxieties always aroused by Holocaust-related fantasies, since there always exist hidden enemies in the world of fantasy and imagination, and the Holocaust is always at the door waiting to occur again. The workshop generated a feeling of helplessness as well as suppressed or repressed anger towards the facilitators, the organizing staff and the group itself. The anger was directed at the group members themselves, both as individuals and as a whole, and this was noticeable in the great nervousness, tension and frustration pervading the group. After some time the pervasive feelings became boredom, restlessness, weariness and a sense of depersonalization. The fear of openly expressing anger against authority was so great that an intense regressive state was generated, and the participants began to confuse themselves with their objects. Here Hopper and Kreeger ask an important question: isn't it possible that the group members, who were unconsciously identifying with the camp prisoners, were unable to express their rage towards the facilitators, just as the camp prisoners were unable to express their rage and helplessness towards their oppressors? Under these circumstances it is not surprising that projective identification was their primary defence mechanism in the face of their feelings of anger, aggression and helplessness. The participants made use of it to control those who seemed to them to be responsible for their fate – the organizing staff and the facilitators.

Chapter 6

Self-esteem and sexual identity

In this chapter we will see how the 'memorial candles' cope with two central elements of their identity: self-esteem and sexual identity. These elements remained static and did not develop during the process of constructing their identity, because of their identification with their survivor parents and their sharing of the parents' emotional world.

'I see,' said Nahum at one of the group sessions, 'two lines moving quickly. It looks like a production line where newspapers come out, many newspapers moving quickly, and when you try to read something that's written on one of them, it's impossible. The letters are rushing very fast. Suddenly I notice that it's not newspapers; it's people. Many, many faces of people pressed one next to another and rushing very fast. I need, and I also want, to identify among the thousands of faces my family that disappeared. I stand there and I want and need to point with my finger, to identify my grandfather and grandmother, my aunts and uncles and all the rest of my relatives. I become very, very tense. I'm standing there with my finger stuck out and I'm not succeeding – there are so many blurred faces rushing very fast and it's hard to stop them. It's impossible to stop next to a familiar face, an image, a face, and to feel the closeness and the fact that in some way and at some time some of them belonged to me, or more correctly I belonged to them. They were something so close and intimate to my parents, and through them also to me. After all, I'm named after my grandfather, and he's one of thousands, millions, of these anonymous faces, so how can I make him less anonymous?'

Nahum stopped talking, looked at the group and turned confusedly and hesitantly to Devora, tears glistening in his eyes and intense emotion in his voice: 'You know, when I saw you at the first session I felt a strange and special feeling towards you. I didn't know you. In reality I knew almost nothing about you, actually nothing at all. But during that time – I don't know if you felt it or not – I would sometimes sit the whole session staring at you. I have often thought that this look is probably unpleasant for you – what do I actually want from you? At first I myself didn't know what I actually wanted from you, what I was looking for in you. I only knew that I was drawn to look, to get to know you, perhaps to identify something, to find something. A few sessions ago, when you were talking about your mother and the beautiful young sister she lost there, whom she loved so much and was so strongly attached to, I suddenly realized that you actually look very much like my mother's younger sister, who was also lost there among thousands of faces.'

Nahum was silent for a long time and then continued: 'There's one wrinkled and faded picture of this young aunt of mine. It's interesting, this is the first time I can call her my aunt, I can utter this word with my mouth.' Tears began to drip slowly from his eyes. 'She was so beautiful. I can describe a little of how she looked: long, flowing black hair, like yours, Devora. A beautiful face. And she was tall and straight like you. The last time my mother saw her she was about eighteen, and she remained there. I'm trying to remember her name now, and suddenly I can't think of it. It's strange – after all, I knew her name.'

Nahum tried to remember the name, but he did not succeed before the end of the session. Meanwhile, Esther began telling a dream she had had the night before the session: 'In my dream I'm standing in front of an open mass grave containing piles of bodies. I don't know if I told you that my mother, in addition to her parents and other relatives, lost ten brothers and sisters in the Holocaust.'

Esther stopped talking, and then Itzhak turned to her and said very warmly: 'You really never told this to us clearly. We always knew that your parents lost everyone there. But all these years you never told us who exactly they lost. Just as I probably never spoke clearly about what my parents went through there. I'm thinking about this: look what a strange coincidence! You're

sitting here with us, and we're a group of eleven, ten besides
you, just like your mother and her ten brothers and sisters.'
Esther sat with her head down and listened quietly. She seemed
   very tense and upset. Suddenly she interrupted Itzhak and said:
   'Yes, I never actually thought about it. I also don't really understand what you mean. What's the connection between the fact
   that I'm sitting here with ten other members of the group and
   that fact that my mother lost ten brothers and sisters there?'
Itzhak answered with a smile: 'We often talked here about the fact
   that the group sometimes feels like a family, and that we serve
   for each other here as sibling figures. It's interesting that you
   never thought about the fact that we are like your brothers and
   sisters.'

Here I intervened and tried to bring Esther back to the dream
narrative, even though I knew it was difficult for her. I reminded
her that she had been standing there in front of the huge mass
grave and looking at the pile of bodies, and I asked her if she was
capable of really looking at them and identifying someone familiar
among them, one of her relatives, perhaps one of her aunts and
uncles. After some hesitation she answered:

'Yes, I'm standing there and I don't really want to look inside, but
   nevertheless I feel that I have to. Something is driving me from
   within. So many years I ran away from it, I didn't know anything
   and I didn't especially want to know. My mother hardly ever told
   me anything about her brothers and sisters. My uncles and
   aunts don't have any form or any clear image for me. There
   aren't even any pictures of them left.' And suddenly she started
   talking directly to them: 'Perhaps now, for the first time, I can
   dare to look at you a little more, to try to imagine you, to see a
   little of how you were when you were alive. But it's still so hard
   for me to call you aunts and uncles and to see you clearly. I only
   know that I'm named after my mother's youngest sister, whom
   they all loved so much.'

Esther began to weep. After having maintained her restraint for
years, she allowed herself for the first time to cry uninhibitedly.
Most of the group seemed very moved and there were tears in the
eyes of some of them. A few people started talking to Esther and
supporting her by identifying with her/their pain. Not only did
Esther succeed in this session in looking for the first time inside

the mass grave and identifying her relatives, but she also succeeded in forming a personal and emotional bond with them and calling them aunts and uncles. Actually, this started a process of encounter with her feelings of loss and mourning, which she was able to achieve only thanks to the support and identification showered upon her by the group. In contrast to her former practice, this time Esther was able to trust the group. She also drew courage and strength from Nahum's daring to expose his feelings on a matter so similar to her own, and from his ability to make use of Devora, their associate in the group, as a 'transitional figure' to his young aunt, whose picture he carried in his heart. Devora helped him raise his aunt's image clearly, work on his feelings towards her, and imprint her image internally; thus he was able to release her from the difficult, conflict-laden emotional burden that was his mother's rather than his.

It's worth spending some time here on a very central topic in the psychological growth and development of every child, the topic of identification. Psychoanalysis considers the concept of identification a central element in the formation and construction of the personality. Many scholars, including Freud (1921, 1923) and Sandler (1960a), stress that identity development is partly dependent on the ability to distinguish between the self and the self-object. An independent self is achieved by a developmental process that includes as its central component a series of identifications vital for the maintenance of an inner sense of continuity, which involves a feeling of secure unity with a figure that gradually becomes familiar. Silvermann (1986) stresses that in general only such a process can permit one to give up one's illusions of unity with the primary object, generally the mother. This enables a separation between the self and the self-object, which permits the beginning of the formation of a separate, distinct self. The identification mechanisms involved in this process play two roles simultaneously: the identification of the distinction between the self and the self-object, and the psychological unification of the self with the self-object through identification and imitation. The identification mechanisms change as one grows: in the first year of the child's life there are very archaic and primitive mechanisms that are derived from unconscious drives such as introjection and assimilation; gradually, in the process of growth and maturation, they are replaced by more mature mechanisms of a distinctive character derived from the ego and the superego.

The success or failure of these developmental processes depends on the extent to which they undergo significant structuralization and internalization. The question may be asked as to which of these identification mechanisms were developed by the 'memorial candles' towards their survivor parents?

In the previous chapters we saw that the survivor parents created, in the transposition process, a shared fantasy world with their children, who were participants in this intrapsychic drama. This narcissistic union of the 'memorial candles' with their parents makes them the rescuers of the objects that died in the Holocaust. The 'memorial candles' also try to heal the narcissistic wounds in their parents' injured psyches by fulfilling the parents' enormous expectations of them, in order to compensate the parents for their great loss.

The shared fantasies of the 'memorial candles' and their parents, and the narcissistic union between them, prevent these children from feeling aggression and hostility towards their parents, weaken their guilt feelings towards them, and strengthen their consistent union with the object. The 'memorial candles' share the feelings of loyalty to the dead and the life styles that have become a substitute for the mourning process, a mourning that the survivor parents are trying to avoid, come what may. The archaic identifications deriving from the superego, which are common to the 'memorial candles' and their parents, are associated with feelings of identification with the victim and with narcissistic wounds, which strengthen the intrapsychic conflict of the children. Out of their need to be special in order to fulfil their parents' unsatisfied wishes and drives, the 'memorial candles' are not free to occupy themselves with the satisfaction of their own personal needs, which retards their individuation in the rapprochement stage (around the age of two) and afterwards, before and after the oedipal stage (ages 4–5).

Sometimes the defective development of the 'memorial candles' generates a symbiotic psychic closing-off in the first year or two of their lives, before there is any separation between the self and the self-object. At this stage are developed the primitive identification mechanisms through which the 'memorial candles' internalized and assimilated parts of their parents' unconscious world, mainly involving their traumatic loss.

The great difficulty the survivor parents had in setting clear limits for their children in the separation-individuation stage of development generally prevented the 'memorial candles' from separating their own self from their parents' self. The primitive identification mechanisms of assimilation and internalization remained dominant in their psyche even at a relatively advanced age. More highly developed mechanisms, derived from the ego and the superego, did not develop in most of the 'memorial candles' before they began therapy, and even then they required extensive therapy and continual contact with the therapy setting. Their growing trust in the therapist and in the therapy group, as well as the respect and positive attitude to the patients' wishes, feelings and limits, led to the weakening of the threat of the disintegration or flooding of the ego. When the processes of therapy are effectively internalized through structuralization, the separation process begins, and the 'memorial candles' succeed in setting clearer boundaries between their own self and that of others, including their parents.

> In the survivor's child [says Bergman (1982)], empathy and identification with the parent as a persecuted victim, or as a Nazi aggressor, lead to mechanisms of splitting in the ego and super-ego representations. Frequently the child cannot idealize the parent who was victimized, particularly if the child has witnessed the latter in a subservient role vis-à-vis an official or authority. . . After devaluation of parental authority, one's superego cannot internalize one's parent as a protective agent on one's own behalf.
>
> (pp. 297–8)

An ego that is independent of parental authority is generally a direct result of the internalization of the superego. The 'memorial candles', however, had great difficulty internalizing the elements of their parents' superego, for three main reasons: (1) the problems inherent in identification with and idealization of their parents; (2) the double messages transmitted by the survivor parents to their children, which originated from the split between the self and the object in the representations of the superego in the parents (sometimes this split stemmed from simultaneous identification with and criticism of Nazi morality); (3) the children's chronic inability to fulfil their parents' enormous expectations.

For these three reasons the characteristics of the superego and the ego ideal were externalized for the 'memorial candles'. The children's involvement in their parents' renewed psychic adaptation to life was concentrated on the elements of the superego and the ego ideal as central organizing elements. Such involvement retards the development of representations of the self in the 'memorial candles' and damages the autonomy of the psyche, which is so important for the development of a superego and an independent personal ego ideal. The emotional need of the 'memorial candles' to compensate their parents for what they lost comes at the cost of the development of an independent self. The relationship between the survivor parents and the 'memorial candles' is thus liable to become an obligation containing great hostility, which cannot be released until the 'memorial candles' can separate themselves intrapsychically from their appointed role. Such a separation may grant the 'memorial candles', for the first time in their lives, the ability to feel healthy narcissistic emotions and to consolidate a sense of autonomy and real independence.

The ability of the 'memorial candle' to separate himself from his role is thus dependent on his ability to break the closed circle he shares with his parents, a circle designed to prevent any real encounter with loss and guilt and with the mourning involved in such an encounter

At this stage, the third stage of therapy, the sense of emotional isolation characterizing many sessions of the previous stages gives way to strong, deep expressions of feeling. The patient's laconic, expressionless, rational-intellectual speech, which has no power to bring about a dialogue, is replaced by warm, emotional speech that comes from the heart and touches the heart. At this stage expressions of support, closeness and identification are heard in the sessions, while the suspicion, hostility and distance which were dominant during the previous stages are now dwindling. Trust in the therapist and in the therapy group increases, partly because the attitude of respect for the patient's feelings and boundaries allows him to feel less threatened with the disintegration or flooding of his ego, and to shed the rigid defence mechanisms that had maintained him until this point.

The inner security of the 'memorial candles', which is strengthened in the therapy process, permits them to feel both the ability and the desire to break the closed circle and deal with the intense painful feelings stemming from the Holocaust that their parents went through. The encounter with loss involves the ability to undergo a real process of mourning, which their parents were incapable of doing. The mourning is simultaneously their parents' mourning and their own. The parents' loss was truly enormous, but they, the children, also lost the sense of continuity, the extended family, and – most important of all – the chance of growing up with secure parents having a sense of self-esteem and a complete sexual identity. The psychological loss suffered by the 'memorial candles' is therefore inherent in the fateful stamp imprinted by the traumas of the Holocaust on the psyches of their parents. The emotional encounter with the images of relatives who had perished, painful as it is, succeeds in freeing the 'memorial candles' from the cycle of guilt and compensation into which they had hitherto been locked with their parents. Until this stage of therapy the 'memorial candles' considered the loss as their parents' loss, in terms such as: 'my father' lost 'his father' or 'his brothers'. The parent deserves to have his pain shared, but the child feels that he has no share in this loss. Just as the parents are unable to truly mourn, so the children were also unable to do so – until this stage.

In the perception of the 'memorial candles' the family tree begins with their parents. They do not see previous generations, or even their parents' brothers and sisters, as part of the texture of their family. They do not feel a sense of belonging or identification with them, and they therefore do not feel their loss directly. The ability to call their mother's sister 'my aunt' and their father's father 'my grandfather' demonstrates a feeling of closeness and belonging to the family, but only in an advanced stage of therapy do these words begin to appear in the mouths of the 'memorial candles'.

Until this point the figures of the dead grandmothers, grandfathers, aunts and uncles were anonymous and faceless. This was the source of the inability of the 'memorial candles' to experience a sense of belonging to them. How does a niece feel? How does a grandson feel? These are new and unfamiliar emotional experiences which the 'memorial candles' finally begin to feel with some hesitation and with the same sense of novelty that the newborn feels when he encounters for the first time the figures that populate his environment. It is thus not surprising that these first experiences are accompanied by a sense of confusion, full of tension and excitement.

At this point the 'memorial candles' are undergoing a double experience: they are beginning to sense their dead relatives as if they were real – that is, they give a face and form to the images that were hitherto blurred and formless, and at the same time they begin to sense the real pain of their loss – they begin to mourn.

When correct therapeutic processes – respect for boundaries and mutual trust with structuralization – are internalized effectively, the separation process begins, and the 'memorial candles' succeed in setting clearer boundaries between their own selves and the selves of others, including their parents. The separation process is a primary corrective factor enabling the development of more mature identification mechanisms. These mechanisms, which are not archaic but derived from the ego and the superego, and possess a well-defined character, permit a mature, well-balanced identification that provides the ability to feel true empathy for others. As mentioned, until this point the 'memorial candles' were unable to identify with their parents' pain and thus feel their own pain.

We will now see how the 'memorial candles' cope with the process of separation between their own selves and the selves of their parents, and how mature, well-balanced identification mechanisms with their parents and with the world in general are constructed within their psyches. The discussion will centre upon two principal components of the identity of the 'memorial candles': self-esteem and sexual identity.

Conflicts involving self-esteem

Within the third stage of group therapy it is possible to distinguish three separate phases in the process of dealing with identification: the identifying phase, which we have been discussing until now, the belonging phase, which we will now discuss, and the phase of working through the traumas, which we will discuss later. In the belonging phase the 'memorial candles' begin to come into contact with the delicate, complex texture of their parents' and families' past, and for the first time in their lives they feel a sense of personal belonging to this texture. Their own personal identity is still rather unstructured and undefined, with many of its components not yet in their proper place. Many other components of their identity are still missing, partly because of the great empty spaces within their lives up until this point. As mentioned, the beginning of their family history was the moment of their birth. Whatever had happened before remained concealed; not only had they never pictured the images of their dead relatives, but they had rarely encountered even a faded photograph of them. Their internal pictures of these relatives, if they had any, were vague and blurred in their consciousness. The 'memorial candles' did not yet have any clear sense of the continuity of their family history or of their place within it.

The eternal dimension of time, the horizontal dimension of the family chain into which we are born, is so natural and obvious to most of us that we generally do not pay any attention to it. We do not grasp its importance as a basic layer in our sense of existence and belonging. On this layer alone can we build the vertical dimension, our separate identity. Only through natural growth, both mental and emotional, and through identification with figures close to us – especially our parents and our siblings – can our selfhood be consolidated. Without the horizontal dimension, the construction of the vertical dimension is much more difficult and it is doubtful whether an identity constructed in its absence can be sufficiently solid and sturdy. Indeed, lacking an intimate acquaintance with the experience of belonging to an extended family and to particular members of this family, the 'memorial candles' are robbed of the ability to experience intimate belonging, and this obviously makes it more difficult for them to achieve healthy mental and emotional development.

Thus, when the 'memorial candles' begin to experience the feeling of immediate contact with their relatives who perished, this experience – like any other first experience – moves them and agitates them greatly. But since it is new and unfamiliar it is also threatening and frightening. Therefore, after an emotionally moving session involving feelings of closeness among the members of the group, the 'memorial candles' are often attacked by feelings of confusion and a sense of threat, and they retreat into their shells, into the emotional disconnection they had become accustomed since their childhood to see as a familiar and secure hiding-place. This stage, like every stage of therapy, involves alternating progress and retreat – getting closer, followed by distancing, followed by getting closer again, and so on.

After the identifying phase the need arises in the 'memorial candles' to begin the work of weaving the complicated network of belonging in their family. Just how back-breaking this work is can be seen from a discussion between myself and Rivka. In the course of our discussion Rivka encountered various family figures for the first time. Although this discussion was held in an individual session, it was possible to sense the presence of the group in the background the whole time. The group was the first real framework of belonging Rivka had had in her life, and it served as a representation of the extended family that had perished. Rivka's complete trust in the group's support granted her the strength to cope with the painful and threatening feelings she had not dared to confront before.

As soon as Rivka arrived she began to report a dream:

'Last night, after the first group meeting after the vacation, I had a dream. In this dream I am coming home. I knew it was my house, but it wasn't the house I live in now, at least it didn't look like it, and there's someone with me, some man, but his image isn't clear. And when I go into the house I see a truck parking and many evil men dressed in uniforms jumping out of it, looking a little like SS officers. They raid my apartment and take everything out of it, all the furniture and all my possessions. And I'm standing there frozen and not saying anything, not reacting, quiet. You know, I didn't feel afraid at all, only that I was not responding. The only thing that bothered me was that they might find my ring.' She stopped the flow of words for a moment. 'Yes, it's the ring I'm wearing now.' And she showed me the ring on her finger. 'I was worrying the whole time what would happen if they would find this ring, but I had hidden it well, and I really hoped they wouldn't find it. All the rest wasn't all that important to me.'

Therapist: 'So what do you think about this dream?'

Rivka: 'It seems significant to me. It's somehow related to the group. There's also the fact that I dreamt it right after the group session.'

Therapist: 'It's interesting that you used the word "evil". What exactly did you mean? It seems to be describing part of your feeling that they are appearing as SS officers, that is, as threatening and aggressive figures. And just yesterday you expressed warm, positive feelings towards the group, and for the first time in three years you called the group a family.'

Rivka: 'Yes, it's strange. Yesterday I felt so close, and in my dream there is paradoxically a feeling of distrust. The suspicion that they are emptying my house and that I will remain without anything.'

Therapist: 'Yes, this is a suspicion that often arises during the course of therapy. Perhaps precisely because there is more closeness and openness between the members of the group. The feeling is that if I will be separated from all my familiar parts, which have been part of me for so many years, then I will be left empty inside, and what will be left of me? What will happen then? And actually, in all these years of therapy it was very hard for you to allow the group, and the therapists as well, to come into your house, into your inner self. I'm talking about your silences and your difficulty in opening up.'

Rivka: 'Yes, it's strange, although now I feel somewhat different, because I'm less afraid, both in the dream and in reality, with the group. Yesterday I was happy to come. Somewhere it's a good thing that they're taking away the furniture, it's only my external scenery. It's such a long time that I've hidden behind it.'

Therapist: 'Yes, we talked about that a lot. It seems that you're ready now to give up this scenery. You already feel that the group can help you separate from some of this scenery. But what about the stress you put on external appearance, which goes together with your closedness? And what about all the feelings of inner pain you hid and repressed all your life? Aren't they also part of the old possessions/parts within you? They're still there, aren't they? They're harsh and they arouse suspicion. You know, what's interesting is that you don't react at all. You stand there on the side as if you're paralysed. But actually that's very familiar to us from many situations.'

Rivka: 'Yes, you know what it reminds me of? My mother's reaction, there, when they separated her from her mother and her sisters and took them to the forest and she heard the shots, she went into some kind of shock. I always felt that she had gone into a state of internal numbness.' Rivka stopped talking and tears gathered in her eyes.

Therapist: 'Then your dream is connected both with your reality of today in the group and your mother, there.'

Rivka: 'It seems so. It seems to me that I actually react in many situations the way my mother reacted there.'

Therapist: 'Then what is the meaning of this picture of the truck and the men who raid your house and empty it?'

Rivka: 'I don't know exactly. . .'

Therapist: 'You know, you actually never told me anything about the ring on your finger.'

Rivka: 'This is a ring that belonged to my mother's grandmother. When they took them to the camps they managed to hide some of the jewelry on the roof of the house opposite their house, which was a kind of hotel. I'm not sure, but I think that it also belonged to the family somehow. When they went back after the war, my mother and my aunt, who were the only ones in the whole family that remained alive, they found this jewelry, and then my mother put on her grandmother's ring. It had three stones in it then, but over the years one of them fell out, and then she made a modern ring out of it and they put in the two stones that were left from the old ring. I remember that even though I was only a little girl then, I was terribly angry with my mother for changing the ring, and I even told her about it. And then, many years later, after it had already lost another stone, she gave me the last stone and I made this ring out of it. You see? Now it looks a little like an ancient ring again.'

Therapist: 'If you were so angry when your mother changed the ring, it seems that it was very important for you that with everything that was lost, at least something belonging to the family should remain, something that would preserve the connection with the grandmother and the continuity. Do you remember anything you ever heard about this grandmother?'

After a long silence Rivka said: 'I'm not sure. I remember something a little vague. I don't know if these stories belong to my mother's grandmother on her mother's side or on her father's side.'

Therapist: 'Have you ever seen a picture of her?'

Rivka: 'Actually, yes. There was a picture. There were a number of old pictures that were left. I didn't actually like the way she looked in the pictures.'

Therapist: 'Why not? What about her didn't you like? How did she look?'

Rivka: 'I don't know. She looked very elegant and respectable, but there was something cold about her, she didn't radiate any warmth. Actually she looked very much like my grandmother, that is, her daughter, who also didn't radiate much warmth. There was always something that bothered me about her when I looked at the pictures.'

Therapist: 'Can you see any similarity between yourself and this grandmother?'

Rivka: 'I don't know. Everyone always told me that I look like my father and his family, although I didn't know any of them either. But there really is something about her that reminds me of myself. It's hard to define it exactly.'

I smiled at her, 'At least in the elegance I can certainly see a similarity.'

Rivka returned my smile and said, 'You know, when I was a child – I think I already told you this – I always fantasized that I had a grandmother and a grandfather, and for the grandfather I always chose the one on my mother's side, who always impressed me in his pictures. He looked like such a handsome and powerful man, very respectable and giving a sense of strength and security. But the grandmother I would choose rather from my father's side. She seemed to me a somewhat simple woman, but very warm. I always imagined them and thought about them as my grandfather and grandmother. I chose these two and put them together.' Rivka's smile was like the smile of a naughty little girl who knows she has done something mischievous, perhaps forbidden, but amusing.

Therapist: 'Do you know anything about what happened to this grandmother when they took your parents to the camps? Was she still alive? How old was she? After all, your mother was only fourteen then.'

Rivka: 'Yes, that's true, I never thought about it. Actually I have no idea what happened to her or how old she was then. I never asked anything about her.' Rivka stopped talking, and after a while she added, 'Like about many other things.'

Therapist: 'This is a square that is still empty in your great internal mosaic of your family – you've filled in part of it already, and it's waiting for you to fill it in too.'

Tears came into Rivka's eyes. She looked simultaneously sad and happy. 'Yes, it still frightens me to really open the family book and read it clearly chapter after chapter.'

Therapist: 'It's a hard book to read. Each chapter is full of pain, but after all you know that it's also full of feeling. It would be very difficult for you to read it by yourself. But, you know, what we've done here today is actually to open the book and read a whole chapter of it together, and more shared reading of many more chapters is waiting for us, and I think that the group also reads it with you sometimes.'

Rivka: 'Yes, that's true. See where we started from today. I had actually planned to tell you other things entirely.'

Therapist: 'All because of the ring.'

We both laughed.

For the first time in her life Rivka was meeting the images of her family figures – grandmothers and grandfathers. It was not enough for her just to identify them, but she went a step further – a very important step. Like an artist drawing one detail after another, until all the details come together to create a whole clear image with all its shades, lines and expressions, so Rivka was beginning to reconstruct the images of her ancestors. She possessed small fragments of information, faded pictures with which to begin building, with much labour, the images of her grandmothers and grandfathers, and even the image of her mother's grandmother. The images were not yet complete, and she would have to return to them, to alter and polish them, until they came out clearly – each one separately and all of them with their relationships to one another.

In the absence of real figures in her life, Rivka tended during her childhood to fantasize an extended family. She was able to select the bits of information she liked and create an imaginary family to suit her taste. This fantasy in which she lived served as a compensation for the enormous void she was actually in.

But Rivka's story also highlights the difficulty she still had in feeling her parents' pain for their loss in their lives as if it were her own pain. At first she spoke as if she was reading a story from a book, and the story sounded detached and without pain, as if it didn't concern her. Gradually she began to grasp the fact that these figures actually existed in reality and that they were lost not only from her parents' lives but from her own life as well, entailing her own loss of the chance of experiencing the feeling of belonging to a whole family. Between the growing cracks in her previously absolute emotional disconnection one can see excitement and confusion, even if they are somewhat restrained. This is thus the beginning of her relationship of belonging, even if only partially, to the lost figures of her family. In addition to identifying them Rivka has begun to see how the figures relate to one another and put them in their places, one beside the other, according to the links between them and their location on the family tree.

A similar picture arises from a dream of Orna's – also the daughter of two survivor parents. Although thirty-five years old, she is not married, and she finds it difficult to create a real, continuing relationship with a partner.

'In this dream I'm about to get married. Everything is ready for the wedding, even though I don't have any idea who the groom is. It's precisely him that I can't see. I can see the hall, and the people, and my mother there. I am getting ready for the wedding and trying on the wedding dress my mother bought me. When I put it on I see that it's a dress made entirely of lace, a sort of antique lace in a cream colour. In general, it's this sort of old dress, in an ancient style. At first it bothers me a little, I wanted a new, modern dress, but after all it's a nice dress and I like it and I agree to wear it.'

When I asked her what the dream meant, Orna answered that she didn't understand it, except for the motif of the wedding, which was very familiar to her. This motif had appeared again and again in her dreams, and it represented the fulfilment of a wish in her heart and in the heart of her parents, who had long been expecting her to finally get married and have a family.

Therapist: 'Then what do you say about this antique lace wedding dress?'

Orna: 'I don't know exactly. Maybe it belongs to someone, to someone in the past. But I don't have any idea what it is.'

I remembered that Orna's mother had been married before World War II and had lost her husband in the Holocaust, so I said: 'You know, I don't think we ever talked about your mother's first wedding. What exactly happened there? Who was there? How did your mother look, and what was the wedding like in general?'

Orna didn't answer immediately, and only after a long pause for thought did she say, 'Right, I never thought about it. Once she actually told me a little about it, a long time ago.'

Therapist: 'And what exactly did she tell you?'

Orna: 'She told me that she was very young, about eighteen, and she was very lucky. She was a very beautiful girl and always surrounded by admirers, and she chose the one who became her husband. When the wedding took place the atmosphere was already very strained. I'm not sure if they were already living in a ghetto, but I think they were, there was already fear in the air. But they held the wedding anyway, and they were all there, her parents and her five sisters – after all, she was the eldest sister – and also her grandfather, who was already quite ill, and her grandmother. And there were aunts and uncles, and the groom's whole family. It's hard for me to imagine such a big family. And everyone there loved her and they were happy about the first daughter and granddaughter to be getting married.'

Therapist: 'And do you know what your mother wore at the wedding?'

Orna hesitated for a moment and then answered, 'She told me that she wore a dress that wasn't really white but rather cream-colour, and that her mother gave her a very beautiful veil of old lace. A sort of very delicate lace, that maybe her grandmother had received from her own mother. I'm not sure of all this, but it's what went through my head, the sort of things that are handed down from one generation to the next, from mother to daughter.'

Therapist: 'And what happened afterwards to your mother and her husband?'

Orna: 'They managed to live together for about a year, in the ghetto. And then they were taken away from the ghetto and put onto trains. She managed to jump off the train and then she pretended to be an Aryan and returned to the ghetto. He never came back, nor did anyone of all the people that were there at the wedding. Only her husband's mother and sister managed to survive, and after a very long time she met them again in the ghetto, but the relationship between them had already become unpleasant. They couldn't forgive her for surviving when their son and brother did not.'

Therapist: 'Let's return to the dream now, to your wedding. Have you ever tried to imagine what your wedding would be like?'

Orna seemed sad and confused. There were tears in her eyes. 'Yes. . . No. . . Once I thought that there wouldn't be anyone standing there at my wedding except for my parents. Oh, and also one uncle, on my father's side. There wouldn't be such a family as at my mother's wedding. This ties in with my lone-liness. On the Seder night, for example, on Passover, my father, my mother and I always sit around a big table, and that's that. It's always so empty, so sad. Suddenly I think that I would have liked so much to see my mother's mother once, that's actually my grandmother, perhaps standing there next to me at my wedding ceremony, but actually it's hard for me to really imagine it.'

Therapist: 'Is there anything in your house that remains from her? Any picture? Any object?'

Orna: 'I don't know. There isn't any picture of her. It's hard for me to see clearly how she looked. All I know is that according to what everyone says my mother looks very much like her, so I can imagine her somewhat.' She was quiet for a moment and then continued, 'You know, suddenly I remembered that at my mother's house there's a pillow with a cover made of very beautiful, very delicate lace, and my mother told me that this is lace that her mother – that is, my grandmother – and my grandmother's mother, embroidered themselves. Marvellous lace. My mother told me that my grandmother was always embroidering marvellous lace like that. Her veil at her wedding was also made of that kind of lace, it was actually the same lace!'

Orna, like Rivka, is occupied with the work of identification. She allows herself to dream and to fantasize about her extended family through associations arising within herself – a large warm tribe, which was once living and breathing. In contrast to her mother, who knew what family warmth was, Orna – the only child of isolated parents – grew up in a vast, cold vacuum that surrounded her from the moment of her birth. But now she is already able to find in her self some sort of link with a few figures: their outlines, however hesitant, are becoming visible.

The outstanding emotion in Orna's attitude towards these blurred figures is the sense of lack deriving from an unsatisfiable longing. With the help of the dream, the lace dress, and her mother's lace veil, she links herself indirectly to the generational chain reaching until her great-grandmother. The very real lace pillow in her mother's house is an anchor – the only real memory she has. Everything else was lost. But in her dream Orna has a wedding dress made of the same lace fabric, made by her great-grandmother, that was handed down from generation to generation. Orna is thus seeking to belong to the figures of the women she was not fortunate enough to know or even to see pictures of.

The next phase that the 'memorial candles' go through involves a direct, painful encounter with their parents' traumatic experiences during the Holocaust. Although the 'memorial candles' can permit themselves to give up some of the over-protectiveness that previously characterized their attitude towards their parents, a direct encounter with what really happened to their parents during the Holocaust generally fills them with feelings of pain, pity and empathy, and simultaneously with a heavy burden of suspicion and anger. The raising of these harsh and contrasting feelings, which have hitherto been repressed, is painful but vital and necessary for the separation and completion of their identity.

As mentioned, many survivors have a damaged sense of self-esteem, and this feeling was internalized by their children. Raising it to the threshold of consciousness involves the readiness and ability on the part of the children to expose problematic feelings like shame, suspicion and humiliation – feelings that had existed in their psyches only unconsciously until this point and had become components of their selves. The need to repress and deny these components directly affected their damaged sense of self-esteem and led to conflicts and insecurity in various areas of life. The possibility of raising these problematic feelings to the threshold of consciousness, talking about them and working on them in the therapeutic setting has a decisive effect on the course of therapy. Many questions disturb the survivors' children, although they dare not ask them aloud: how was it just my parents who survived? What price did the Germans force them to pay in exchange for their lives? And how are they capable, after everything they experienced, of returning to living an outwardly normal life, bearing and raising children, without losing their sanity?

And this isn't all. The psyches of the 'memorial candles' are still full of intense, disturbing conflicts directly derived from their parents' experiences in the Holocaust. These conflicts are centred around two foci: one connected with the pain, torture and humiliation suffered by their parents, which caused them to lose their sense of self-esteem; and the other involving their parents' sexuality during the Holocaust, especially as concerns such questions as how they were able to cope 'there' with their sexual maturation and their sexual drives, and whether they used their sexuality in any way, directly or indirectly, in order to survive. These questions, if not clarified, will never allow the 'memorial candles' to separate from their unconscious symbiotic identification, or from the archaic identification derived from the superego they share with their parents, in order to attain a mature, balanced identification with the parents.

Now, in this phase of therapy, the 'memorial candles' are beginning to gradually give up some of their defence mechanisms, and they are filled with the drive to dare to raise these disturbing questions to consciousness and to expose their feelings to the light. They now perceive the therapy setting as more secure and supportive than in the past, and they also feel this way about the mutual identifications and the dialogue taking place between the group and themselves and between the therapists and themselves; all these perceptions help them cope with their feelings and serve to lessen the strength of the threat and the anxiety involved in their self-exposure.

In one of the group therapy sessions a dialogue took place between Michal and Nira, each the 'memorial candle' of her family. Nira, about thirty years old, is an only child. Michal, also about thirty, has two sisters. At this session they exposed for the first time a fraction of the traumas suffered by their mothers, who had both been adolescents when the war broke out – Michal's mother had been about eleven, Nira's mother about fourteen. During the course of the discussion Michal and Nira revealed to each other their feelings about their mothers and about the various things they went through during the Holocaust, with the rest of the group remaining in the background and serving as a supporting element.

At the beginning of the session Nira had related how, after her mother and aunt had been sent from one concentration camp to another, and had suffered terrible torture and countless humiliations, and even marched in death marches, they succeeded in escaping and hiding in a granary next to a Polish peasant's home. Nira had said in a restrained voice and with a frozen expression:

'Even today I can't go into this granary, and every time I don't go in it becomes more difficult to enter.'

Therapist: 'You keep trying all the time to go into the granary by yourself. You could go in with Michal, or with us. Perhaps it would be easier.'

Mordechai: 'You know, you were always an only child and you carried everything by yourself your whole life, and even here you act the same way. You never really trust us. You don't let us get close to you, help you, be with you.'

Nira turned her chair towards Michal and spoke to her, still in a restrained voice: 'My mother told me how she put her sister in a corner of the granary and covered her, both to warm her and so that no one should see her. At this point her feet were already completely frozen and she wasn't able to move at all. Then she went out and milked some goat that she found, and dripped drops of milk into her mouth. And what happened after that? Her sister was lying there frozen and half-dead, and she was left alone in the dark, frightening granary. Those hours, after they succeeded in escaping from the camp and hid in the forest for hours, in the snow and ice, and the Nazis with their wolfhounds. They looked for them in the forest for hours, and they didn't manage to find them, and now, when it seemed as if everything was finally alright, but actually nothing was alright. How could they stand it? How could they stop and think and be afraid, and be hungry and cold, after everything they had gone through already, the death march, the forced labour camp, the frozen mud, hours after hours. . .'

Nira's voice became weak and she started to tremble. She stopped talking. After a while she continued, 'I can't imagine that if I were in the situation that she was in then, that I would be really able to stand it and get out of it alive, and that's that.'

Mordechai: 'And that's what? Are you referring to what you feel after such experiences?'

Nira: 'Yes. Actually, it's impossible to feel anything then. Because feeling means placing your life itself in danger. I feel this very strongly.'

I tried to lessen the tension: 'Say this sentence to everyone in the group here.'

Nira turned to Yaakov: 'I feel that if I feel too much then I won't able to stand it.'

Therapist: 'Actually, you are telling Yaakov that if you show him what you really feel, it will be hard for you to continue to keep up your image in his eyes. Since what you don't express clearly – it's as if it doesn't obligate you and it doesn't really exist.'

Nira began to cry quietly, and Michal spoke instead of her: 'From that moment, there in the granary, if I had been in your mother's place, I wouldn't have been able to continue at all. I wouldn't have been able to give any more. She was in the midst of death, in the midst of the snow and the ice, and she actually saved her own life and her sister's life. I've often thought about would happen if my parents died and I and my two sisters would be left. I thought about how I would take care that there should be a little money for each of them, something very elemental. When there were bombs during the Six-Day War my mother would give us a canteen and send us to a shelter in a house rather far away, because we didn't have a shelter. I held my older sister's hand on one side, and my younger sister's on the other side, and so we marched to the shelter. Even then I felt responsible, that I needed to take care of them. I was only nine years old. When I was with my mother in Europe, in the country where she was born, she only took me with her out of the whole family. We saw the house that had belonged to her family, they had lived there for eight generations. We walked down the street and we were silent. We stopped by one house and she said, "Here lived the Cohens, and they had a girl the same age as me." And I thought that my mother's life had frozen there. All her illnesses and headaches and nightmares, they all came from there. When we got to her family's house, she went down to the cellar one evening. She said she wanted to get rid of everything that was left there. . . I stayed upstairs and started to cry terribly. But right away I told myself, "You have to stop, it's hard enough for Mother even without your crying." A few hours later my mother came up from the cellar, and she looked as white as a ghost.' Michal began to cry quietly, her tears flowed but she did not stop talking: 'She put a package on the table. In the evening I looked at it. There were some pictures of the family and some notebooks.'

Michal bent her head down. She seemed immersed within herself, and silence reigned in the room. After a few moments had passed I addressed her: 'Michal, when you tell this story now, are you able to feel that you're telling it to Nira and that you're close to her?'

Michal: 'I don't know, I don't really think so.'

Therapist: 'Actually, when you're with your mother in that cellar, in the hiding-place where she hid for three years, there isn't any room left for anyone else. None of us here with you can participate and really be with you, just as it was hard for Nira to really share her experience with us.'

Michal looked pensive and somewhat confused, and she turned to

Nira: 'When you told us the story about your mother, I really felt your mother in the snow, her loneliness, her suffering, everything. . .'

Nira finally came back to participating in the discussion: 'But I felt almost nothing, I didn't dare to really feel my mother. I was envious before that you were so moved, I don't dare to feel it. I only felt pain held back inside. It doesn't even peek out.'

Michal: 'When you spoke last time about how emotionally closed your mother is, I felt something strong. I didn't make the connection with my own mother directly, but perhaps it is connected. When other people here in the group showed me how I speak apathetically and disconnectedly, I knew that you knew that something happened to me inside.'

Nira: 'I always knew that if my mother hadn't saved her sister and hadn't needed to take care of her, she wouldn't have come out of it alive. I also often feel, as I do now, that when I have to take care of someone or something, then I exist.'

Therapist: 'Then try again to go back to the granary. Your aunt is lying there under the pile of straw and her feet are frozen. What happens next?'

Nira: 'It seems so hard to me, it's impossible to feel it. How can one be a human being and go through this?'

Therapist: 'Yes, it's really very hard. But if you hold everything inside and cover it up well, does that make it easier? That's what your mother had to do in order to survive, in order to remain alive. It's also what you often do. But you weren't really there. . .'

Nira: 'If I'll start to cry it won't stop. In our house there was no crying. It was actually forbidden to cry. My mother couldn't see me crying. When it breaks out here sometimes, I don't know where it's coming from.'

Therapist: 'Undoubtedly it was very hard for your mother to see you crying because it aroused in her all the pain and crying that she held back and suppressed all the years. If she sees you crying, maybe she'll also start to cry, and that's too threatening.'

Michal: 'If you like, Nira, I could go into the granary with you.'

Nira: 'Yes, I would like that, but it's so hard for me to tell what happened there. There's something there that's very frightening to reconstruct and to feel. In emergencies, when something physically difficult happens to me, in the first moment I feel a general collapse, but afterwards I get organized right away.'

Michal: 'Yes, you really need a lot of courage and strength, but you say that your mother had strength, not only to go through all that, but also to save her sister.'

Therapist: 'I think that you too, Nira, have this strength.'

Michal: 'You know, there, in the granary, if I were your mother I would have taken the straw off my sister and rubbed her frozen feet and cried and cried and cried.'

Tears appeared in Nira's eyes and flowed slowly down her cheeks. 'Yes, it seems that this is what I couldn't see by myself.'

After Michal spoke, Nira allowed herself to really cry this time, and she cried and cried.

Nira and Michal identify with each other and feel closeness and sharing of the contents and conflicts of their inner worlds. As mentioned, their mothers had been adolescent girls when the war broke out, and the feelings of loss in their psyches, stemming from the cutting-off of the process of their emotional growth, were apparently very similar, as the emotions they transmitted to their daughters are not essentially different, even though each of them internalized them in her own way.

It is interesting to see how Nira and Michal assist each other in finding links with their painful emotional worlds – both their own and their mothers'. This process expresses a mechanism of mutual projective identification. Michal is able to feel Nira's mother's pain and even to express it aloud. Michal's emotional ventilation and verbalization give Nira legitimation to identify with her mother's pain and to feel a bit of the sadness that surrounded her in the granary – and through her mother's pain to feel her own pain as well. Michal, on the other hand, through her identification with the pain of Nira and her mother, succeeds in getting close for the first time in her life to her own mother's pain, which she had internalized and repressed many years earlier. The group as a whole now had a higher threshold for holding, which gives it the ability to cope with stronger expressions of feeling and with the exposure of harsher traumas. It is therefore able to grant Michal and Nira the sense of calmness and security so necessary for their difficult work.

In their dialogue Michal and Nira gradually become aware of the parts of their mothers' egos which were projected and that they had absorbed and internalized during their childhood as parts of their own personalities. This awareness, although only tentative and partial, is very important because it involves the possibility of identifying borrowed parts of their personalities. Although these parts were internalized in their egos, they actually belonged to their mothers and their past. As therapy progressed Nira and Michal would still have to deal with their separation from these borrowed parts of their egos, in order to reach a new internal integration that would allow them a separate and independent identity. But in order to attain separation and integration they must first come to grips with these borrowed, internalized parts of the ego, which is the reason for the importance of the initial stage of awareness for their very existence. Michal, for example, went through a traumatic experience at the age of nine, when she went to the bomb shelter with her sisters. At nearly the same age her mother had gone into hiding. There is no doubt that, if not for the internalized experience borrowed from her mother's past, the walk to the bomb shelter would not have been so traumatic. Michal had lived for years in a state of psychic closing-off, and in stressful situations she became helpless: this is nothing if not a reconstruction of her mother's inner feelings which had become set in her psyche when she lived in hiding for three years.

I remember the group session in which Michal first succeeded in freeing herself from some of the psychic stress and closing-off that had dominated her life. This occurred in a real emotional encounter with the reality of her mother's life in hiding. Michal had dared to enter the hiding-place and to sense her mother there, with the group surrounding her and protecting her.

Michal: 'This week I asked my mother a little about what happened to her there in the hiding-place, how she studied and what she did exactly. The part of her story that touched me most was when she described how she would get dressed and comb her hair every morning, getting ready for "school". Then she would put her briefcase on her back and her father would take her to school. That is, they would have this sort of ceremony. They would walk the few steps that were possible along the length of this little room, and then she would step over the threshold of the room, and this was the sign that she was entering school. . . Then she would sit down on a chair and her father, with infinite patience, would sit for hours every morning teaching her all the subjects. It's really amazing, but when they left the hiding-place, three years later, she knew all the subjects perfectly, she wasn't missing anything. . .'

At this stage of therapy the 'memorial candles' begin to deal with their parents' humiliation during the Holocaust, and besides the pain and the pity feelings of shame and anger arise in them. The marathon session reported here took place after about three years of group therapy.

A few hours had already passed since the session had started and Martha was still sitting enclosed within herself and had not opened her mouth; actually, she had been sitting this way in most of the group sessions during the previous months. Suddenly she started talking:

'I feel choked. During the last two hours I've been feeling that I actually don't have any air to breathe. I've been almost choking and I haven't had any air, especially when I heard Yair, who spoke about his birth on the way to Palestine, and how his parents smuggled him in on a ship of illegal immigrants in a basket full of fruit and rags that covered him. Then I really felt this choking.'

Yehuda: 'Yes, you know, in many situations, especially if I'm under tension or stress, I also feel choked, and it's hard for me to breathe, and recently I've really been thinking that perhaps it's connected somehow with that time of my birth and when I was on the ship.'

Martha: 'I don't know exactly when I started getting these attacks of shortness of breath, but it was a long time ago, many years ago.'

Therapist: 'I remember your telling us that when you were about fourteen you had a severe asthma attack. Where was this?'

Martha didn't answer. After a long time had passed she bent her head down and started murmuring in a whisper: 'It's strange how I forgot. It was when my parents and I were travelling to Europe for the first time, when I was fourteen – back to the city they had lived in and run away from. I very much did not want to go there, but my father insisted and we went. They didn't say anything special. When we got there and started walking around, I don't remember any special reactions of theirs, but after we were there for two days I had such a severe attack of asthma that they had to put me in hospital there for ten days.

Then I didn't understand anything. Now I realize that what happened to me was associated with what my parents felt when they went back to their homeland, which was also the place where disaster had struck them. After all, they had lost more or less everything. My father had had a sister who had been about fourteen when she died. I'm named Martha after her. And my mother was about the same age when they escaped in the middle of the night, she and her parents, and tried to find the way to the border. . . My father told me what happened to them the night they escaped. They got lost there in the forest, it was completely dark. They were wearing backpacks with some water and some bread – this simple kind of bread that my grandmother had managed to bake before they set out. They were very hungry and attacked the bread, but my grandfather said they had to save some for the next day. They were very hungry and tired. At a certain point my grandfather told my father that he should stay in charge of his mother and sister for the meantime and he himself would go to look for the road. He went away and they waited for hours and hours. My father, who was about sixteen, stayed there alone with his mother and sister, in this total darkness in the middle of the forest, but his father never came back. He didn't know what to do, where to go, and suddenly from far away they heard dogs barking, voices of Germans and shots. Apparently my grandfather had been caught.'

Yehuda: 'And how do you think he felt? Did he ever tell you?'

Martha: 'I don't know, he never said it outright. It's hard for me to see my father afraid. But now I feel that I'm all trembling inside, my belly was so tense all this time. Now I really feel these cramps.'

Martha looked very pale. Her teeth chattered and her whole body trembled; it seemed as though she was incapable of controlling the trembling that had seized her body. She nevertheless continued to speak in a weak, hesitant voice: 'Now I feel real fear. I don't know, I'm not sure how he felt there in the forest. It's very hard for me to imagine the state he was in, it's so frightening. I can't actually get into it.' She stopped talking for a moment, but immediately continued in a somewhat more confident voice: 'This anxiety, this terrible helplessness at that moment in the forest, and also afterwards, later, in a thousand situations during all the years of running away and hiding. Now I remember that even nowadays he still gets into such anxiety at every stupid thing that happens, it's really funny. Out of every little thing he makes a catastrophe and he's always getting into stress and anxiety states. And this is also what he transmitted to me and to my mother all these years. After all, I'm the anxiety champion, as I told you a few weeks ago, and now I think it's all connected somehow.'

Tears began to flow from her eyes and she wept softly. Zvia, who had been sitting immobile, spoke to her gently and with tears in her eyes: 'You know, all these months in the group I had a problem with your silence. I know you're carrying all sorts of things around inside you, but you're so closed, you don't let anything out. Now that you've spoken and told your story, I feel a lot of closeness and warmth towards you. What you told about your father, I don't know why exactly, reminded me of what my father told me a few weeks ago, when I was home. He said that in the camp they worked for hours and hours in the mud and the cold, and they dug and dug and dug some ditches or pits or whatever there. I try to imagine him there, marching in a row like a powerless skeleton. I can't stay with this picture. My stomach gets all cramped, and suddenly it's hard for me to breathe.'

Zvia did not stop talking but her breathing became heavy and tears continued to run down her cheeks: 'The hardest thing for me to think about him is what he told me at the end. He was injured from all the work, in the foot or the knees, I don't know. And when he couldn't work any more, he decided to go to the infirmary. He described how he actually crawled, how he went on all fours the whole way in the frozen mud to the infirmary. He crawled and crawled without any strength. And a Nazi officer who saw him on the way shouted and cursed him and even added some kicks, but he kept crawling. Like that, like a dog that's been kicked.'

Zvia broke out in loud sobs and was unable to continue her story. The group sat frozen in their places. The atmosphere was full of tension, and some of the people cried quietly.

Afterwards Baruch began speaking, his voice choked with tears. His face was very white and his eyes expressed horror: 'The story you told just now, Zvia, was very hard for me to hear. At first I didn't understand why I really wasn't listening to you but was thinking about other things, but then I started to listen. My own mother and father also told me some of the things they went through. I was reminded of my mother's description of the time when she was in Auschwitz. Every morning she would go out to work in the mud and the cold, like your father, in a long line outside the camp. But, you know, it's hard for me even now to really feel it. I see you crying, and the others, but I can't even cry. My father told me that the day the Americans came and liberated their camp, Bergen-Belsen I think it was, everyone who was still alive went outside. There was a sack of potatoes there, and they all ran and attacked it and grabbed whatever they could. My father, whose feet were injured, with gangrene already spreading along the toes. . .he couldn't run, and could hardly walk, at most he could crawl. So he crawled very slowly to the sack, and when he got there he was the last one and there wasn't even one potato left.'

A note of anger had crept into Baruch's voice. But anger with whom? With his humiliated father crawling there, or with whoever had brought him to this humiliating state?

The 'memorial candles' thus finally dare to open up and to share with the group these stories of the traumatic events that occurred to their parents. Some of the stories project an image of the parent as persecuted and humiliated. This arouses identi-fication and pain in the children, but also repulsion and anger. Zvia and Martha expressed mainly pain and pity, and even the humiliation aroused in them now, for the first time, empathic identification. For Baruch it was more difficult. Although he could feel his father's pain, he was struggling with him and even allowed himself some degree of anger and repulsion towards him; it is perhaps more difficult for a son than for a daughter to identify with the humiliated father. The image of his humiliated mother wallowing in the mud is also too threatening, and he cannot find in his heart any emotional link with the terrible picture that is beginning to form before his eyes. Baruch's fear of the emotional flooding that might undermine his defence system and his psychic equilibrium is very strong.

In this session it is clear that the feeling of threat is beginning to weaken gradually in the group matrix and that the group members are managing to identify with one another's pain and to share their feelings with one another. When one of them opens up his closed heart, the others immediately join him. The group's capacity to hold higher levels of feeling opens the door for the exposure of the humiliating situations suffered by their parents.

The exposure of the parents' weakness and helplessness sheds light on their children's feelings of insecurity and low self-esteem, as well as on their body images. For this reason none of the group members except Martha, who can discern the link between her fears and her father's anxieties, is able as yet to make the connection between their parents' humiliation and the feelings that disturb them.

Breaking the rigid defence system protecting the parent's image (both the real and the internalized one) involves the readiness to stop protecting oneself excessively against other people in general and the group members and the therapists in particular. Only when this defence mechanism is broken can the 'memorial candles' achieve full exposure of their parents' humiliation, and thus understand its influence on their distorted self- images. The working-through of these painful contents gives them the ability to understand their parents and to feel real empathy for them – to accept and feel their pain, and at the same time to distinguish it from their own pain. It seems that only facing and working through these contents can bring about the separation of the ego of the 'memorial candles' from those elements that were borrowed from their parents' inner world; for, after all, they did not actually live through the Holocaust themselves.

Conflicts concerning sexual identity

In the process of constructing a mature identity, masculine or feminine, the 'memorial candles' are confronted with the traumas that damaged their parents' sexual identity. As mentioned, the survivors who went through the Holocaust during their childhood or youth became prematurely adult. Most of them reached puberty under conditions of isolation and lack of privacy or intimacy. Many of them were the victims of sexual abuse and humiliation or witnessed it among the people in their vicinity. Thus the emotional maturation which normally accompanies physical maturation did not take place for them. Even the sexual identity of older survivors was undermined and remained fixated at a younger emotional age than their actual age, although outwardly they functioned as adult men and women in every respect.

The 'memorial candles' generally knew nothing of their parents' sexual experience during the Holocaust or previous to it. They might perhaps know that their father had got married and had children before the war, and had lost them all in the end. Their mother, it seems, had also been married once, or had she only been engaged? What had been the nature of the relationship between the parents and their previous spouses? How had they coped with their sexuality during and after the years of terror? All this remained vague and misty.

Even people who did not live through the Holocaust do not tend to share the most intimate details of their lives with their children, and this is all the more true of the survivors. They were unable even to tell their children the usual sorts of information that every parent shares with his children at one point or another. In this matter too the 'memorial candles' are placed in an ambivalent and conflictual situation. On the one hand they share their parents' emotional world through the process of transposition; they live in the fantasies they share with their parents through an intense narcissistic conjunction that began during their early childhood. In the area of sexual identity, as in the area of self-esteem, archaic identifications with their parents were formed in the 'memorial candles' – identifications stemming from the narcissistic injuries created by the damage to their body image and their sense of self-esteem. On the other hand, however, the survivors created a myth including past memories, whose purpose was to maintain a traumatic screen over the harsh feelings, including feelings of hostility and anxiety, that were associated with the brutal experiences, both physical and psychological, they had gone through (H. Klein 1987). The maintenance of this myth required the most massive repression of all memories of the past, in such a way that any exposure to them or sharing of them with their children was perceived as impossible or extremely threatening. It is thus not surprising that the heads of the 'memorial candles' were filled from early childhood with all these unanswered questions, and at the same time with vague fantasies about their parents' sexuality during the Holocaust, all of which disturbed them greatly.

This intrapsychic situation strengthens the oedipal (incestuous) fantasies of the 'memorial candles'; instead of strengthening its repression it prevents individuation during and after the oedipal stage, as well as the construction of an independent superego. Moreover, the topics of aggression and sexuality, drawn both from myths and from the reality of their parents' past, continue to exist in their oedipal fantasies.

It must be remembered that the initial dialogues between the survivor mothers and fathers and their infants were saturated with anxieties, depression and guilt, with very little room left for joy, pleasure or intimacy. Therefore the 'triangle' of the 'memorial candle', his mother and his father is necessarily disturbed, and its formation is retarded. The 'memorial candles' thus find it difficult to identify with their parents, and this difficulty is partially associated with the fact that in representations of the survivors' superegos there is a split between the self and the object, which causes the survivors to transmit double messages to their children in the area of sexuality as well as in other areas. Therefore the identification mechanisms of the 'memorial candles' with respect to their parents in the area of sexual identity have remained primitive, archaic mechanisms deriving from the id or from those archaic mechanisms of the superego that were described above. The 'memorial candles' find it difficult to develop more mature mechanisms that would enable an intrapsychic separation from their parents and the consolidation of a discrete, independent sexual identity. The lack of consolidation and discreteness of their sexual identity is expressed in difficulties and conflicts that they report during the first stage of therapy, with respect to their inability to establish an intimate relationship with their spouses – a relationship blending the emotional level and the sexual level.

Indeed, the 'memorial candles' have many difficulties in the area of sexual relations. These difficulties increase when they enter an intimate and committed emotional relationship such as marriage. Sometimes their sex lives are normal, but they frequently change partners, and their relationships are superficial and emotionally uncommitted. It must also be remembered that the relationship between the survivor parents themselves as a couple was dominated by a symbiotic pattern of dependency and control. Thus most of the 'memorial candles' were not exposed to an equal intimate relationship that could serve as a model for identification. Affection, warmth and physical closeness of any sort were rare in the families of survivors, and the children had no choice but to internalize damaged identity parts, which then became part of their own selves.

Out of their inner need, and out of their greater capacity and security, the 'memorial candles' are ready at this stage of therapy to try to break the myths surrounding their parents' sexuality and to begin to expose the conflicts, the internal confusion, and the complex emotions that have been disturbing them for years in this area.

At first one of the 'memorial candles' raises out of the twilight of his consciousness all the fears and fantasies connected with his parents' sexual experiences during the Holocaust. It often becomes clear that the main questions disturbing him are those surrounding the 'family secrets' that were carefully hidden from him yet nevertheless were always floating around inside the house. These secrets come up to awareness during the therapy sessions.

Nira: 'There's something bothering me that I've never spoken about. My aunt told me once that when they were in the camp, and they were all waiting in line and were put on the trucks, after they had already put their mother on, they almost put them on too. And then one of the Nazi officers looked at her and at my mother and said that he needed two laundresses for the camp laundry, and so they didn't put them on the truck. They asked for their mother to be taken off the truck as well, but some woman said to them, "Leave her, be thankful that they let you stay. If you want to live, leave her."'

Nira stopped talking for a moment, confused and wrapped in thought, and then continued: 'I don't understand exactly what happened there. My mother looked very good then. She was young and pretty, but my aunt was thin and not particularly good-looking. How is it that they let her stay as well? What actually happened there? I've never let myself imagine or think about it until this moment. Was there perhaps something sexual there? Did they perhaps have to do something in order to survive? I've never wanted to think about my mother's sexuality. Recently she's been appearing in my dreams, very pretty, feminine and sexy, and when she appears with a strange man it's clear that there's something sexual between them. I try to separate them, or I turn her again into the sick, weak person I perceived her to be all these years. It's very hard for me to see her as a woman and to grasp her sexuality. I see this as connected with what happened when I matured and became a woman. On the one hand she was very happy, but on the other hand she completely stopped taking care of her own femininity. I also see it as connected with another thing: When I accompanied my mother to Germany, when she went to give evidence against some Nazi criminal, I was already eighteen. My mother was afraid to travel alone, so she took me along to accompany her and to support her. We didn't talk about anything, not even about the significance of this journey, what it was doing to her, as if it were a vacation or a pleasure trip. I remember that there was an officer of the Italian staff on the ship, a very good-looking boy, who was trying to chat me up, and my mother enjoyed it very much and encouraged it. And when he offered to give us a better cabin, she accepted it gladly.'

Therapist: 'How did it seem to you then? And now?'

Nira: 'Then I didn't react at all. As usual, I didn't say anything. But when I think about it now, it seems rather strange of her.'

Itzhak: 'It's actually very much like the use of sexuality and femininity for instrumental purposes, in order to get all sorts of things. Often when you were speaking here in the group about your recent relationships with men, I had a similar feeling. You also use your sexuality for this type of purpose.'

Nira: 'Yes, I think I know what you're talking about.'

Itzhak: 'This week I finished reading Primo Levi's book. The whole time I had pictures in my head of how he looked and what he did. I asked myself if he ever felt any sexual desire in the camp. But the hardest part is the insults, the way they humiliated him. And yet he succeeded in maintaining his humanity. He didn't become totally blunted. The whole time he searched for human contact. Nira's story reminds me now that I've been having a difficult time lately with Noa, with our intimate relationship. It's difficult for me to see her naked. I remember that all the years, even at home, if it ever happened that I saw my mother naked, or half-dressed, it was very difficult for me to take. When I would look at the pictures from the Holocaust and see the naked women standing there, I always had the same feeling. . . My father once said that there are many things that my mother never tells anyone. She became pregnant before the wedding.'

Therapist: 'What did you think about what your father said? Did it arouse fantasies in you?'

Itzhak: 'Yes. I often thought about whether something had happened to her in the sexual sphere, rape or something like that. Once I thought that she might have been compelled to engage in prostitution. She was with the partisans, and later she worked as a maid for some Ukrainians. She had to go to church every Sunday to prove that she was a Christian. She had a false name and counterfeit documents. The hard part is thinking about her submission, her humiliation. My mother came from a religious family. My grandfather, her father, was very religious, so all these things must have been impressed upon her very deeply – it must have been a real trauma for her.'

Arnona: 'In my job I work with some crippled girls and I identify very much with their handicap. One of them is paralysed in the lower half of her body. I have often thought that I would not be able to cope so well with such a handicap. My mother always does everything perfectly, in spite of her advanced age. She always tries to maintain her fitness, she even does exercises. But I still can't perceive her as a sexual being. She hides her sexuality. I always had the feeling that she was hiding all sorts of things. I don't know what happened to her in these areas during the war. She was about twenty-four then, young and pretty. I never consciously thought about this, but now, while Itzhak and Nira were talking, it suddenly became more apparent to me that my mother might also have been exposed to such experiences.'

At this point Nehama joined the discussion: 'On the last Holocaust Memorial Day, when I was home, my mother told me about her five sisters, none of whom survived. The oldest was very beautiful, and when they went out of the ghetto there were some SS officers standing there and they made their own selection. Or perhaps it was after they had already got to the camp, I don't know exactly. At any rate, they selected my mother's eldest sister together with some other girls, all of them young and pretty, putting them on one side. Afterwards they heard that they had been taken to be prostitutes for the SS officers. She never came back from there and no one knows exactly what happened to her. The younger sisters went with their mother straight to the gas chambers. Not even a picture of them is left, or of their parents.'

Therapist: 'And do you know how your mother's eldest sister looked?'

Nehama: 'Not exactly. All I know is that she had black hair and green eyes and she was very beautiful. In general, my mother and all her sisters were all very beautiful, but the eldest sister was especially beautiful.'

Therapist: 'Can you actually imagine her?'

Nehama: 'Yes, now I can do it. The whole week it was on my mind, everywhere I went, at work, even on the road, when I was driving, the whole time her face accompanied me. I couldn't stop looking and seeing her. It was as if she was running after me. Perhaps she wanted to tell me something.'

Arnona: 'It must have been very hard to hear this story from your mother. It's true that it wasn't your mother but only your aunt, but still. . . What do you think she wanted to tell you all week?'

Nehama: 'I don't know exactly. . .' She stopped talking for a moment and she seemed confused. 'Maybe she wanted to ask me not to erase her, not to ignore her, perhaps to forgive her. There's a good reason that my mother couldn't tell me anything about her all these years. I don't know what exactly my mother feels about her after everything that happened to them. For myself I feel that she is actually very important.'

Therapist: 'Perhaps at this point it's somewhat easier for you to accept your aunt than it is for your mother. After all, you don't have to blame her and you don't have to feel guilty about the fact that in the end you survived and she didn't.'

The mutual trust between the group members had increased during the course of therapy, and at this advanced stage the members no longer avoided exposing their secrets in front of the group. Even the difficult contents connected with family secrets no longer needed protection, as within this setting everyone was carrying the same burden. The group and the therapists thus succeeded in getting to know another layer of the inner world of the 'memorial candles', a layer saturated with painful intimate contents that had been hidden until this point. To be honest, not all the questions they raised could be answered. Sometimes their parents' lips remained sealed and their secrets were not revealed. Few mothers are willing to reveal such painful secrets to their children, when the exposure of these secrets threatens their image in the children's eyes. But it was not the events themselves – if they occurred at all – that left their imprint on the psyches of the 'memorial candles'. As mentioned, the children could not know what really happened; it is the fragments of information and the fantasies they wove in their childhood around these fragments that disturbed them and created the conflicts in their psyches. The ability of the 'memorial candles' to bring these fantasies about their parents' sexuality during the Holocaust into the penetrating light of consciousness is one of the main curative elements in the course of therapy.

The nightmarish experiences of the parents – whether real or fantasized – thus became part of the inner world of the 'memorial candles' as if they were their own experiences: they repeatedly re-experienced them in dreams or fantasies.

Since the age of sixteen Aliza has had a recurrent dream with variations. She is now about thirty, unmarried, and having difficulties in forming an intimate relationship. In a rather hesitant voice she reported one such dream:

'It's hard for me to tell this, I'm somewhat embarrassed, but I feel that I can't keep it inside any more. I've already been keeping it for such a long time. At the last session some of the group members talked about their fantasies involving what their parents went through in the sexual area. It may be due to this that I can dare to open up a little today. Even though this dream is about me and not about my mother, I think that it's really somehow connected with what my mother went through. In my dream I'm in a concentration camp and the Germans are making a selection among the girls and they are choosing who will be taken to be a prostitute. I am chosen. But most of the dream is about the evening before they take us. I'm tense, hysterical, crying all the time. They don't tell us what we've been chosen for, but I know. That evening I think that if it's really true, then I'll commit suicide. The next evening they take us to a huge hall, where there are rows and rows of tables full of food. Something like a kind of party. And the hall is full of drunken German soldiers.'

Rahel interrupted Aliza and said that her dream reminded her of a dream of her own that she had had recently but had been too embarrassed to relate. Now she was less embarrassed.

'We're in a big building with auditoriums and long corridors. It's a European building. It reminds me a little of the church in the film *Holocaust*, where they gathered the Jews together. We're all there together, the whole family: me, my brother and sister-in-law and their children, and my parents are also there. They're somewhat in the background. There's a feeling of great stress, it's forbidden to leave. Something is about to happen. In the next building, which looks like a palace, there is much light, noise and music. One can hear the Germans celebrating, drinking and acting wild. The palace has an outer staircase, where SS officers in shiny boots and pressed uniforms are going up and down. They're going up to the party hall. We hear loud dance music coming out of the palace. We're hiding there in the house, very frightened. We don't know what's going to happen to us. Will they take us and send us to the gas chambers? There's a feeling of terror. At some point my brother tells me that he's going to talk to the Germans, to find out what can be done, and then we decide to run away. This is the end of the dream, but another time it had a continuation, like a second act. . . We're riding on a wagon of some farmers. They look like Polish peasants, again like the faces I saw in the film *Holocaust*. We're sitting on a wagon full of straw pulled by a horse. I'm lying there on the straw, half-dressed, half-naked. The torn dress I'm wearing doesn't really cover my body. I feel that something terrible is about to happen. They're going to do something to me, maybe kill me, maybe rape me, I'm not exactly sure. I'm lying there and my whole body is cramped with fear, but there's no choice, it has to happen.'

Rahel stopped talking and Ora began. During the war years Ora's mother had hidden with her own parents in a small dark room. She reached puberty in the hiding-place.

'In my dream I saw myself entering a large, clean public restroom. The floor was shiny and the doors of the cubicles were white. I tried to go into some of the cubicles, but all the doors were locked. Finally I found one door that wasn't locked. When I opened the door, I found next to the toilet the figure of a woman who had been murdered. She had the body of a child of about twelve, but the face of an adult woman. She had been thrown onto the toilet and everything all around was full of blood. I screamed terribly and ran out. My head was full of the picture of the dead woman the whole time and I ran to find a telephone to call the police.'

Aliza, Rahel and Ora experienced in their nightmares the terror of sexual abuse by the SS. The figures in their dreams are themselves and not their mothers. Their identification with their mothers is total, although it's plausible that the contents of the dreams are drawn from stories they read or films they saw, and not necessarily from real stories they heard from their mothers. But emotion 'abhors a vacuum', and so whatever is not provided by the facts it makes up and completes by itself. The parents concealed from their children the sexual traumas they went through during the Holocaust. Their silence left a terrible vacuum in the children's hearts, and they had no choice but to fill it with fantasies and

dreams that they wove out of fragments of information. Occasionally the figure of the SS officer appearing in the dreams of the
survivors' children – mainly those of the daughters – arouses
mixed feelings. The tall officer, polished and pressed, is a
threatening and frightening figure, an omnipotent tyrant capable
of humiliating his victims thoroughly and doing whatever he wants
to them, but at the same time his abundant masculinity attracts
and seduces women, and hidden in his power is a spark of hope for
survival. Their lives are in his hands for cruelty or for mercy, for life
or for death. Which of them will he finally save? The answer may
be hidden in the dreams themselves: the tyrant will save the beautiful girl who finds favour in his eyes, and she is the one who will
serve as the victim for satisfying his desires. It seems that this
conflict – between the forbidden attraction to the aggressor and
the terrible guilt feelings accompanying this attraction — is latent
and repressed deep in the hearts of many survivors. Who knows
how many of them owe their lives to their beauty, their sexuality,
the attraction they aroused in the hearts of the officers, who with
one nod of the head sentenced them to life while sending their
mothers and sisters to their deaths? The survivor mothers' guilt
feelings are double: not only were their lives saved while all their
dear ones were murdered, but the possibility exists that they felt,
for a fraction of a second, an insane attraction towards the tyrant
who saved their lives. Terror and attraction, aggression and sex,
are the eternal motif that appear in myths and legends, contrasting
yet interwoven with one another. But in the hell established by the
Nazi ideology these motifs became actual. The SS soldiers behaved
according to the rules of an archetypal world in which the boundaries between good and evil, between sexuality and aggression,
between attraction and repulsion, were all blurred. In the death
camps the darkest drives took the place of civilization. It is therefore no wonder that these motifs creep so often into the dreams
and imaginings of the survivors' daughters, even if they did not
actually exist in the reality of their mothers' past.

In Rahel's dream the drunken SS officers were celebrating in a
story palace, while she and her family were in mortal terror in the
adjacent house. In the second part of the dream she's lying in a
farmer's hay wagon and waiting for a cruel act that will soon be
done to her: murder, or perhaps rape; she is engulfed in mortal
terror, yet her surrender borders on devotion. Rahel doesn't even

try to resist, escape or voice any sort of protest. She identifies both with the figure of the victim and with the figure of the aggressor. She feels a certain degree of admiration for the aggressor, and perhaps even a dark, unconscious desire to experience the most forbidden act of all: the SS officer and the Polish peasant represent the eternal oedipal figure of the father, which is always perceived as attractive, forbidden and frightening.

If this is so, then the oedipal conflict so common among girls is concretized in the psyches of the survivors' daughters and is loaded with unique contents and symbols drawn from the terrors of the Holocaust.

Ora experienced in her dream the trauma of hiding that her mother had lived through. Undoubtedly the figure of the girl/ woman represents her mother. Just as the girl was murdered in a cubicle of a public restroom, so her mother's emotional life was murdered in the dim room she hid in. Although Ora's mother overcame this ordeal, became a woman, married and had three children, her emotional world was fixated at the age at which she entered the hiding-place, and so her sexual and feminine identity was injured and distorted for the rest of her life. The gap between her physical maturity and her emotional immaturity led to severe emotional defects in her functioning as a wife and mother. In this Ora's mother is no different from many other survivors whose adolescence took place under the shadow of the Holocaust.

At the end of the stage of therapy in which the 'memorial candles' encounter and deal with the fantasy part of their inner world, a new phase of therapy begins, in which they learn about their parents' actual experiences in the Holocaust. The place of the mythic visions and archaic fantasies is now taken by the various shades and tones of historical reality. This new phase reflects progress in therapy; the 'memorial candles' are beginning to take real steps towards emotional maturity, and they are learning to separate the parts of their own identity from their parents'. The ability to come face to face with their parents' experiences during the Holocaust years is generally acquired together with the increasing ability to deal with their true difficulties in the area of emotional and sexual life.

In one of the group sessions that took place during this stage of therapy Ruth opened the discussion. For quite some time she had been in an emotional relationship with a man that had been causing her many difficulties. She seemed very pale and tense when she began telling us her dream:

'This week I had a dream that stayed with me for some days, and then I had another dream. I think the two dreams are somehow connected. In the first dream I'm at home. The house looks like my parents' home. My stomach hurts very much and I feel as though I'm about to get my period. I look and I see that I am actually covered with blood. Not only are my clothes dirty but there's also a bloodstain on the sheet. This is something that doesn't usually happen to me. I take the sheet and show it to my mother and she says: "That's okay, I'll wash it." Later in the dream I'm lying in bed, actually on this sort of bench, and I see that the next room is a sort of large, grey hall, all full of wooden benches. Many grey figures are lying on the benches. They look like dead people, dead bodies. In the second dream I'm with Alex, my former boyfriend, and I know I'm going to die, perhaps in order to come back to life afterwards, but it's not certain. He – but sometimes it's not him at all but the figure of some large, frightening man, perhaps my father or perhaps someone else – at any rate, he takes a big knife, somewhat like a surgeon's lancet, and he comes near me with the knife held out in his hand. He's supposed to cut my arm, to make a very deep cut. I'm lying there, and I'm all this grey colour, actually as if I were already dead or at least half-dead. He really cuts my arm and under the grey layer there appears a thin red layer. I suddenly realize that something new is supposed to be born from me, but I'm not sure yet what it is that's coming out of me. What comes out is a thick, rather revolting liquid.'

Ziona: 'You know, your dreams are so charged! I don't know exactly how you understand them, but to me it's clear that they keep returning to the topic of sexuality and death, which I know so well, perhaps from a slightly different angle. The fear of sexuality, which is sometimes felt as a fear of death, and also the confusion that often existed in the Holocaust between death and sexuality. You've told us recently that you've been having difficulties with your boyfriend, in the relationship between you. I don't know if the problem is specifically in your sexual relationship, or in being close in general. I know, even though I've been married for several years already, and I'm even a mother, still whenever I've even thought about sex recently, it's not simple for me. I feel terribly pressured. This week, when it happened, I was aware of the fact that I felt pressured. This intimacy, I don't know why it's so hard for me to deal with it. Our bedroom door wasn't locked, because with us, just like with my parents, the doors are always open. My mother, when the door is closed and the room is closed, that is, in an intimate situation, always says that she feels choked. She brought it from there. There they were closed in and they couldn't go out. So in my mother's house there's no privacy. There isn't even a corner in which to be quiet and intimate, or to get dressed in peace. I remember that as a child the only place I felt a little privacy was in the bathroom. I would close myself in there for hours and stay there as long as possible. The terrible thing is that I've brought all these patterns into my own home now, with my husband and children. I too, when I'm in an intimate situation, I feel very choked.'

Ziona began to weep quietly, but she continued speaking: 'I hardly feel anything, as if I'm half-frozen. Sometimes I feel the need to provoke Sefi [her husband] so that we'll have a fight and he'll shout. In my imagination perhaps I even want him to hit me, just so I'll feel something.'

Her facial expression became frozen and her look glassy.

'To feel strongly is so frightening. I never saw my mother really sharing anyone's feelings. There, in the camp, she did survive, but the price was that she killed all her feelings for everyone, and here I'm following in her footsteps. To everyone, even to Sefi, I say, "Don't come too close to me, because if you come close I might feel you, and that's too threatening to me." And that's how it is with all kinds of closeness, including sexual closeness.'

Ziona's voice faded away and she stopped talking. The thread of her thought was taken up immediately by Nurit: 'All the years I've been married, I too always tried and even succeeded in avoiding having sex as much as possible. This closeness, I don't know exactly why, always gives me a strong feeling of stress and fear. This week I was a little closer to Gadi. I felt this feeling of choking, just the way you describe it with your mother, and maybe even with you yourself. I tried to fight it. I said to myself, "You're not going to get up now and walk away from it, you have to deal with it, it's enough already." And I really did succeed a little bit, but the next day I felt so tense that in the evening, when I had some more closeness with Gadi, this time also sexually, I actually felt very nauseous and I couldn't go through with it. But, you know, I remember that before I was married, and I had all sorts of contacts, each time with someone else – then it wasn't like that. Then I felt much freer and sometimes I even succeeded in enjoying it, the sex certainly, but also the closeness. The problems began in marriage. Perhaps it's connected, perhaps it's because of the feeling that marriage is a committed relationship. I don't know.'

Ruth: 'This fear of feeling is something I know quite well. My second dream may be related to it. When I'm lying there all grey I'm indeed alive, but really I'm half-dead. You know what? That's how I'm actually living my whole life. Only recently, actually with the help of the man I was with last, I saw a little better how much it frightens me. And sex, after all, is feeling as strongly as can be.'

Ruth stopped talking for a moment, lifted up her eyes, and looked first at the therapist and then at Ziona: 'But how is it connected with my mother? Or to the first part of my dream or maybe to you, Ziona?'

Therapist: 'What stands out both in your dreams, Ruth, and in what Ziona told us about her parents' house, is that there aren't any boundaries, there isn't any intimacy, everything is wide open and there are no boundaries between you and your mothers. As if you don't know who's getting her period. When you get your period, the first sign of your maturing femininity, of your separate personal identity as a woman, what do you do? You bring the sheet to your mother. And what does she do? Does she perhaps teach you how to deal with it? No. She simply responds immediately by agreeing to wash it for you as if she was the one who had got her period, as if it were hers. And what about you, Ziona? You're simply telling us how you're reconstructing, in your home, with your husband, the same pattern that existed in your parents' home: everything is wide open and there's no intimacy.'

Ziona: 'I remember that I too, when I got my period for the first time, I also left everything covered with blood, and my mother washed it for me, but it seemed so natural to me then. Actually, this arrangement lasted for years, not once or twice. My blood was my mother's concern, she took care of it. Now it might bother me, but then? Not at all. I've often thought about my mother as a fifteen-year-old girl in the camp. I especially remember an almost compulsive question that bothered me for years: how did she manage when she got her period? What did she do about it? Did she have what to use to take care of herself? After all, they went around in rags there, and that's all there was. And what happened? Was she covered with blood? This thought never left me. I don't know exactly why. Even now it sometimes occurs to me. But right now, after what Ruth told us, this is the first time I've dared to talk about it.'

Ora: 'I was also very much bothered by the question of how my mother managed with it there, in the hiding-place. She was in the hiding-place during her adolescence, that is, she reached puberty in that stifling place, closed up with her parents, without privacy, without a corner of her own. My mother once told me that when she got her period there for the first time, it was actually her father who spoke to her and helped her, because her mother was in such a bad psychological state that she could hardly function. It certainly wasn't simple: particularly her father who's alone with her in such an intimate matter, and she didn't have any girlfriends or sisters, or anyone of her own age to tell it to and to share it with. Often when I'd read Anne Frank's diary I'd think of my mother. What she went through was really similar, but it was also different. Anne had other people around in the hiding-place. There was at least this boy, to whom she could direct all her longing, and her dreams and feelings. That's so important at this age. . . You know, it's strange, but I too, my whole life, with the most intimate matters, even sexual ones, if I spoke to anyone at all it was always to my father or maybe sometimes my sisters, but with my mother it was impossible even to touch on these topics. Even now the road is blocked. I never thought about it: it's actually exactly the same as what happened to my mother there in the hiding-place.'

Hava began speaking in a very tense and quiet voice: 'What you're telling reminds me that I also had a similar dream once. I dreamt that I had to have sex with an older man, perhaps looking a little bit like my father in his body build. In my family I've always maintained an asexual image, and everyone treats me that way, especially my mother. With my brothers it's somewhat less. When I was sixteen and I told her about my first kiss, she said it was forbidden. When I came home late at night, when

I was already pretty old, she would always shout at me. I was eleven when I got my first period. My mother rang up the school secretary and gave me a book to read on the topic, but she never talked to me about it at all. It was she who found the bloodstains on my pyjamas, I didn't know anything about it, I didn't feel that anything was happening to me. It was as if it was happening to someone else.'

Therapist: 'Could it be that you were very disconnected from your body then?'

Hava: 'Yes. I've always got my period on time, without pain and without feelings. Only now, recently, has it been somewhat different. Now I've been feeling more and more that it's really my body and that I'm a woman. I even have pains when I get my period. It's not so easy any more for me to deal with it.'

Therapist: 'And how is this connected with your parents or your dream?'

Hava: 'It's hard for me to look at them. Their sexuality, my mother's I mean, I can't look. It's hard for me to separate myself from her. Perhaps this also explains many of my problems. Actually, I don't know what exactly my mother feels about herself as a woman. She was about nine or ten when she found herself alone there in the Holocaust with some distant aunt. I don't know how she got through adolescence, I mean in those conditions there, how she felt when she became a woman in that terrible isolation, without any support or encouragement and with the continual fear of death.'

Thus it is not easy for the survivors' daughters to imagine their mothers' situation when they reached sexual maturity under the conditions of life during the Holocaust. It is especially difficult for them to sense how their mothers felt at the time. And yet they must make the effort to do so, as without this difficult experience they cannot separate themselves from their unpleasant imaginings and from their absolute identification with their mothers' femininity and sexuality, or distinguish between them and their own personal experiences. This separation is doubly difficult because of the confusion of realms – the lack of both external and internal boundaries between the different identities in the family.

Because of the isolation and terror their mothers experienced during adolescence, it is doubtful whether they could have acted otherwise with their daughters. But the daughters were not there, after all – the experiences in their psyches are borrowed, and they actually experienced totally different events. At this stage of therapy begins the internal separation between the identity components belonging to the self of their mothers, which were assimilated into their psyches, and the components of their own independent feminine and sexual identities.

It is undoubtedly still difficult and even frightening for the survivors' children to feel any sort of closeness or intimacy, or to give themselves over to feelings that are almost new to them. Although they are finally able, in the atmosphere of sharing that is created in the group, to open up what was closed inside them and to feel identification with the group, this is a gradual, extended process. It is still difficult for them to express their feelings at full strength. Here and there they begin to reveal feelings of understanding, warmth and even love. These feelings are still very hesitant and restrained, but for the 'memorial candles' they are something of a revelation that they could not even imagine before they achieved it. Only now do they dare to speak somewhat freely about their intimate relationships with their spouses and their difficulties in maintaining a close relationship for an extended period of time.

As mentioned, until this point the group members had not expressed feelings of closeness, love or sexual attraction, nor even feelings of competitiveness, aggression or hatred. It seems that the group members considered themselves bound to a convent accord of mutual protection: 'You protect me and I'll protect you – don't expect overly emotional expressions from me and I won't expect them from you.' They still dare not appear in the group matrix as men and women with a separate and distinct personal and sexual identity. The blurring of identities in their families is still dominant, and they find it difficult to free themselves of it even in the hothouse of the group. In the last stage of therapy this difficulty gradually lessens, and the group members begin to express more clearly their feelings of competitiveness and attraction, aggression and sexuality, hatred and love. These feelings are first expressed in dreams, but soon they are revealed in the group dialogue as well. Most people go through the stage of separation, one of the most important stages in the process of maturation, during their adolescence. The 'memorial candles' go through this stage relatively late, when they reach the appropriate emotional age with the help of therapy – many years after they were supposed to have gone through this stage from the standpoint of their chronological age.

At one of the group meetings Yaakov described a dream he had had recently:

'I and some other people grab some person and question him. I grab him by the throat and stop his breathing with my hand. Afterwards they talk about the fact that this was someone who was coming to be the head of the department I'm working in. If he's dead, this means that now I can be the head of the department. I woke up in the middle of the night very disturbed, and I couldn't go back to sleep. But a few days later I had another dream of this sort. I saw a boy lying, without any genital region, as if it had all been cut off, he'd been castrated of all his genital organs. I don't know exactly what it's connected with, but it's been difficult for me recently to feel any physical attraction toward Malka. I feel that I'm very critical of her, of how she looks, of her body and her figure. Nothing is good enough for me. Her muscles aren't solid enough, she's slightly fat, and so on and so on. I've lost all feeling of attraction to her. I'm aware that my criticism has a lot of aggression in it, but I remember that with previous girlfriends as well I used to express a lot of hostility in my venomous criticisms, and this was always expressed with respect to their body, their face, their breasts, and so on. There was always something that wasn't good enough for me. Now, sometimes, I shout, I curse, I lose control. I've been feeling very asexual lately. Always, if I was attracted to a woman, I could only express it with actions. I could invite her to dance or something like that, but I couldn't express anything in words before I expressed it in actions. At home, I remember, my mother never talked about close relationships or about sex in any form, and my father ignored this entirely, as if the whole matter didn't exist at all. I never saw my parents touch each other intimately, with feeling, or with any sort of sexuality. My mother would at least try to talk to me a little sometimes. In my heart I felt her need, her deprivation. After all, she was left completely alone out of her entire family. And my father, I don't know how much he was actually able to give her. He was always so closed, never emotional and never crying and never showing any sign of feeling. Always in complete control. In general, he feels secure and comfortable only when he's in control. He never touched me or my sisters. When I was four I used to wake up at night with fears and then he would come to me. He would give me a little whisky and tell me stories about the children there, in the camps, who were eaten by rats, and then he would tell me to go back to sleep. He never hugged me or tried to calm me, or sat me on his lap. I could never really feel him, his inside, what he was really feeling inside when he was there in the camps and the wandering, or afterwards in his everyday life. I doubt whether he even shared anything especially personal or intimate with my mother. It could not have helped my mother very much, as she was already so depressed anyway. The fact that I keep reading Primo Levi's books over again is possibly because he's a man. He really opens himself up and describes exactly what he felt in every situation he was in. His emotional world is open to me, and this is exactly what I missed so much in my father. In Primo Levi I'm searching for all the answers to the questions that always bothered me all my life, and sometimes I find them.'

Yehuda: 'What you've told us about your home reminds me so much of my parents' home! Not only that, but my parents actually slept in separate beds and later even in separate rooms. I too have become more aware of my difficulties lately. If I feel in full control over myself, over the girl who's with me, even in a sexual situation, then everything is all right. Maybe it's a little bit like what you describe with your father. But if things are open and fluid and I feel that I'm not in complete control, then I shrink and I lose all my confidence, and then I sort of close up inside and express some flinching away, even if not in words. The girl who's with me generally feels this flinching, and then a gap is created. Each time after I get a little closer, I seem to become frightened and again I distance myself and cut myself off. I remember that a little while ago my mother told me that they had once taken a trip for a few days' holiday, and she and my father had a chance to stay together at a hotel for the weekend. She herself wanted this very much, but my father emphatically refused. He said it was a waste of money and in the end they didn't do it.'

Therapist: 'And how do you understand it? Do you think the reason he refused was really the money, or that other things were involved? That perhaps he felt something threatening him, and maybe her as well?'

Yehuda: 'Perhaps. . . I don't know. At first I bought the theory that it was the money. But now, on second thoughts, I think that maybe my father was afraid of being with my mother at the hotel. A hotel is something different, sort of intimate. In a hotel you spend time together, you're in an intimate and sort of sexual situation, it's different than usual. I think that this is what threatened him, and she, as usual, collaborated with him. I too feel this way sometimes in new situations, when I'm not in my secure and familiar territory. Intimacy is somewhat frightening, like what I told you that happens to me with girls. I feel very choked and threatened inside, as if something terrible is going to happen to me. And then I have to run away. It seems to be rather like what Ziona once described as happening to her when she's in a sexually intimate situation of closeness with her husband, this choking feeling. . .'

Yaakov: 'Yes, I also have this feeling. I also worked on myself for years to control my sexual reactions. I remember that once, when I was maybe twelve, I was at the seashore with my friends and my sisters, and we all went wild and everyone tickled everyone else. I worked on myself with all my strength not to react – that they should touch me and I shouldn't feel anything. When I remember my home I shudder. Everything was closed and locked there. Any touch of any sort was actually taboo. In any intimate situation, when I'm sitting with a woman alone in a room, even if the situation is not necessarily sexual, I immediately become formal and serious.'

Therapist: 'And how is this expressed here in the group? The denial and the control of your sexuality? The fear of intimacy, and the aggression and competitiveness you expressed in your dream towards male authority figures? How does all this connect with the dream in which you're punished, castrated, as if it's forbidden for you to be really masculine?'

Yaakov: 'I don't know exactly. . .I haven't thought about it. I only know that on those rare occasions when I actually allowed myself to feel something strongly, something sexual or competitive, I immediately closed up and sealed it off inside myself. Even here I've been afraid of bringing up such feelings and maybe losing control again. . .'

Yehuda: 'You know, I've often thought about the connection between us, that is, between you and me, even though I've never dared to mention it aloud, and neither have you. I feel very great identification and closeness with you, especially when you tell us about your home, your parents, the Holocaust. But it seems to me that that isn't all. Here in the group there's also some competition between us. Competition for place, for everyone's attention, and perhaps also as men – who's more masculine and who's more dominant. When you told your dream it moved me but it also made me feel tense. I've also had many dreams recently with lots of aggression and violence towards men and between men. In general I attack forcefully, I hit, I wound and I even kill. It really scares me to tell you this here in the group. I don't know why with you and with me as well our competitiveness comes out so violently and aggressively.'

Therapist: 'It's really been very clear for some time that both you two and some other members of the group have been afraid to bring up feelings and to deal with them openly. Apparently your fear was too great. Competitiveness and aggression are, after all, natural feelings that everyone has, but in your dreams they appear in an extreme form. Perhaps it's connected somehow with your parents' past, with the aggression and violence they were exposed to there and because of which they always had great difficulty in coping with their own aggression and with yours – the children's. But here, at this stage, it's different than in the family.'

Yehuda: 'Perhaps. Perhaps there's something in it, in what you've said, but in any case, now I feel that I can dare to tell Yaakov what I feel towards him about this. Very often, here in the group, I was envious of you because of your special place in the group. I always felt that everyone likes you and sympathizes with you, especially the women in the group. I felt this especially last month, when you missed a few sessions. Suddenly I felt that there was a place for me and that I was daring to express myself more freely and even to stand out more. I remember that once, a few sessions ago, I allowed myself to take this place in a very decisive way, and apparently this frightened me and caused me stress, because afterwards I had a dream which seems somehow connected with this. In my dream I saw a square cell, closed, without windows, and with many people in it. They are just about to close the doors, and finally the doors are actually closed and the air is getting used up and it's becoming clear that everyone will suffocate in the end. Then I quickly make a sort of calculation: would it be better for me to breathe all the oxygen quickly, and then perhaps I might live a little longer, even though it's clear that I'll be breathing some of the other

people's oxygen; or would it be better for me to breathe normally, like everyone else, and simply wait to die, and when it
comes, it comes?'

Itamar: 'Your dream reminds me of a recurrent nightmare of mine.
A sort of shack, like the blocks you see in films of the camps. The
shack is full of men and they're all walking skeletons. Very very
thin, with striped shirts. And I'm lying there on one of the
bunks, very very weak. I haven't the strength to get up. And I
feel that I'm suffocating. Then I say to myself: if you won't get
up you'll simply suffocate and die here very very slowly. I started
having this dream when I was about fifteen, when my father had
actually been lying in bed for nearly three years and refusing to
get up or even to eat. He went down to less than ninety pounds
then. My mother would feed him some sort of cereal with a
spoon. He hardly spoke, he'd be quiet for hours and hours. Now
I think that he was simply in a deep depression, that he had
actually returned to the period when he was in the blocks, in the
camp. This happened when I was an adolescent, just when I
really needed him. I didn't have anyone to talk to, or to argue
with, or to do all sorts of things. He was there with his Holocaust, with his death and his depression, and my mother was a
wreck, constantly busy just trying to keep him alive somehow. I
would wander around by myself without knowing what to do
with everything that was buzzing in my head.'

Martha: 'It's really hard to get through adolescence that way,
without a father, really, and with a mother who has no one but
you to turn to with her frustration, and even that only with some
difficulty. It reminds me of the period when my mother was so
immersed in herself and her depression, as I too didn't know
how to deal with it. It wasn't as bad as with you, but it was hard.
What right did I have to dress up nicely and to take care of
myself, to go out with boys, to dance and enjoy myself, when my
mother was drowning in her depression? If I would go out and
have a good time, it would be as if I were leaving her, abandoning her. . . And right away I would feel guilty, at least that's how
it was all those years. . .'

Yehuda: 'This reminds me of a story that I may have told you
before. My parents told me that when they came to Israel, when
I was a baby only a few months old, they hid me in a basket and
covered me with vegetables and with rags and smuggled me in,
because I didn't have a certificate. I imagine that I had very little

air there. Undoubtedly I almost suffocated. This feeling of suffocation has apparently stayed with me all my life, just as it has stayed with Itamar.'

Therapist: 'Everything you've said is right, but besides the connection with the Holocaust and with your childhood, the feelings of suffocation and threat are also connected to your present reality in the group. Yehuda expressed this rather clearly, both for himself and for the others, when he spoke to Yaakov before. When you have to share it with so many other people, is there enough oxygen for all of you? There, in the original womb he came from, there apparently wasn't very much oxygen. Your feeling is that you're always being threatened, as if you have to struggle all the time with life and death in order to survive, and if someone takes something, then it's at someone else's expense, even at the expense of your lives. It's hard for you to feel that you can express yourselves and take your place without this being a threat for the others.'

As mentioned, the 'memorial candles' internalized many parts of their parents' psyches, and in their psyches, as in their parents', there is a struggle between the dead, emotionless part and the live, feeling part. In his youth Itamar was in a state of unbearable conflict: if he allowed himself to live and enjoy his life, to take his place in the house as a young man, then he would actually be taking his father's place, while his father was fighting with depression and death. There is no doubt that such a situation would enchant any young boy, yet at the same time it's scary and threatening – and this is the conflict that Itamar has been in until now. He still doesn't know how a person can take his place in his family and in society without this being at someone else's expense. And it's the same with Yehuda: when Yaakov was away for a few sessions, Yehuda immediately hurried to take his place in the group. But when Yaakov came back, he returned to his former place and even accepted the contents of his dream as a form of self-punishment. In his world-view there isn't enough room for two men together either in the family or in the group. The group members' guilt feelings towards their parents and siblings are reawakened – Itamar's towards his father, Martha's towards her mother – and the imagined threat is always greater than the reality. Thus Yehuda's speech to Yaakov constitutes a great step forward. He has come to realize, as have some of the others, that what he says does not lead to catastrophe. On the contrary, their talk places their imagined fears in the light of reality and relieves much of their sense of tension and threat. The 'memorial candles' thus dare at this stage to expose the feelings they've carried in their hearts for years, and, after all, their liberation from their parents' internal world depends on this exposure.

The speakers at the previous session were men who were seeking a place for their masculinity in the group. The following group dialogue shows how the survivors' daughters deal with the shaping of their identity as adult women in their families and in the group.

Dalia: 'Some time ago I bought myself a very pretty, very feminine wool robe. But I still don't feel able to wear it. I don't feel comfortable with it. I remember that my mother never had a robe. She never buys herself pretty clothes. She's always wearing a torn shirt under her sweater and she's proud of the fact that she's saving money by wearing old clothes. I also remember that since I grew up the only one who cared how I look was always my father. My feminine appearance was important to him and he would support it. It wasn't easy for her to accept this – it threatened her. In general, in any sensitive situation, for instance when I had an operation once, it was he who sat with me in the hospital. And in general, when I was still a child and I would call out at night, or if my brothers would call out, it was always he who got up for us, never my mother. I actually can't remember my mother with me in these situations. My father also took care of the garden and the flowers next to the house. He had a part that was alive and he succeeded in transmitting it to me and to the family in general. Perhaps because he wasn't actually in Auschwitz like my mother. My mother I remember as always wearing these worn-out clothes, never taking care of herself or concerned about her femininity. Because of this, I think, I felt this week that the robe I bought for myself I would really like to give to her.'

Ariela: 'You know, Dalia, this reminds me so much of my own mother. She too never puts on any makeup. On the contrary, she totally refuses to do so. When she's home she hardly ever really gets dressed. She says it's hard for her to get dressed because of her illness, and she sits around all the time in her pyjamas with some robe on top. I've often suggested that she use a cream for her face or body, and I've even brought her some, but she always refuses. She says the creams are unpleasant, that they have an unpleasant smell. But, in contrast, she always dressed me very well and with good taste. My dresses, when I was a little girl, were always the prettiest and the most starched. She just didn't want to look nice herself. Once she was a very beautiful woman, and it's still possible to see it a little, but now she's erasing it and blurring it.'

Dalia: 'Then our mothers are quite similar, but you always look so well-groomed, and you always come here made-up and well-dressed, it's really impressive. In the group I'm always looking at you and I'm really impressed and even a little envious. But I never dared to tell you this. I was embarrassed. You also always get so much attention from the men here. For me, on the other hand, it's always so difficult to allow myself to appear too feminine or sexy. I'm like my mother. I too have to blur and erase my femininity.'

Yael: 'Right. I've never spoken about it openly here, but actually I've noticed that I've been spending much more time on my looks lately. Before I go out somewhere I sometimes spend hours on every detail of my appearance — my clothes, shoes, makeup. Like Ariela perhaps, I don't know. The two of us have never spoken about it here. Shlomo sometimes gets angry with me because of this, it really bothers him. Because of these ceremonies of preparation that I perform, I'm always late everywhere, and because of me he's late too. But I can't do without it. I still don't understand it completely, but just this week something started to become clearer. I understood a little of where it's coming from.'

Ariela: 'What for instance became clearer to you? I find it interesting. For me too outward appearance is very important, even though I don't devote as much time to it as you do.'

Yael: 'I was at my grandmother's this week. As you know, I've been visiting my grandmother again very often recently, after a period when I went to her much less often. So this week, when I was there, I don't know exactly how, the topic of conversation came around to my asking her a little about what it was like there in the camp, and what she and my mother really went through there. I don't know exactly why, but this time my grandmother was really ready to talk. Perhaps she felt that this time I was really ready to listen, and that I didn't just want to run away, as usual. She told me that when they arrived at the camp, first of all they separated them, the men on one side and the women on the other side. Then they divided the women into rows of five, and a Nazi officer stood there and examined them, and took from each row the one that looked best to him, that is, the ones who were younger and prettier. My mother was sixteen years old then, and very beautiful. So my grandmother pushed her to stand at the end of the line, so they would see her. The German officer shouted at her to leave the line. Then my mother started crying terribly that she wouldn't leave without her mother. Why and how, I don't know, but a miracle occurred: they agreed that my grandmother too should leave the line. In the same line, together with them, stood my grandmother's mother and sisters as well. They remained there in the line and that was the last time my mother and grandmother saw them. They took them straight to die.'

Yael's voice became choked and she began to sob. After a long while she succeeded in controlling herself, and she continued with tears running down her cheeks: 'You know, it's as if always, my whole life, I've known this story. I knew and I didn't know. But really I knew it very well. I knew it and I learned it. I knew and I drew my own conclusion: if I want to survive, to remain alive, then I have to be beautiful. That's what will save me. I know that this need becomes stronger mainly when I don't feel so self-confident. When I feel more confident again, I can let myself not pay so much attention and not be so fanatically concerned about every little detail of my appearance. You understand? One might after all say that it was my mother's beauty that saved the two of them. When my grandmother told me this she was a little more emotional than usual, but she didn't actually cry. I think she's still afraid to feel it completely. But I cried terribly, I really sobbed. Afterwards she told me that until now she had been afraid to tell me all this, perhaps it might shake me up too much. She didn't know that I hadn't asked her before because I was afraid that it would shake her up too much. From my mother I've never heard so much as one word.'

Therapist: 'Outwardly you are all very different from one another. Ariela and Yael, for instance, are very well-groomed externally, while Dalia has trouble with this. But after all you know that what one sees outwardly doesn't always reflect the inner feelings, and as we have heard from Yael, behind her concern for her appearance are hidden things that are loaded with the traumatic history of her family.'

Ariela: 'For me too it's not just the way it seems. Perhaps it's easier for me to get dressed up and to pay attention to my outward appearance, but you, Dalia, already have an anchor. You're married, and you're even a mother. Even though I'm older than you, it's still very difficult for me to build a real relationship. In general, I'm still very far from seeing myself married. The truth is that at an early age I promised myself somehow that I would not be like my mother, but actually that's only on the outside. Inside I'm so confused. I have no idea what I am and who I am and how I want to live in various areas of life.'

Ruth: 'I actually identify very greatly with this confusion of yours. This week I noticed that I don't speak very clearly, I mix up the genders, masculine and feminine and so on. I think that this confusion is very deep inside. My mother actually always dressed very elegantly. A real glamour girl. But I, inside, have never felt her confidence and calmness as a woman. I felt as if she had remained a girl, even a little girl, as she was there in the Holocaust. At the age of eighteen she already had me, and this was already after everything. So when did she have a chance to grow up? When I was growing up she gave me all sorts of double messages. On the one hand she acted happy, but on the other hand I felt her distance. She couldn't give me warmth or support or the feeling that she was really with me. I see her as a woman on the outside, but there's this distortion on the inside. On the inside I see her as a confused little girl. Actually it's very hard for me to see her as a woman, because this means competing with her as a woman and this frightens me too much. It's like the time I made the doll out of plasticine, and the group showed me that my doll looked like a cross between a little girl and a woman, with very blurred features and body shape. Actually, even then I wasn't sure if it was her or me. And perhaps the doll really symbolized both her and me. Now I'm trying to fight very hard within myself to become a woman and go out into the world a little less confused, but it's not easy. The last time my mother and I met, she told me that when she was young she had nicer legs than I have. Since I was a little girl she's always been telling me that I'm not pretty. Doesn't that mean that we really are competing with each other? After all, it takes two to compete, so I really am competing with her. I know that my body

isn't bad, it's even rather beautiful. I even get many compliments from all sorts of men, but actually I feel uncomfortable
with it. I don't know exactly what to do with this. I feel as if my
body doesn't really belong to me.'

Ariela: 'I'm happy you said what you said today, because you've
generally been very quiet lately when we talk about these things.
You know, I've often felt your competitiveness, but under the
table. You never gave it a clear expression. You've always hidden
your true feelings. But after all you really look very good, and
people react to this, even if you deny it and don't accept any
responsibility. Today for the first time I felt that I could understand where you got this difficulty with this whole topic. And,
you know, I'm grateful to you. It frees me of a lot of tension
towards you. I too, at home with my mother, felt something
similar sometimes, even if it was perhaps in a slightly different
way. I think you once told us that you felt very close to your
father, and you even had a sexual dream about him, didn't you?
You're the only daughter in your family, since you have brothers
but no sisters, but I'm an only child. My relationship with my
father was also very complicated. He often looked for closeness
with me, alone. He wanted to complain, to cry to me about all
sorts of things, including my mother and the trouble he had
with her. And I, for my part, cooperated with him, and it seems
to me that you do the same thing with your father.'

Dalia: 'My father too was always looking for intimate spots to catch
me for a few moments alone. He too always wanted to talk to me
about my mother, how bad he had it with her. He even told me
about their sexual relations. It was very difficult for me to deal
with this. It put a lot of pressure on me, but I never dared to
refuse to listen. So you're right, I too cooperated. I never
thought about what it was doing to my mother, this coalition
between us.'

Ahuva: 'My father always treated me as his partner in many re-
spects. On my last birthday he insisted on coming with me to
buy me a present, and guess what he bought me! A pair of
earrings.' She smiled an embarrassed smile. 'When I was a little
girl, I would be afraid at night and go to my parents' bed. Then
my mother would get up and go to sleep in my bed and I would
stay and sleep next to my father. This lasted for years and I liked
it very much. Only recently did I begin to feel uncomfortable
about it. Because of her. After all, she actually gave up her place

as a wife for me. She would always wear black and she was very fat. I'm always shouting at her that she has to reduce, to go on a diet, but it doesn't do any good. She also hardly puts on any makeup. Only once in a while does she put on something more dressy and wear heels. But perfume, heaven forbid. And speaking of creams, she never puts on any cream. I remember that when I used to touch her, it wasn't so pleasant. Her skin was always hard and rough. I actually couldn't touch her. And she always had this unpleasant odour, as if for the purpose of keeping people away. I've often thought about how she was when she was a girl, before the Holocaust. Was she that way even then, or was she perhaps different then? My mother keeps telling me that my father bothers her, that she has no strength for him, that he's so aggressive and bossy. When she tells me this I always have the feeling that she's talking about sex, even though she never says it explicitly. Here in the group I feel that you all have a place here. I don't. I'm the last one in line. I also connect this with my femininity and my sexuality. It's very difficult for me to really feel them and to show them on the outside.'

Therapist: 'It seems to me that not only did you all communicate with one another somewhat better today, but you also all talked about variations on the same theme, each of you from your own angle. And the theme is your mother's identity as a woman as you experienced and internalized it during your childhood and adolescence, up to the present time. We heard descriptions of mothers who aren't able to dress up or put on makeup, or are always dressed in black or in old clothes. Women who can't allow themselves to demonstrate their femininity or sexuality or who don't know how to feel good with themselves and their bodies. These descriptions raise an important question: how is this connected with what your mothers went through there, in the Holocaust, when they were girls or young women? How is it connected with the fact that their mothers and sisters and everyone they loved disappeared from their lives at the same time, and they remained alone in fear and hunger and terrible humiliation, with bodies that shrank and gradually turned into walking skeletons; and – who knows? – perhaps even indescribable sexual traumas?'

From the time of her liberation from the camp, Ahuva's mother has almost always worn black. Ariela's mother hardly ever gets dressed at all. Makeup, perfume, and other cosmetics don't even come into the picture. Mourning, depression and guilt feelings killed their joy in life. How could they possibly be with their daughters in spirit during their adolescence? How could they support them and be happy with them when they turned from little girls into young women? These are the central questions that the survivors' daughters keep raising at the sessions taking place at this stage of therapy.

One of the greatest problems involved in the late maturation of the survivors' daughters is their difficulty in rebelling, in becoming angry with their mothers and competing with them openly. Indeed, how is it possible to stand up openly against mothers who experienced the Holocaust on their flesh? Dalia has finally dared to buy herself a pretty woollen robe, but she doesn't dare to wear it and she wants to give it as a present to her mother. It seems that there is a wish buried deep in her heart to compensate her mother, if only symbolically, for all she suffered. Ahuva brings her mother perfumes and cosmetics and tries to convince her to lose weight and to dress nicely, as if she is trying to tell her to have done with death and depression and mourning, to be like other mothers. These are desperate attempts to restore a bit of happiness to their mothers and to provide themselves with mothers with whom they can compete, and even be angry, and yet learn things from in the realm of femininity – that is, to attain that balanced identification with a mature womanly figure so necessary to every adolescent girl. But this way is closed to them, and they have no choice but to make peace with the situation, to stop hoping for the impossible, to leave behind the pain and the anger and to separate themselves from their hopes and illusions that their mothers will really be able to be with them and help them without taking control of their intimate world. The daughters of the survivors must give up their complicated identification with the confused identities of their mothers, who are still little girls that haven't grown up sufficiently and are still in need of support and holding themselves, and they must acquire their own separate and distinct feminine identity. But giving up one's identification with one's mother is difficult – not only because of the lack of boundaries between the children's and the parents' identities, but also because in reality there still exists both material and emotional dependence between the parents and the children.

The relationships between the survivors' daughters and their fathers have a special place in this essay. This relationship also lacks clear boundaries. As described in the daughters' stories, many fathers seek intimate closeness with their daughters, a closeness that sometimes contains a note of seduction. The relationship between father and daughter sharpens the oedipal conflict in the daughter–father–mother triangle. Sometimes there is a desire – generally unconscious – in the daughter's heart to maintain this forbidden intimate relationship with her father, not only because of her aspiration and fantasy of compensating the father for his real or imaginary unsatisfying relationship with his wife, which is a very common oedipal phenomenon, but also because of her need to compensate her parents in every possible way for the losses and the narcissistic injuries caused them by the Holocaust, which never ceases to trouble the 'memorial candles'. Because of this subterranean intimacy with the father the relationship between the mother and the daughter becomes fraught with unbearable tension and stress, and so the daughter wants to come closer to her mother – and at the same time to separate from her. It is not easy for any young woman to complete the process of her maturation while her father is trying to use her to fill the vast emotional void within himself, and the mother is willing to give the daughter her own place at his side because of her own difficulties. How much more difficult is it, then, for a daughter of survivors, who bears the great load of her parents' – especially her father's – expectation that she will compensate them for the close feminine figures they lost and the feminine nurturance and holding that were lost with them. In order to complete their maturation the survivors' daughters need to fill many more missing parts in their identities. In order to do this they must separate from their childhood, from their mother, from their family's traumatic past, and also from the emotionally fraught relationship with their father, who has often, as mentioned, unconsciously transferred to his daughter the expectation that she will hold him emotionally in place of his mother, sisters, and sometimes wife as well.

Last and Klein (1974) found no direct correlation between the father's degree of traumatization and the relationship between mother and daughter. On the other hand, it has been demonstrated in various ways that the degree of traumatization has affected the relationship between mother and son, as well as the relationship of the father with both sons and daughters. The lack of sufficient emotional nurturance from her husband, and her inability to reveal her frustration to him directly, causes the wife of a survivor to turn her feelings of deprivation and frustration primarily towards her sons. The son is thus compelled to absorb, in place of his father, the frustration and anger that overwhelm his mother's feelings. In his distress he turns to his father to seek comfort and identification, but the father, because of the severe traumas he has suffered, is not only unable to be open to his son's feelings or to allow him to penetrate his inner world, but is also unable to be the sort of confident and strong father figure that would arouse in his son the wish to identify with him. The son therefore lacks an object for emotional identification that he could emulate and internalize.

And this is not all. Not only does the son feel during his entire period of adolescence the heavy demand of his environment to hold his father, with all his emotional deprivation, within himself, but because of this demand he cannot compete and struggle against his father as does every adolescent boy. The father is perceived as a weak figure; he must be pitied and protected rather than competed with. The feelings of anger, aggression and competitiveness, the natural desire to rebel – all these remain locked up in the son's psyche without discharge.

Although, as mentioned, no direct effects of the traumas undergone by the father during the Holocaust were found in the relationships between mother and daughters in survivor families, it should not be concluded from this that the tension-laden family structure does not have an indirect effect on these relationships. Even if the mother's rage and frustration are not discharged openly, in many survivor families the father's low status in the mother's intimate perception is not concealed from the daughter. In order to compensate her father, the daughter identifies with his weak, humiliated image and feels the need to protect him and to fill the emotional void surrounding him. At the same time, however, she also feels identification with her frustrated mother, and so in the end she is driven into a conflict of identifications with two objects whose relationship to each other is saturated with tension.

Last and Klein (1974) also say that the degree of the mother's traumatization does not affect the relationship between father and son or between mother and daughter, but only the paternal socialization patterns with respect to their daughters, and the maternal ones with respect to their sons. Indeed, many of the stories we heard from both sons and daughters support this finding. The more severely the mothers were injured, the lower is their ability to function emotionally and sexually in their relationship with their husband. Here too the father is surrounded by a great emotional void, especially if he was less severely affected by the Holocaust than his wife. The father tries to fill this void through his daughters, who serve as a kind of substitute. The first intention of the father who turns to his daughter in this way is of course mainly emotional, but it is not entirely lacking in any element of seduction, and it contains an unconscious desire for the daughter to hold his frustration and the pain of his loneliness and not to leave him. The daughter, who is fixated in the archaic identifications derived from the superego that are common to herself and her father, remains in an oedipal conflict whose incestuous content is maintained within it instead of being repressed, and which therefore cannot be resolved. She therefore develops fantasies and sensations in which sexuality is indeed interwoven. On the other hand, the more severe the mother's psychic injuries, the lower is her ability to serve as an appropriate feminine figure for her daughter to emulate and identify with.

The mother's inability to clearly and directly provide her daughter with all the love and feeling she needs during her childhood and adolescence, and the emotional deprivation which prevents the mother from holding her daughter's feelings – including those of pain, anger, aggression or the desire to compete and rebel against her mother – combine to decrease the daughter's ability to perceive the mother as a strong, independent figure existing in her own right. Obviously the lack of such a figure in the life of an adolescent girl damages the process of her maturation and retards the stage of individuation and separation from the parents' identities. As mentioned, the daughter's identification with her mother's suffering and her need to protect and compensate the mother are internalized deep within her psyche and become part of her personality. But this internalization occurs at such an early age that a difficult and extended inner struggle is required to resolve it. It is not easy for the daughter to acquire the realization that maturation and internal separation from her mother and father do not involve death or final and absolute abandonment like that suffered by the parents. The acquisition of this realization requires great readiness, determination and strength on the part of the 'memorial candles', and much patience and perseverance on the part of the therapists. The 'memorial candles' do finally succeed in facing their parents' real identity as men and women, with all the difficulties, defects and conflicts filling the parents' psyches, which are reflected in their shaky sexual identity. This is a gradual and difficult encounter, but it enables the 'memorial candles' to consolidate a distinct independent identity, and to separate themselves from that part of the parents' self that was assimilated into their own self. Thus the 'memorial candles' succeed – some more and some less – in separating from their archaic identifications with their parents and consolidating an independent identity of their own by revealing and working through the difficulties and conflicts that are disturbing them in the present, especially on the plane of the creation of an intimate relationship with a partner.

The cooperation, closeness and mutual identification in the group serve as a curative and facilitative factor of primary importance in this difficult process, in which mature, independent identification mechanisms towards parents and environment are formed and internalized. For the 'memorial candles' this is a crucial step on the long road towards the formation of a mature identity.

Chapter 7

Parting from the role of 'memorial candle'

'Yesterday I felt very intensely that I'm tired of being a symbol of the Holocaust,' said Devora, 'that this time I'm not giving in. I decided to share the burden with my sister and to talk openly with my parents. And, unbelievably, it happened! I don't want to carry the dead around by myself any more, I don't want them all on my back, I don't want to carry the dead around for them as well any more. I won't just be a burial hearse any more, as I have been all these years. I'll open up the graves of the dead and we'll all be with them together. I want to separate myself from these dead people, who have always been stuck to me, inside my soul. I want to see them and talk to them and even begin to love them, but I don't want to be buried with them any more! Enough! I don't have any more strength or will for this. I collaborated for forty years and now it's enough. I really feel that a new period is beginning for me.'

The integration of the personality takes place during the last stage of therapy, when the 'memorial candles' overcome a considerable portion of their inhibitions and the feelings of threat that have filled their internal world. Their defences are gradually weakened and they begin to express more clearly their emotional needs and their sense of trust in the therapists and the group. They accept the therapists' interpretations of their dreams, and these interpretations are gradually internalized into their personalities as positive elements that support and strengthen them, and not – as at first – as a frightening threat that had better be rejected out of hand. The suspicion and aggressiveness and the silences that characterized the earlier stages of therapy gradually disappear.

Now, as the 'memorial candles' begin to realize that revealing their inner world and working through its contents do not damage it, but rather strengthen it, they are able to continue progressing together along the last part of their journey. As mentioned, in the early stages of therapy the children of survivors generally avoid expressing feelings of anger and frustration, jealousy and competitiveness, love and sexual attraction; in the third stage they begin to express these feelings, with the support and encouragement of the therapist and the group. In spite of the difficulties and anxieties that initially accompany the open expression of feelings, it becomes a significant curative experience for the 'memorial candles', as it is very different from what was customary in their families. In the last stage of therapy the contents that arose during the previous stages arise once again, but their intensity and the type of emotions that accompany them are different. Of course, the struggle between their attraction to the images of the past – especially to the feelings of emptiness and death that dominated their inner world – and their desire to shake them off and to experience the reality of inner and outer life with its joys and pains, continues as in the previous stages, but now extensive islands of desire and ability for self-expression have crystallized in their personality and tip the balance towards the side of life. Happiness and sadness, joy and pain, competitiveness, love and attraction begin to populate their inner world and gradually take the place of the feelings of depression, inner emptiness and vague anxieties. With the growth of self-trust and trust in others, the emotions of the survivors' children become clearer and more focused. Their ability to express their emotions increases together with their ability to express their wishes clearly. This provides evidence of an ego that is being consolidated, with the boundaries between their own self and that of their parents becoming sharper.

In the last stage of therapy the survivors' children leave the role assigned them by their parents – the role of 'memorial candles' for the Holocaust, for the family history and for the lost relatives. The 'memorial candles' are on the verge of becoming able to drop the burden of unworked grief and depression, and to realize their parents' unconscious expectation that they will serve as a link joining their family's past with its future and will be able to endow the coming generations with a living rather than dead historical memory of the relatives who perished. The 'memorial candles' are now involved in searching for their parents' and their families' roots. They are discovering that the towns, villages and houses they heard fragmented stories about actually existed, with real people living in them. They no longer have trouble imagining past figures, families and communities. The world of the past acquires gestalt and meaning. This search for their roots arouses a more extensive feeling of identification in the 'memorial candles', and they experience a sense of belonging to the Jewish people. This feeling arises mainly in their dreams, which now contain symbols and motifs from Jewish history, religion and culture.

Baruch: 'The inner poverty I've lived with all these years is becoming clearer and clearer to me – how I didn't know what it was to love spontaneously, without calculation. Recently, especially in the group. I sometimes succeed in being warm and giving. But it's still with a feeling of some sort of open eye behind me that watches over me. Most of the time it's still not really uncalculated. As if all I can really give is seriousness, anger and suffering. I'm not free enough for anything else.'

Therapist: 'Who is saying this inside of you? Who has signed this statement?'

Baruch: 'Perhaps me. . .perhaps my mother or my father. It's a kind of family signature. This week I called my father and went to visit him. This is something I haven't done very much on my own initiative. There was more conversation between us. He told me about the trouble he's having with his feet. These are problems connected with the fact that in the camp both his feet froze and since then they hurt sometimes. I felt that even though we talked he wasn't really free to listen to me. Actually, I too wasn't completely free, it's very much like what happens to me in the group. I'm not satisfied with myself. I want to know how to really be with other people, to be freer inside. But I don't always know how and I don't always succeed.'

Hava: 'When I hear you speak, Baruch, I feel so choked. I feel that I'm still afraid to show all the warmth I have inside me for the group, and now also for you. I want to love, but I'm afraid to become free and to give myself. For instance, I want to hug you now. This is something I've really wanted to do for some time now, because I didn't know how to give you or show you all the warmth I've been feeling towards you. After all the years when I was so passive and paralysed in the group, now I feel for the first time that I want to give. I've always been afraid to connect with myself, because then I would really feel the pain and the sadness and the love we both felt. I was afraid that if they sensed me, if they sensed that I'm feeling, then they would still be able to hurt me. I don't want to be hurt. I hear what I'm saying and I know it's for myself and also for my mother. I see her again as a little girl in the camp. I don't want her to be hurt. She needs to be strong. She must never show them what she feels inside, because she needs to survive.'

Hava looked around, confused and embarrassed: 'Here I may possibly be able to dare now to feel and to tell you what I'm feeling, but all the time I also keep going back and reconnecting with my mother, there. . .'

Baruch: 'Right, I also do something like that. On Saturday I began asking my father again about his family and about the Holocaust. He wasn't exactly in the mood to talk about it.'

Therapist: 'It seems that only when you begin talking to your father about this topic and you reopen the old wound do you really feel together with him, and this is important. When you try to talk to him about present concerns, you don't feel that they have any significance. Hava too can dare to feel strongly only when she's connected to her mother there in the camp. Even when she wants to express warmth towards you or others, she still feels too threatened and it's more comfortable for her to return "there". On the one hand it's very stressful, but on the other hand it's familiar and safe. Still, now you're able to talk about it more openly, and this is a big step forward.'

Baruch: 'Right, as rotten as it was there, at least it's familiar territory. I'm fixated on suffering. What else do I have? Joy of life? Love? Merriment? Everyday life? There's always this heaviness in my guts.'

Therapist: 'It seems as though you're remaining attached to the Holocaust. This heaviness is also your best and strongest defence against life.'

Baruch: 'Yes, sometimes I feel absolutely unwilling to leave and to say goodbye. Not to my mother or my father or all of this past of theirs. To cut it off and to free myself of all these contents – that means being independent, and that's what still frightens me. After all, that's what held me together all these years.'

Hava: 'What contents exactly are you talking about?'

Baruch: 'The blaming, the anger, the depression. After all, if I won't have them any more, that will mean starting to really see and live in the world. It will mean starting to function in the world as it exists, without having my own different story that makes me something unique. My uniqueness has always protected me. Because of it I haven't had to cope with responsibility like everyone else when it comes to functioning in all sorts of situations. There are areas in life in which I've always excelled easily, but in the areas where it was difficult for me I always allowed myself to give up. For example, when I don't go to study, that is, when I don't get to the university on some particular day, I immediately say to myself, "Well, I have so many other things on my mind. I'm occupied with the concentration camps, with my father who was away from home for long periods, with my mother who dominated me but didn't see me." So then what do I do? I masturbate in my head with all these things, and meanwhile the whole outside world gets further and further away from me. To leave all this also means to give up and forgive my father and mother, and this is still difficult, even though I already feel closer and readier to do it.'

Therapist: 'You're still not ready to give up this defence completely, but you are ready to make peace to some extent with your parents and their past, as well as with your own past – to make peace to a greater extent within yourself with what they didn't have. And perhaps this is an opportunity for you to see more of what they did have as well – all the strengths they actually had, which enabled them to function and continue the struggle in spite of everything.'

Baruch looked thoughtful and answered hesitantly: 'Yes. . .I think that's right. Actually, these days my father is much more alive and even somewhat happier than he used to be, and I also see that my mother accomplishes more and enjoys her work. I can see this for a moment, but then I repress it again and return to the way it was before, and that's how it is all the time, back and forth, back and forth.'

Ruth: 'What Baruch just said reminds me of a dream I had this week. In the dream I'm in some place surrounded by people. They seem familiar to me, but I can't identify them exactly; perhaps they're members of the group, or my friends in school, or my family, but the main thing is that I know I have to be buried in the earth. They have to bury me and I have no idea if I will get out of it alive, but I do have some chance. I have to be buried in the earth and then get out of it and return to life. I think it would be better for me to lie on my stomach, because if I lie on my back the dirt will get into my nose and eyes, and I might also suffocate. In the last part of the dream I'm walking in a dark tunnel with a group of girls. The whole time there are more trains and more trains passing by, and we have to get out of there. We jump up and run someplace, but it's terribly dark there in the tunnel and I don't know where we're going. Finally we get to a very dark room and I feel that I have to get out of it in order to survive. I search for the light, and I search and search for the light switch, but the dream ends and I'm not sure if I found it in the end. When I woke up from the dream I was still searching.'

Rachel: 'And how did you feel when you woke up?'

Ruth answered in a choked and monotonous voice: 'I felt a lot of pressure. I woke up early and there was already some light from the window, and this relieved me a little. But the pressure didn't leave me all day. I feel that now I have a lot of anger and pain inside, and not only anxiety as usual. But I don't know exactly what this anger is about. I'm not sure who it's directed at. To some extent at the whole world.'

Ruth's anger infected Rachel: 'But now, as you're talking, this anger doesn't come out so clearly. Didn't you say you want to get the anger out? I feel that my head is already splitting and you're still talking quietly.'

Avraham, who generally identifies with Ruth, didn't give in to her this time: 'Every time you say something about your parents, you immediately start understanding them and justifying them. It drives me crazy. The more you speak, the more I feel that I am sinking and sinking. A feeling of a sort of weakness and helplessness.'

Therapist: 'It seems that it's still hard for you to really express all the anger inside you. It seems that the other members of the group, like Avraham and Rachel, are doing it for you. But in your dreams you're beginning to struggle and search, to find the light at the end of the dark tunnel. In order to return to life and light you have to face darkness and death. And you have the will to begin breaking down the wall of darkness, the helplessness or inability to express your wishes or feelings clearly. And it seems that you have some helpers here.'

Ruth: 'You're right. It's still hard for me to express anger strongly and clearly like Rachel or Avraham. At home I was always the good girl who wouldn't dare to rebel, or get angry, or object to anything. My brother, on the other hand, always did whatever he wanted and allowed himself to do all sorts of things that I never did.'

Avraham: 'Just as here, in the group, you've always played the role of the nice, smiling, quiet one, who never gets irritated and never says any harsh words to anyone. But recently you actually have been talking in a much stronger and clearer voice, not in that tiny, weak, choked voice that really used to drive us all crazy. You're finally beginning to permit yourself to disagree openly sometimes, to object once in a while and to express your wishes clearly. You should know that this makes everyone feel better and easier. Before it was as if you were made of pink cotton-wool, and when someone tried to hit you his hand would remain in the air. Now there's finally a feeling of being confronted by something real.'

Ruth: 'You know, two weeks ago was the first time I didn't tell my parents in advance that I was going to take an important test. I only told them after the test. My mother was astounded. She couldn't digest it for hours. This time I felt very clearly that I didn't want her involved in my affairs, that it would only bother me and spoil things for me. Recently I've been feeling that I don't want anything from them. With all this dependence of mine all these years, both financial and emotional, I feel it's enough.'

Rivka: 'I had a similar encounter with my mother this week. She tried again, as usual, to get involved and take control over something in my life, in the area of work actually, but this time I didn't give in to her as I always do, and I didn't cooperate with her. I reacted immediately, on the spot, and I told her very assertively that she couldn't intervene in this area, that these are my limits.'

Miriam: 'The fact that Ruth can express her feelings much more clearly now, and if she gets angry then the anger comes out clearly, and the same if she's sad – this is similar to what I've been feeling lately. I have a clear feeling of when I'm alive and when I'm not. But even when I feel that I'm not alive, I feel this lifelessness very actively.'

Miriam stopped talking for a moment, then continued with a shy smile: 'I know that what I'm saying now sounds somewhat strange and paradoxical, but that's the way it really is. It's different to feel the loneliness or the pain clearly and strongly than to be the way I was all my life, in a depression and not wanting, and actually not being able, to do anything. Just to sit for hours and stare at the four walls around me. This time it's totally clear where the pain belongs. I thought about a lot of people I would have called if I could, because I really wanted to, but in the end I felt that I just couldn't do it at that time. But at least the clear desire already exists, and I believe that the ability will come in the end. What will I tell them? The feeling of optimism, even a tiny bit of optimism, is already something very new.'

The inner world of the 'memorial candles' thus begins to stir into life. It's still difficult for them to overcome their anxieties completely, and to feel overwhelming joy or poignant sadness in their full intensity, just as it's still difficult for them to draw clear boundaries for their personalities and to separate them from the personalities of their parents and other family figures. The ability to cry and to feel pain and anger permits the 'memorial candles' to grasp the extent of their parents' loss. Now, having entered into its depths, they are finally able to separate and free themselves from the burden that was placed on their shoulders. But the separation from the faded, suffering figures they internalized during their childhood frees them for a renewed encounter with the essence of their parents' real past, and they raise poignant questions they had never asked before: what exactly happened to Father in the camps? Where exactly was Mother on some particular day? How and where did Grandmother and Grandfather perish? The separation from the role of 'memorial candle' thus enables them to come into contact with reality itself, even with the most painful reality. Although the pain hidden in their family's history is extremely intense, the ability to feel it is also the ability to live a full emotional life.

The 'memorial candles' are now able to work through their new feelings and internalize the ability to feel clear and intense emotions. In a previous chapter we heard the story of Baruch, who described how he came to be chosen as the 'memorial candle' in his family. In one of the individual sessions at the last stage of therapy Baruch returned to this scene, but this time his reactions were totally different.

Baruch: 'I began feeling this intense anger towards everything –
towards the Holocaust, towards the tasks I was given, towards my
father, who on the one hand was so active and organized everything in the underground, and then afterwards, when he board-
ed the train, thought that everything was wonderful and that the
train would take him to freedom, and then in the end when they
arrived at Bergen-Belsen, the same thing all over again.'

Therapist: 'And there they made you.'

Baruch: 'Yes, and towards that irresponsibility. . .'

Full of rage, he stopped the flow of words, and after a long silence
he continued: 'I'm so angry with my father, for what he did. For
it wasn't me that he made. He tricked me. He did indeed father
me, but he didn't have me in mind at all. He actually had his
younger brother in mind – the one he helped raise before the
war. The fact that my father didn't have me in mind made me
live all sorts of roles except for my own life. I was my father's
father, I was his brother, I was his opposite, whatever you want,
except for really being myself.'

'All these years in therapy I've told you that I don't feel myself, that
what I feel is a frozen void. Whenever something happened to
me with some woman, or something else, at the beginning I
would feel a little, and then I would immediately go back to this
inner immobility and death, which I called my tomb. There, in
the tomb, I felt calm. I always went back there. I spent so many
of those years in that tomb. It's not surprising that now, at
the age of forty, I hardly feel twenty. I haven't built myself a life,
I haven't got married, I haven't had children. So why shouldn't
I be angry? My mother simply closed her eyes and accepted all
of my father's decisions, passively and with her eyes closed, and
I'm not supposed to be angry about that? But what's the use?
Actually I'm just like her. I bought my father's stories just as she
did. When I was living with Tzafrira, I often felt that in all sorts
of situations it was my father who was responding to her, that it
was he who was there with her, not I.'

'It's so hard for me to separate. I feel that I am angry but at the
same time I'm also hurt. Last time we spoke about the fact that
I'm named after my father's younger brother, who was shot to
death there, next to the river, when he was scarcely twenty.
Perhaps I'm living instead of him. Do you remember? I was sort
of confused, and I called my uncle my brother instead of my
uncle. But after all I never actually knew him. I don't know how

it could be that I'm living him. I've often felt that my father expected me to be what he couldn't be, what he transferred to me from his two brothers. Perhaps he transferred to me what my uncle was, or what he expected him to be. This uncle, who my father always spoke about with respect and admiration, was very intelligent. When we were children my father would force me to study very compulsively and rigidly. He was never satisfied with me, that is, with my achievements. His attitude towards me,' here Baruch suddenly began to stammer, 'his attitude towards me was that he taught me compulsively and aggressively. I hated this so much as a boy that then, exactly at that age, I began to stammer. I wouldn't be surprised if it was connected somehow to my attitude towards his brother who was killed. I don't know how, but I have the feeling that it's connected. You know, one of the reasons I came to therapy was my stammering, but lately there have been long periods when it has disappeared. But when I just touch on these topics it comes back very strongly.'

'My father always loved this younger brother of his very much and he never stopped talking about him admiringly. I was never good enough for him. Now I finally feel some relief. When I came here today I was very pressured. When I talked with Tzafrira yesterday, I was able for the first time to tell her clearly how I've felt all these years with her, how I've played all sorts of roles with her, all sorts of roles that I know from home, which I've transferred to my relationship with her. How it wasn't really me at all, perhaps it was my father. I felt clearly that I myself hadn't been there at all. And so when we parted I came away with this feeling of ease. It's amazing, but I don't even miss what there was between us.'

'My parents' closeness is less threatening now. They can be closer to me now without making me feel so pressured. They are already less mixed up with me. They are they, and I am I. They do their thing and I do mine.'

Therapist: 'It seems that this anger, which was locked up inside for forty years, is finally coming out strongly and clearly – something that was too threatening before.'

Baruch: 'Yes, exactly. Now I see that if I come into contact with my real self, it's easier for me to express my own personality, I can speak more clearly.'

Therapist: 'This is because now your personality is already separate and not so mixed up with the other parts and roles.'

Baruch: 'You're right. But listen, I had a dream last night, I forget exactly what about. In the dream some people are re-constructing my uncle's death, and I agree to cooperate with them. There's a figure of a man with a long sword in his hand, and he plunges the sword into the area of my heart. I don't know if he finally penetrated it or not, but I felt the pain in my heart. When I woke up in the morning I still felt pain in my chest, and my heart was also beating rapidly. Well, you know that the heart is the symbol of emotion in general.'

'I feel sadness and pain for this uncle who was twenty years old when he was shot there and for the grandfather who died. All these years I've always talked about the emptiness inside and about the feeling of death and nothingness. Now the emotions have become interchanged: the sadness and the pain have become mixed up with emotionality and life. But this is so different from the feeling of depression. I think that the figure with the sword is my father, who rebelled against his own father and became a Zionist and left him there to die. He even got a postcard from his father asking him to come and rescue them, but he decided not to go back. My grandfather was already in a detention camp, on the way, you know where. In his day my grandfather had been an officer in the Austro-Hungarian army. I've seen photos of him with this sword in his hand. My father greatly admired him. He himself was never a real soldier, and he always greatly admired officers. Now I feel, on the one hand, true grief for my uncle and grandfather who remained there, but I also feel that I am separate from them and perhaps also from parts of myself. And at the same time I feel relief. I want to unload this burden from my shoulders. I feel like saying to my father, "Take it away from me, it's yours", and to my mother, "Take it away from me, it's yours", and to my uncle, "Take it away from me, it's yours", and to all of them together, "Let me finally be myself". For the first time in my life I feel that I'm at the beginning of a new process. Death and life – I am wavering between them. There were a few days when I was terribly tired. The house was neglected and I couldn't do anything – that was apparently death. But after I got the anger out, I got out of it to some extent, and some more energy was flowing through me – these seem to be signs of life.'

A few days after this session Baruch related a dream in which one can clearly see the struggle taking place within him between the desire to live and the attraction towards death, the intense competition between his identification with the role of 'memorial candle', with the death and loss involved in it, and his desire to free himself of this role out of inner choice and the ability to make independent decisions.

Baruch: 'Last night I had a dream that seemed very significant to me, at least I thought you would think so. . . I dreamt that some important monk had died, and I wanted to be buried with him, or perhaps instead of him, it's not so clear. When the time for the funeral arrived, my friend Arye – you know, he's also a son of survivors and always occupied with the topic of the Holocaust – then I asked Arye and his wife Varda to come and help me, and they came. On the way Varda fell into a puddle of water. It was I who helped her get out, while he didn't show any signs of concern. I lie down on the monument and they wrap me in wide strips of plastic, like shrouds. The ceremony is very impressive, but I can't move. Arye arranges my appearance well and the moment is approaching. Suddenly I realize that I haven't asked what kind of ceremony this is, what is customary in a case like mine, do they put me to sleep first or what? At the very last moment I decide to get out of it. Enough, I don't want to die. I tell Arye to get me out and he actually disconnects the electricity the way you're supposed to, and he cuts the plastic strips I am wrapped in and I get out. Now we're running away in a Transit. By the way, a Transit was the car we rode in together in the summer, I and my sisters and my parents, on that famous journey to our roots that I told you about, to Budapest, the city where my parents were born. But let's get back to the dream. I start crying very hard, and Arye becomes very tense. Then I tell them with much feeling that crying in a situation like this is like being connected with my parents' feelings and with the Holocaust, and that the only way to become free is to become connected first.'

Baruch's dream is a clear, concise dream about death and the return to life. The dream reflects Baruch's life as well as that of his parents, who appear here in the disguise of a friend and his wife. The monk in the dream represents both his father and Jewish tradition, which plays a central role in his life and his father's. Baruch is supposed to die instead of the monk, who is his father – that is, bear in his place his losses in the Holocaust. But in the end Baruch arises from the grave. Just as in reality Baruch bore in his heart for so many years the burden of emptiness, depression and emotional death, and the figures of his dead uncle and grand-father that his father loaded onto him, so in the beginning of the dream he accepted the role imposed on him by the monk. Arye, who represents his father, as mentioned, is not free in the dream to help his wife when she falls in the puddle. It is Baruch who is called to help her, just as throughout his life he has been com-pelled to care for his mother's emotional needs.

Baruch escapes from death in a car of the type in which he and his family rode in their visit to his parents' birthplace. The only way to become free is to become connected first, says Baruch in his dream; and so the search for roots, a symbol of coming back to life, which was a liberating task for Baruch, is closely connected with the burial ceremony in the dream, which is the encounter with death.

But this is not all. In the dream there's a scene associated with a very primary stage in Baruch's life. He lies wrapped in plastic strips, which remind one of the swaddling clothes in which a baby is wrapped when he has just emerged from his mother's womb and is not yet able to move voluntarily. Baruch's mother became preg-nant while his parents were in the camp, when their lives were in danger at every moment. In his dream Baruch is lying in the grave/womb and waiting for the fateful event: death/birth. In the end it is birth that takes place, but not without the help of Arye, who apparently represents, in the performance of this task, the therapy group and the therapist. At the last moment Baruch chooses life and does not surrender to death. When he comes out of the grave he immediately breaks out in strong crying, which reminds one of the first cry of the infant bursting out of his mother's womb and announcing that he is alive and already able to breathe by himself. But Baruch is also crying for the emotional death he was immersed in for forty years, as well as the cry of his father, who never cried for the dear ones he lost. Thus death and life are interwoven in Baruch's crying. This cry is the clearest expression of the catharsis of his feelings of pain and mourning. Unlike his parents, who do not cry because the mourning is locked up within them and cannot come out, Baruch has now succeeded in really mourning. Parting from the role of 'memorial candle' thus involves the ability to complete the mourning process; only then can the birth, the escape to freedom, take place.

Devora, who we also met in the early stages of therapy, told me the following during one of her last individual sessions:

'I've felt sad and choked during the past weeks. I thought that my restlessness, and my continuous discomfort with the emptiness and anxiety, are connected with all the symbols, roles and meanings that all my relatives have imposed on me – my mother and father, and even my sister, to a certain extent.'

Tears gathered in her eyes. She continued: 'I cry sometimes, and not only feel more and more anger inside. I cry because nobody saw me just as an ordinary human creature that needs attention and love. They buried me with the dead while I was still alive. It's hard for me to drag around the dead and their messages all the time. "Don't put them down," they tell me. "We're comfortable this way." I want them to take back their dead. I'm not the family hearse. I think I already said this sentence or a similar one, but now I feel that I have much more strength inside, not just to say it but also to stand by my words.'

'For so many years there was always an uncomfortable atmosphere around me in the family. I always felt that I existed for them as some kind of shell, pretty but without any content. The trouble is that I also lived this way for myself all those years. Now, after all the years of therapy and the group, I feel that I actually do have a lot of content, that I'm definitely not just a pretty shell. At work I felt this very clearly. I felt that I was taking care of things and doing them with much more responsibility. Recently I've had a lot of energy, and not only at work. In general I feel that I've stopped hovering above things with that "unbearable lightness" that was always so characteristic of me. After all, that was my main defence. Wherever there could have been something deep, a feeling or a thought or a commitment, I would immediately begin flying in the air. It was my luck that I was always talented enough and somehow managed to study and accomplish things in spite of all this. Now I feel that I'm able, and also want, to get more deeply into things, to get to the bottom of them, without being afraid.'

'Perhaps the end of all this is death, this nothingness that I've really been facing recently. At least that's how it seems to me at the moment. And I'm not afraid of it any more. It also affected me in another way: yesterday I was at my parent's home and I asked my father and mother about their family that remained there. Who exactly they were and what they were. . . My mother told me about her whole family and I wrote down their names and ages. This is the first time I've tried to organize it. Suddenly I also have a family tree, even if it's made up mostly of black squares rather than golden or green ones. But it's still a family tree that organizes things somewhat inside my head. Yesterday I also found out for the first time that my father's family was in the Warsaw Ghetto, and his sister's son, that is, my cousin, was in the revolt there. When I heard this yesterday I felt very strange. I felt pain, of course, but the pain was mixed with a lot of pride, and this is a totally new feeling for me in connection with 'there'. It was always just this vague sort of depression, or sadness and heaviness, and suddenly I can imagine my cousin fighting actively there in the ghetto.'

'My father told me that the thing that disturbed him the most was the thought of the way they sent his parents to die. Packed like cattle in a freight train, unable even to breathe or to sit down, or even to perform their natural functions like human beings. With such humiliating torture. I cried, and even my father had some tears in his eyes. You won't believe it, but this is the first time in forty years that we could be together with this and feel really together. To be sad together openly and not only to be together in stress and tension and depression, which only makes you anxious and nothing else, and at the end each one continues to feel completely alone. He told me about two cousins who remained alone in the Warsaw Ghetto, and about the look in the eyes of one of them, a little boy, who was only eight when they took him away from his mother, who died there in the ghetto, and then from his father as well, who was also killed, and finally also from his brother, and sent him to die alone. I think that this look in his eyes, full of fear, was transmitted to me. I cried and cried and couldn't stop. They've told me in the group so many times that I have such a fearful look in my eyes. This means that the people here managed to receive this look through the mask that I usually succeeded in putting on my face, my laughing mask. Here I didn't succeed in hiding it. I feel that recently there are periods, which are becoming longer and longer, in which I'm free from this terror and I can go out into the world without the mask.'

'Then I went to my sister and told her that Father had read me parts of the diary our cousin kept in the Warsaw Ghetto. She told me that there were years when this diary and the stories about the Holocaust ruined her life, and that since then she's been afraid of doctors and of bosses, and just generally afraid. This diary reached my parents right after the war, in 1946. My sister told me that when they received it, Mother went into such a depression that she could hardly function, and Father too was depressed. I was about a year old then, but they sent me to an institution for nearly a year, until Mother recovered somewhat.'

'Yesterday I felt that my sister too was closer to me. For the first time we were able to talk about these things really together. There was a partnership. I started talking to her just as I've done over the years with the group. I'm sure that without what I went through in the group I would never have been able to open up this topic and share it with anyone.'

'After I left my parents' home yesterday I walked around the streets and cried and cried. Even at home I continued crying a little. My mother saw even there that I was crying, and she completely ignored it, but this doesn't matter to me any more. The main thing is that I didn't have to hide anything any more and to wear this damned mask even there. Yesterday I succeeded in taking it off both with my parents and with my sister – it's unbelievable.'

Arye, also in the stage of parting from the role of 'memorial candle', said something similar:

'Lately I've been feeling very preoccupied. For a few weeks now nothing has been loosening up in me. Friends don't interest me. I went to a Purim[1] party and I didn't manage to enjoy it. I walk in the street with Shoshi, I see nice things, but I don't enjoy it. I don't sleep well at night and I often wake up with a terrible restlessness. At work I actually feel a little better. There's a new boss at the department where I work, and I spoke to him very clearly. We clarified his expectations from me and what I want. This is the first time I've been able to define the relationship and the expectations between myself and my boss. This time I was ready to do this and I even felt good about it. In the past I never knew how to do it. During these weeks I've been thinking and dreaming about death again. I realize where it's coming from: I have something sad inside me that can't be happy, but I can't call it mourning.'

Therapist: 'Why can't you call it mourning?'

Arye: 'Last week there were two days when I felt happiness returning, but afterwards it disappeared again. To call it mourning is to stay with it, to think about my parents, to read about the topic in books and to be with it again all the time – that is, to be in it and not to get out of it for a long time.'

Therapist: 'But isn't that precisely what's been happening to you these past weeks?'

Arye: 'Yes, it seems that you're right. This week I thought I wanted to go and see my parents, to be together somehow with the whole family. I remembered that in my childhood, on Passover, I would go to the synagogue with my father, and my mother would invite guests, always the same people: two families we knew, who came every year. After all, we didn't have any family. My father had some things he always did – for example, he would play with the *afikoman* [a Passover game in which a piece of matzo is hidden by a member of the family and other members of the family search for it], and sometimes he would manage to be a bit happy, the only day in the year. He would tell us a little about his home. And my mother would cook an egg soup, the way they ate it there in Poland before the war. Suddenly I realized that I'm searching once again for the warmth that we had and we didn't have at home. For the tiny drop of warmth that there was in our house on Passover I'm willing to go through many hurdles.' Arye's face clouded over and his eyes became wet. 'Actually, it's like searching my whole life for the kind of father I always wanted him to be. Passover was the only time I remember my father as I wanted him to be. You understand? The difference is simply between a live father and a dead father. I feel this pressure in my head again.'

Therapist: 'But now you're allowing yourself to feel not only the pressure and the tension but also the sadness, especially the longing for something you hardly ever had in your daily life with your father, and perhaps with your mother either.'

Arye: 'Do you remember that we once talked about all the names I have? This week I thought about this again. I have three names

– not only Arye but also Tzvi and Moshe, and in addition I also have three family names. The names are for my father's brother, for my father's father and for my mother's father. You see, I actually carry the whole family on my shoulders. Until recently I never really considered the significance of this – what a heavy burden they put on me without thinking about me at all or about what it would do to me. All in all, it makes me very angry. Only death and nothing else. It's very complicated and I don't really get along with death very well. Why couldn't they try to balance it so each of us would carry the same amount? A little for my sisters, a little for my parents, and a little for me. Such a negative burden was placed on me, as if they said to me, "You just have to carry the dead." Last Passover, when I was with the whole family, I felt somewhat different. First of all, there was a slightly more lively atmosphere in the house. Moreover, my father started to tell me stories about the family in the past, and I felt that he was taking away part of my burden and taking it upon himself, and was even giving me something positive in return. My sisters were there too, and they also heard the stories, and listened and asked questions. I had the feeling that even though they are still somewhat emotionally detached from the whole thing, they still belong to it and are participating in some way. Perhaps, or rather certainly, something has changed in me as well. I am willing to involve my sisters more, to share all the immense burden with them – this difficult, oppressive thing that only I have, like the Holy of Holies that no one else is allowed to touch. This is the precious burden they gave me, with the names and with the fact that I was born in 1946. I've definitely been feeling lately that this is a precious burden with immense emotional value for me. It contains my history and that of my family and my ancestry, and I want to be connected with it, but in a completely different way from the way I was until now.'

Therapist: 'What exactly do you mean when you say "in a different way"? And how is all this connected with the dead and the live parts of your father that you mentioned before?'

Arye: 'My father, because of his inner insecurity, in contrast with his total outward control, and because of his deadness and depression, was never able to give me what I really needed and what I searched for in vain all those years.'

Therapist: 'You're describing the emotional handicaps your father suffered from, which were expressed in all sort of ways and in all sorts of situations where he was with you. Your mourning reaction this week, and lately in general, means that you're actually beginning to accept the fact that the depressed side of your father is really part of him, and that, on the other hand, the alive and happy side appears only rarely, and will apparently never be enough to satisfy you.'

Tears gathered in Arye's eyes once more, and he said: 'Yes, I know, that's exactly how it is. But it hurts so much.'

Therapist: 'You needed years of therapy to begin to accept this situation and to be able to make peace with it. But you already know that mourning is actually part of the pain involved in making peace.'

Arye: 'Yes, you're right, but there's something more than that, something even more complicated. Maybe it's like an umbilical cord. My father and I, I and my father, for many years it was like something symbiotic. What he felt, I felt, and what he went through, I went through, and if he was happy, then I was happy.'

Greatly moved, Arye addressed his father in the second person: 'Only now am I capable of seeing you as not being the father I always hoped for, and for the first time my moods are not like yours. So how do I see you now? The only relationship I know how to form, with a man or with a woman, is a symbiotic one, so how will you seem to me when you are no longer a part of me? And how will my mother seem when she is separate from me? I have two umbilical cords. It's new to be able to see it so clearly, and it's somewhat frightening, but perhaps it means that I'm really beginning to detach myself.'

Therapist: 'Exactly. For you to face the situation is also to leave it. Now you see and feel things more intensely than you ever did before. It seems to me that you're also ready inside to take another step forward. This symbiotic relationship, as you called it, began with the names your father and mother gave you, and now the time has come to choose from among them the name that will be yours, the name that suits your present feeling. This doesn't mean that you can't let the other names remain beside it, as a decoration or addition.'

Another point which is very important for the understanding of the therapy process is directly connected with the experience of group therapy. In the group setting the 'memorial candles' experience the process of the gradual formation of a relationship of trust, cooperation and mutuality. The central topic common to the group is their family background. All the group members have secrets from their families' past, secrets they have avoided revealing and sharing with others for many years – even with their closest relatives. In the group setting these secrets are brought up for discussion again and again, each time more openly than before. Moreover, these secrets are kept continually at the crossing points of all the relationships and as the focus of all the identifications between the members of the group. In the group the 'memorial candles' experience the breaking of their family and individual taboos on discussions touching upon the Holocaust, and the pressure and tension generally aroused in them by these topics gradually fade away.

The healing experience that the group is capable of providing for its members bears fruit in the last stage of therapy, when many 'memorial candles' are ready to transfer to their families some of the behaviour patterns they practised in the group. Their ability to speak openly with their parents, to ask them direct and penetrating questions, and not to leave them alone until they give satisfactory answers – coupled with their willingness to listen to these answers and deal with them, and to share their parents' pain and mourning – seem to be the most important achievements of their therapy. In the group they learn that it's possible to experience shared pain together, and if this is possible with the members of the group, why shouldn't it be possible with their families as well?

As mentioned, many brothers and sisters who are children of survivors find it very difficult to share their feelings with one another or to feel true equality with one another. The explanation of this difficulty is very complicated and cannot be discussed here. At any rate, during the last stage of therapy an important change takes place in these distorted relationships as well. The group experience serves to change the members' habitual attitudes towards their peers, thus enabling the 'memorial candles' to break the wall of emotional isolation surrounding them since their early childhood, which they wittingly or unwittingly helped to build and maintain. The ability they acquire to speak openly with their brothers and sisters about their parents' past and its effect on their lives is based on the sense of inner strength and security they are able to draw from their new independent identity. This ability enables them to take an important step towards their liberation from the task of 'memorial candle' for their entire family. From this point on the 'memorial candle' can say to himself, 'I am only one member of my family, and like all the other members I carry only part of its burden on my shoulders, not all of it any more.'

This change is reflected in a statement made by Miriam at a group session held close to Holocaust Day: 'This year I feel that I don't want to go alone to the Yad Vashem memorial as I do every year, and to immerse myself once more in the whole thing. At any rate, I won't be the only one going out of my whole family. Besides, I don't have much free time. I'm busy with other things in my life – my work, the boyfriend I have now. I told my brother openly that perhaps this time he should go to the ceremony at Yad Vashem, or that the two of us should go together. I really feel that I'm more or less done with this pressure that was inside of me all the years.'

At the same time that the 'memorial candles' become interested in finding out substantive facts about their family history, many of them also begin to feel the desire, at this stage, to visit their parents' birthplace together with their parents and siblings – to see with their own eyes the city or town or village in which their parents grew up, and, if possible, the houses they lived in.[2] Obviously, this 'journey to one's roots' arouses mixed feelings at first: curiosity and interest are mixed with avoidance and fear. For both the parents the children this is a journey fraught with intense emotions and conflicts. Some of the parents are totally unwilling to attempt such a journey. They refuse to go back and step on the ground where their families were murdered. Some of them agree to go, while others even initiate the journey. Impressions from these journeys, with the complicated emotions they arouse, are expressed in the group discussions.

Arnona: 'This week, when I came home, my parents brought up the idea of a trip together with me to Poland. Their friends had gone there recently and told them about it, and it seems that this made them begin thinking about going there. But afterwards, when we talked about it, they said they wouldn't even consider going there without me, and that actually it wasn't for themselves that they wanted to go, but for me, in order to show me the places where they were born and grew up, there in Poland before the Holocaust. It came out all mixed up. My mother said that she was willing to go because my father wanted to go. My father, on the other hand, said that he was only going because of my mother, but actually they wouldn't go without me. I came out all mixed up about the whole thing, about who really wanted to go in the end and for whom. It was almost grotesque, I didn't know if I should laugh or cry. My mother said that she really wanted to go because she wanted to see the beautiful castles in her home town once more, that she had heard that after the war they had built a new museum that she hadn't seen yet, etc., etc. It was really absurd. I told them that I thought they wanted to go to Poland because of the Holocaust. After all, millions of Jews were murdered there, and I've often thought that wherever you step on the ground there, you're stepping on the ashes of the dead, and whatever grows there is growing from that "fertilizer". I knew that if I went there in the end, I wouldn't be able to eat anything that grew on this land of theirs. I would bring all my food from home. When I told them that so many Jews had been murdered there, including their own families, my father suddenly seemed rather embarrassed. He began to tell me that yes. . .and that no. . .and that actually they themselves had not gone through the Holocaust in the most terrible way; on the contrary, they had gone through it relatively easily, and there were others who had had a much harder time and who suffered from it to this day and had nightmares from it.'

Arnona suddenly stopped talking and an oppressive silence reigned. After a while she continued:

'You see, it sounded as if they were going there on a trip, to have a good time and see castles and museums, as if they had no connection whatsover with the Holocaust. But as for me, because of this I've been having nightmares all night about the Nazis and the concentration camps, and feelings of terrible fear that I'm being pursued.'

Therapist: 'If I'm not mistaken you once told us that when you were a little girl you also suffered from fears and nightmares.'

Arnona: 'Yes, that's right, about skeletons and dead people. I would lie in bed and wait trembling for the skeletons to come out of the closets and the bookshelves. But lately an even stranger thing has been happening to me. I suddenly smell this strange smell, it comes in waves and makes me really nauseous.'

Avraham: 'Can you say what sort of smell it is?'

Arnona: 'I don't know exactly. . . It's a sort of sweetish smell. I remember that I read in some books, where people described what they went through in camps like Auschwitz and Treblinka, where there were crematoria, that they were continuously enveloped, both by day and by night, by this sort of smell that came from the crematoria, where they burnt the Jews. It seems to me that the smell I'm smelling is like that smell.'

Avraham: 'But that's really fantastic. After all, you weren't actually there at all, yet not only do you fantasize and dream about skeletons and dead people and Nazis running after you at night, but you even smell the smell that came from the crematoria. It's really unbelievable. You're carrying around the entire Holocaust on your back and they're totally free of it. It drove me crazy when you described the conversation about the idea of going to Poland. I'm not at all sure if you really want it or if it's really appropriate for you now. I, for instance, am certain that I would definitely not be willing to do such a thing with my mother at present. She would drive me completely crazy. I wouldn't be able to stand it. It seems that they've once again dumped the responsibility for this very important decision on you. And you, for about the millionth time, cooperated with them. Or, as I hope very much, were you perhaps able to detach yourself from them somewhat and see things as they really are?'

Arnona, embarrassed by Avraham's question, answered hesitantly: 'Yes. . . No. . . I think that this time I managed to respond a little bit differently, but perhaps not enough. After the conversation with them I felt really dizzy. I felt that the way this conversation had taken place between me and my parents was really strange, that there was something crooked and crazy about it. But it was, of course, not much different from most of the conversations in our house. Still, this time I managed to see it and grasp it in time, and to stop the conversation instead of agreeing immediately, almost mechanically, like a robot, as I always used to do. I told them that I needed time to think and deliberate about it, and that I would only answer them later. That's the reason I brought it up here today, in the group – so you could all help me get it clear. It's very important for me to know what your reactions are to this whole idea. . .'

Martha: 'I myself can understand very well what you're going through, all these mixed up feelings about the trip – yes or no. I remember that I once told you about it, but it seems as if it has still remained inside me. When I went with my parents to Zagreb, the town they were born in, I was about fourteen. My parents didn't prepare me emotionally or mentally for the trip.

I think they didn't prepare themselves either. We didn't speak about anything of importance beforehand – not about what they left there and not about what they felt then, and especially not about how they felt about going back there after all those years. We wandered around the streets, and my father showed me the house that had belonged to his family for generations. His grandfather's grandfather had built it and he himself had been born and raised and lived there until he had to run away in the middle of the night. He showed me the house and all he said was, "Here, in this doorway, I saw my parents and my sister for the last time, when my sister was exactly fourteen years old." It's amazing. At the time I didn't understand and I didn't make any connections. My mother told me that when they left the town (my mother and my father are both from the same town) – she and her brothers and both her parents – she was about fourteen, maybe fifteen. And here I was going back there with them, and I was exactly the same age as my father's sister, that he was so close to, and also the same age as my mother when she was uprooted from there so cruelly. At the time I didn't understand any of this, but three days later when we were walking around there I began to feel ill. I simply felt that I couldn't breathe. And in the end I had such a bad asthma attack that they had to put me in hospital there for ten days.'

Arnona: 'They simply transferred to you, unintentionally, the immense burden of feelings that belonged to both of them together and to each of them separately. You couldn't carry it, of course, especially since you had no one to talk to, and at the time you certainly didn't have the capacity to deal with it. Your asthma is like my nightmares. When I wake up I also feel rather choked.'

Martha: 'Yes, you're right, but it's interesting to imagine how it would be if I were to go there now. Now that I'm older and have more awareness and confidence, would I react the same way, or would it be different? It seems to me that even now, as I was speaking and telling you what I went through during that trip, it's already different. I feel it differently in comparison to last year, the first time I told you about the trip.'

Yoel: 'I was actually born in Poland, and I was still rather young, about nine, when we left. In all the years that have passed since then, I've wiped Poland completely out of my consciousness. I haven't thought about it, I haven't been reminded of it, I haven't missed it, as if it was a part of my life that was completely closed, without any need or desire to return to it. But recently I've actually had several dreams about Poland. It's very strange. In my dreams I return to the house I grew up in until the age of nine, I see the house very clearly, in all its details. There's also some old woman appearing in the dream, the landlady apparently, who still remembers my mother. Recently I've simply been feeling that I miss Poland and that I want to go back there to see and to remember, and I don't know exactly what else. Obviously for me to go to Poland would be different than for Arnona, or even for Martha, since she went back to her parents' town, not her own.'

Therapist: 'It's true that from a certain standpoint it's different, since for you it's your own past, and for them it's their parents' past. But they carry their parents' past within themselves. It has become a part of their inner world and it keeps bothering and disturbing them. As we've said here a thousand times already: in order to part it's necessary to meet. But here the parting is only from the nightmarish aspect, from the fears and the pressure and the tension that give Arnona nightmares and gave Martha asthma attacks.'

The encounter with their parents' roots, with the places their families had lived in for generations, whether it occurs in reality or only in the imagination, may well calm the souls of the survivors' children at this stage and fill up the empty spaces in their inner world. During the course of therapy the 'memorial candles' often compare themselves to uprooted trees. This association is undoubtedly a direct result of their having grown up without a family history. Now their hearts are filled with the need to find the missing links in the family chain. The journey to the past, if it fits the emotional needs of the survivors' children, may free them of stress and help them consolidate and integrate their identity.

At a group session Ziona related the story of her trip to Hungary with her parents:

'When we went to visit Hungary – that is, my parents and I, my sister didn't come with us, she already had her own family, and in general it was always I who went everywhere with my parents and shared with them everything associated with the Holocaust. My sister, at least outwardly, had washed her hands of all that; she always said that it didn't interest or concern her, although recently I've begun to think and to see that maybe this isn't exactly so. . .'

'Anyway, what I remember best from the whole trip was the rather miserable village my mother grew up in. When we approached it my mother told me more and more about her eight brothers and sisters, all of whom remained in the village and eventually reached the crematoria, so she never saw them again. Since the financial situation in the house wasn't particularly good even before the war broke out, my mother and her sister moved to Budapest to work, and that's how they survived.'

'When we reached the outskirts of the village there was a sort of wooden fence, where my mother had parted from her family when she went to the big city, and since then she hadn't seen them or gone back there again. So there, next to this fence, my mother was very moved and she cried. Actually, she hadn't really wanted so much to go on the trip. It was actually my father who put pressure on her and wanted to go there. During the entire trip my mother hardly ate anything. She was truly unable to swallow a thing. There, in the village where she was born, some farmer's wife, who remembered my grandmother and all my mother's brothers and sisters very well, and even remembered my mother as a little girl, gave us some red cherries and we ate them. After all, we couldn't refuse! At night my mother woke up and began to vomit over and over again – something sort of red. We were very frightened, we thought it was blood. We thought it would be the end of her there, that she couldn't take it any more. We felt somewhat guilty, both my father and I. After all, she had said she didn't want to go there, maybe it was too much for her. Then it was I who insisted that if we had already got that far we should also go and see the village and the house. This whole house was actually a kind of wooden hut they had lived in. My mother was very moved. She got into a sort of childish state and began laughing and crying and talking like a little girl. Apparently being there brought her back to those years, when she was still a little girl and she lived in this wooden hut with her parents and grandparents and all her sisters and brothers – a whole tribe.'

Ziona began sobbing and couldn't continue her story.

Ahuva: 'My mother and I also went to Hungary. This was a few years ago. Only the two of us went. I think she took me with her because it was important to her that I should be the one to go with her. I really don't know why my father didn't come along. Altogether I felt a great emotional overload on this trip, even though the significance of each thing we did and every situation we were in wasn't clear to me. Now it seems to me that I received my mother's emotional overload, but without the ability to consider the matter, or to understand it, or to talk about it. But this trip was nevertheless important for me as well. The whole time I had this feeling that it was important for me to go back there with my mother. There was one incident that remains engraved in my memory. It was our visit to the ghetto, or more precisely what remained of it. There my mother told me a little about what she went through, or more precisely what they went through, during the time they were there. One morning she asked me to stay in the hotel while she went to visit the grave of her little girl, the baby who died of hunger there in the ghetto, at the age of three months. I wanted very much to go along, and I begged and pleaded with her to take me with her, but she refused absolutely. This disturbed me very much. Why wasn't she willing to let me go there and share it with her? As if it were something that belonged only to her and she wasn't willing to share it with me. After all, the baby buried there in the ghetto was my sister, at least on my mother's side. The whole morning, which was grey and rainy, I remained stuck to the window, and I cried and cried and waited for my mother to come back. It was a terrible morning.'

I had the following discussion with Yael after she and her boyfriend came back from a European tour.

Yael: 'In general, the European tour with Zvika was very successful. I almost forgot to tell you that we also went to Dachau.'

Therapist: 'When you told me your plans for the trip you didn't say a word about it!'

Yael didn't respond immediately. She hesitated and then said, 'What? I really didn't tell you? Strange. Actually, we originally planned to travel along a different route, but in the end, because of problems with the planes, it turned out that we started the tour in Munich, and from there we visited Dachau. I felt complete acceptance of the tour of the camp. I really wanted to be there. I felt that this time I was really prepared for it emotionally. I think something happened to me there that's connected with my mother, that's been ripening inside me for some time. When we got there, it was. . .you know. . .by train. We could actually have gone in our car or by bus, but I insisted that it should be by train.'

Suddenly Yael began to cry. She continued talking with the tears streaming down her cheeks: 'On the train I sat and looked at all the people around, at all those faces each of which seemed to me as if it belonged to "there". That old woman there looking at me, she must have known what happened there. The ticket seller who spoke to me not very nicely really brought me back forcefully to what happened there. And then. . .you know, I felt that I had to travel on that train.'

Therapist: 'Actually, you wanted to go on the same route that your mother went on.'

Yael: 'Yes, yes.'

Her crying became stronger, and she was unable to continue talking. Finally she calmed down, but for a long time she didn't open her mouth. I tried to encourage her to continue the story by asking her what happened afterwards.

Yael picked up her head and stared at me in surprise, as if she had completely forgotten that I was there at her side. She looked at me silently for a few moments, and finally pulled herself together.

'We got down at the train station and took a special bus. You know, there's a special bus that goes to the camp. Dachau itself is a lovely, well-cared-for town. There are well-dressed people walking in the streets, talking and laughing as if nothing ever happened. This was really a very strange feeling. I walked in the streets with shivers running up and down my spine.'

'On the bus there was a group of blonde German children who were taking their annual school trip – to Dachau. Happy, mischievous. The driver put on the radio and the whole way this very loud disco music was roaring in my ears. You understand, I thought I would die! I sat there frozen the whole way. I couldn't say a word. In the camp itself, they had actually destroyed everything! Of all the shacks and all the barracks they only left one. We went into this shack. Inside they had left those wooden beds, just as they were there, and also one wooden table, one striped suit and one pair of wooden shoes. Those strange wooden shoes, you know, like the ones my mother wore there and her toes froze, and even now they're still sensitive and not really alright. You know, it seemed so real. Those wooden beds, one on top of the other. My mother hadn't been in Dachau at all, but rather in Auschwitz, but it's basically the same thing, isn't it? There, in Dachau, they left the crematoria the way they were. Someone told us that because of some technical difficulty they never actually succeeded in using those crematoria. When we approached them I thought of my grandfather who was burned in Auschwitz, but I was absolutely incapable of going into the installation itself. I felt that that would be too much for me, and I stayed in the doorway, only peeking inside. I couldn't go on with it.'

'When we came back to the shack I sat down on one of those wooden beds. I felt that I was there together with her, that I was like her. I sat and sat and couldn't get up. I felt that I could sit there for whole days without getting up.'

Yael began crying again. In a few moments she calmed down a little and continued: 'You know, now, while I was crying, I felt something strange, as if my whole body was responding to my crying – my feet, my hands, my chest. But I didn't let it really reach my belly, only a little. My belly remained empty. I hear what I'm saying and it's even more paradoxical, because actually the strongest feeling I had there was some sort of closeness with my mother – this new sort of feeling that had been unfamiliar until then – the feeling that after all I was born from her and it was she who made me.'

Therapist: 'At the last few sessions you spoke quite a bit about your difficulties in deciding about motherhood, about the desire you have and the doubts you also have about getting pregnant and giving birth in the near future. Do you think there's any sort of relationship between these things?'

Yael looked at me in wonder, and through her tears a small smile appeared on her face. 'Yes, it seems that there is some relationship between my connection with my mother, and this feeling in my belly, and my thoughts about motherhood.'

Therapist: 'These thoughts of yours about motherhood have become much more real and practical lately. Undoubtedly this is somehow connected with your mother and her maternity – the way she experienced her pregnancy with you and your birth and infancy so few years after Auschwitz.'

Yael: 'Yes, I understand. I only wanted to say that this was a totally new feeling, that my mother had after all given birth to me.'

Therapist: 'And how did you feel about your mother when you returned to Israel after this journey? Were you able to tell her about it, to share it with her to some extent?'

Yael: 'Not so much. I looked at her and I did feel somewhat different inside, but to actually talk to her about all this – that is still very difficult. The events were still too fresh inside me. I felt that I couldn't let them out yet. I wanted to, but at the same time the words stuck in my throat. I felt rather disappointed by this.'

Therapist: 'I understand. Apparently it's still too difficult. Perhaps you'll be able to talk to her after the feelings inside you cool off a little and you get more of a perspective on them. But there's no doubt that this trip was very important for you, as well as the very fact that you wanted to do it and that you also had the strength to go through with it while experiencing intense feelings and not detaching yourself. The only thing left for us to do is to see what effect these two journeys, the internal one and the external one, will have on your future.'

Thus, at the last stage of therapy, the integration of the most extreme parts of the self is completed. Together with the ability to withstand intense emotions, the 'memorial candles' develop the ability to give up the split in their ego. When they feel the need to express positive and negative feelings simultaneously, as occurred in the previous stage of therapy, the group members are able to perceive themselves and the others as multi-faceted individuals embracing varied and opposing traits, leading to a moderation of the polarity that previously existed between various subgroups within the therapy group. From this point it's not a long way to the intensification of the feelings of closeness and love between the group members, and they speak much more clearly and securely now, with more shades and tones in their speech.

Rina: 'All week I've been preoccupied with what happened in the group at our last session, especially with the question of whether or not there is love here in the group, both among the group members and between us and the therapists. I thought a lot about what I received from the therapists, but I wasn't always sure if what they give also includes love. It's important for me to tell everyone that I've actually been feeling very good in the group lately. I feel that I'm getting a lot of warmth and support, which I never got from my disjointed and scattered family. I feel that I can now trust both the group – each person individually and all of you together – and the therapists, that there's a framework here and I feel very good in it. I'm reminded now of a scene in a funny dream I had this week. In the dream the whole group was sitting in a circle, and I could actually see each person's face very clearly. The therapists were also sitting there, and they too were very clear. But the group members weren't dressed as usual, but they were all wearing flannel winter pyjamas, like the kind children wear. I don't remember exactly what was said, but I remember that everyone was crowded together very closely in the circle and there was this good feeling of warmth and closeness, like children after a bath who have been dried and dressed in warm pyjamas and are sitting close together. . .'

'This week my brother called me from abroad and spoke to me for the millionth time about family problems – about my sisters, who I haven't heard from in a long time, and about the family home, which has been locked up and neglected since our parents died, without anyone taking care of anything. But I think that perhaps I'll finally manage to get something going about this. I told him yesterday that he's very important to me, and that in general all the family affairs have become much more important to me lately. From the day I arrived in Israel I ignored everything, for years I closed up and cut off and erased it. Now I realize that it's actually impossible. After all, inside myself I've remained connected to my family and my roots, even though I repressed it all for years and cut myself off from all that. I've been thinking that what I really want to do, when I'll just have a little more time, is to write the family history. This is a long, complicated history, as you know.'

Rina smiled and looked around at all the people in the group: 'You know, it actually all began with those dreams about the antique brooch my mother gave me that she herself had got from her own mother, who got it from *her* mother, and so on. Through these dreams I began to understand and also to feel my connection with the heritage my mother transmitted to me, and the continuity between the past and the present, and I hope the future as well. These grandmothers that I never knew – after all, the brooch was once theirs, and before that it belonged to their mothers. This is really quite amazing!'

Mordechai: 'What Rina has been telling us now about love reminds me of a dream I had this week, which seems somehow connected with this. In the dream the group is sitting in a circle. Some of the people are very clear while others are less clear, but the figure of the therapist is very clear and colourful. I look and see that everyone is sitting in the circle and each person has a Torah scroll in their hand. These are somewhat old scrolls, covered with writing that looks like ancient Hebrew writing. The therapist is sitting in the middle of the circle and pointing to a place in the scroll with her finger, and everyone is searching for this place with their own finger. I think it's part of the Book of Proverbs. . . No, I'm not sure – it seems more like part of the Song of Songs. Everyone has already found the verse the therapist was pointing out, except me. All I remember about what has to be searched for is the word "love". And I search and search and I don't understand why it's so hard for me to find it. Finally they help me and I find it too. All the people in the group smile at one another and especially at me, as if they're telling me, "We're happy that after all your anger and suspicion has finally come out of you, you too are joining us here in our circle of love."'

Leah: 'You surely remember that a few months ago, when I got married, I received a present from the group – a passage from the Song of Songs written on parchment. After all, that's really like a scroll. Ziona and Itzhak chose it in the name of the group, and I felt that this present contained much love that the group has given me.'

Mordechai: 'You're right. I totally forgot. But you should know, Leah, that your wedding affected me very much. A wedding is, after all, an embodiment of connectedness and love. I feel that I too want very much to achieve this already. Lately I've been thinking all the time about my relationship with my girlfriend, and I feel much better and hope that this time it will work.'

Miriam: 'I too dreamt about love. This dream took place in the ghetto, in some grey, dreary city in Europe. The ghetto was enclosed between high walls and the Jews were forbidden to go outside. There were a boy and a girl there, who were friends, or actually lovers, and they managed to love and to be together even in the ghetto. At some point they decide to try to escape and break out of the walls. In their attempt to escape they go through all sorts of dangers, but eventually they manage to find some small opening, and they go out of the walls and run outside. There are green grass, sunlit hills, and a running stream. They have left the dreariness of the ghetto for a world full of life and colour. I think this is an optimistic dream that expresses the feelings I've had lately, in the past few months. Actually, it's already quiet a long while that I haven't been depressed and I even feel some joy in life. I'm also much more optimistic about my chances to find love at last. It seems to me that in this dream my wish is fulfilled.'

Itzhak: 'I had a somewhat similar dream, but first I want to tell you, Miriam, that when I was fifteen I once read a book about the Warsaw Ghetto. There was a chapter there about a couple who got married in the ghetto, and the girl even became pregnant. In spite of the terrible situation there, they managed to find time to be together and I remember that I was very curious then to know how they did it. Your dream reminded me of this story.'

'In my dream I was with Nurit, in some sort of two-level pool with a covering that had rectangular holes in it. I dived into the first pool and at the bottom I found all sorts of old Hebrew coins. Then I went into the second pool with Nurit, even though she wasn't very enthusiastic about it. There were airholes at the top. Suddenly Nurit says she has no more strength to swim and she also feels she has no air left. We start swimming towards one of these airholes, but it's closed. She begins to faint, but I encourage her to go on to the next opening, and then I woke up. You know, this reminds me of a description I once read of the gas chambers with the fake windows they had. Still, in the dream I managed to reach a real window, with air. Besides, I also found a lot of old coins. This means that I found things with great monetary value, but not only monetary. My father told me once that he managed to get through the war mainly with the help of his belt, which was full of gold coins. He succeeded in bribing whoever had to be bribed and in many cases bought his life. Yesterday, when we were talking about something having to do with money, I suddenly had the thought that perhaps it would be better to hide part of it, in case we should have to escape from Israel someday. . . What a strange thought!'

Therapist: 'I have a different association to the dream. The ancient Israeli coins are actually connected with what you've found within yourself lately, that is, roots, belonging, the past, and so on.'

Itzhak: 'Yes. Perhaps. You're referring to what I experienced here in therapy. You know, a lot of the therapy was like going up to the attic and finding pictures, letters and all sorts of old things from your grandfather and grandmother – something that I obviously never had the chance to do in reality.'

Miriam: 'What you're saying moves me very much, especially since I've been feeling something similar lately.'

Itzhak: 'Don't think that I'm not moved. I didn't tell you yet that I planted a grove of trees, here in the hills near Jerusalem, in memory of all those who died from my family – actually both families. Each tree in the grove is named after one of them – one for my grandfather, my father's father, and one for my grandmother, my father's mother, and one for my grandfather, my mother's father, and so on and so on. Yes, very many of these fresh green pine trees. Since I planted this grove I feel that I've found them again and that I'm encountering them much more clearly. I really feel relief and liberation, and also this sort of joy inside, a joy that is still sometimes mixed with sadness.'

Therapist: 'In the dream you were able to go into the second pool, that is the gas chambers, only after you found your roots – the ancient Israeli coins. Isn't that what actually occurred here in the past months?'

Itzhak looked pale and emotionally moved. 'Why did you say that? Now I feel tense again. It's connected with the gas chambers, which I've never actually succeeded in really going into.'

Therapist: 'Then could you perhaps try now?'

Itzhak: 'Primo Levi, whose books I've been reading again lately, says somewhere something like this: "They took everything away from me there, my human image, clothes, hair, family, identity, everything." He says that it gave him such a feeling of shame that he often thought the lucky ones were those who went straight to the gas chambers. I'm trying now to imagine my grandmother and my two aunts standing there naked, in line, in the middle of the camp. It's still hard for me, but, as you see, I'm succeeding.'

The test of the success of integration at the last stage of therapy are intimate situations. And indeed, at this stage the group members do express closeness and intimacy towards one another, towards the therapists, and towards the group in general. They gradually acquire the ability to express closeness and love in direct, open conversation, thus reducing their need to make use of the symbolic language of dreams, which is, despite its intensity, an indirect way of expressing feelings.

At the last group session described above, the two levels of intra-group communication – direct speech and symbolic language – are intertwined.

The word 'love' is used explicitly both in Mordechai's dream and in the exchanges between the people in the group. The feeling of intimacy is interwoven with symbols drawn from Jewish tradition, symbols reflecting identification with a wider entity – the Jewish people. The picture in Mordechai's dream could have been taken from the Jewish *cheder*[3]: a group of pupils sitting in a circle with a *chumash*[4], in their hands, and the teacher teaching them the Torah; or *yeshiva*[5] students sitting in a circle and studying a page of the Talmud. The teacher appears in the guise of the therapist teaching Torah to the group (even if it is quite a different sort of teaching) and pointing with her finger to the appropriate verse.

The motif of the circle appears in both dreams, Mordechai's and Rina's, and symbolizes maternal holding, femininity, and even perhaps the womb – the infant's first home. In both dreams the womb and the maternal holding inspire feelings of warmth, closeness and love. In Rina's dream the children, clad in warm pyjamas, are sitting curled up inside a circle of warmth, security and intimacy, with the parents – the therapists – in the background taking care of them.

Rina and Mordechai see the various figures in the perfect circle of the group clearly and distinctly. This seeing reflects the ability the group members have acquired to relate to each of their fellow members separately. In spite of the closeness they feel towards the other members of the group, each one has his own clear personal boundaries – even if Rina is still dressing all the people in the same clothing, without a personal touch. As mentioned, the group in the dream constitutes a perfect circle; indeed, at this stage of therapy the division of the group into different subgroups has moderated greatly.

In Miriam's and Itzhak's dreams sombre Holocaust motifs still appear in the background. The principal subject of these dreams, however, is pairing and intimacy, with the Holocaust and its terrors forming the background. The central struggle taking place at this time in the inner world of the 'memorial candles' is for the achievement and realization of the ability to build and maintain an intimate relationship. The intimacy in the fabric of the group reflects the integration that is being consolidated in their personalities, and this is expressed in parallel in their increasing ability to deal with intimate relationships of various sorts, both with their parents and siblings and with their partners.

In Miriam's dream there's a chance of getting out of the ghetto walls – the walls of her internal defences and inhibitions, which have hitherto prevented her from realizing any sort of intimate relationship. The couple in the dream succeed in maintaining their relationship inside the walls, and eventually they manage to break out into the open, to a place drenched in light and warmth. This optimistic dream reflects Miriam's new feelings and her ability to express and realize herself in the area of intimate relationships.

Itzhak too is still struggling with his feeling of emotional deadness and choking, but now he is no longer struggling alone – in his dream he's with his girlfriend (his future wife). He's free now to see her, to consider her, to help her, and the focus of the major conflicts within his self are the various dimensions of the intimate couple relationship.

In Mordechai's dream as well the central topic is love and its intimate realization, both emotional and sexual. Mordechai was undecided for a moment as to whether the group was reading a chapter from the Book of Proverbs, but then he immediately noticed that the chapter was from the Song of Songs. In the love songs sung by the Shulamite and her lover there are very strong, clear motifs of youthful love and devotion. Optimism and the continuity of life may now be seen to reign in the inner world of the 'memorial candles'.

The following group session continues the dialogue on the topic of searching for one's roots.

Yoel: 'I too have been very preoccupied lately with this topic of identity and roots. I always envied you, Mordechai. I saw you as the embodiment of rootedness, of belonging to Israel and to Judaism, as far as I know anything about it. You once told us that you're not really Orthodox but rather traditional – observing the Sabbath, going to the synagogue and so on. Even in your dreams there are ancient Torah scrolls. I, on the other hand, have roamed around in all sorts of countries during my lifetime, and even today I don't know exactly who I am or to whom I belong. Even at present I hardly know the Bible. Each time we moved from one country to another, I never missed the old country or dreamed about it. Even here, in Jerusalem, many years went by before I began to feel anything. All the years that I lived here, I had the feeling that I was always on the road –

here today and somewhere else tomorrow. At the last session, when we talked about roots, I sat and listened but I didn't say anything. I never had any roots. I never knew or felt what it was. I never even felt anything clear about the fact that I'm Jewish. What does it actually mean to be a Jew? For many years I was happy that my parents had given me a Polish, non-Jewish name. I don't know if I was actually ashamed of being a Jewish boy in postwar Poland. I was the only Jewish boy, but I would hit the Polish boys if they even dared to say anything to me. I hit them murderously, I wasn't afraid of anyone. The fact that I wasn't circumcised didn't bother me at all – quite the contrary. When I decided at the age of fourteen that I wanted to be circumcised, it was connected with the fact that we had moved to another country, to a city that had a large Jewish community. Only then did I begin to feel anything connected with being Jewish. When I heard you, Gideon, talking last time about your childhood in Russia, and about the identity problems you had there, I felt very very close to you. I suddenly realized what we have in common. I seem to remember that you too were not circumcised as a baby. Our parents, in Eastern Europe right after the war, were still under the influence of the terrible fear and trauma of the years before we were born. They wanted to save their children's lives at any price, the way they put Moses in the basket and sent him onto the Nile.

'You see,' laughed Yoel apologetically, 'something from the Torah *has* stuck with me, except that I heard this story from my son, who learned it in a Torah class. But lately I have somehow been feeling a bit more rooted here, or a bit more belonging. Much of this is because I've been sitting here in the group for five straight years, and except for my time on reserve duty I don't think I missed a single session. And if this is so, then it's apparently more important to me than I thought. But I still feel that I don't identify completely with Judaism. Orthodox Jews, especially those of Meah She'arim [the prototypical ultra-Orthodox neighborhood in Jerusalem], with their long black coats, have always disgusted and angered me. Recently my little son has been asking me questions about my past, about the years in Poland, and also about Judaism. For his sake, and actually with his help as well, I've been forced to begin thinking and clarifying for myself many questions that have remained open. It's not so easy any more for me to remain on the fence with my feelings of belonging and identity, and this is undoubtedly also connected with my experiences here in the group, with what I said and heard. On the eve of the last holiday I found myself strolling with my little son in the streets of Meah She'arim, and I think I felt different from usual. Not that I'm planning to become religious, God forbid, but still I felt a bit closer to them and perhaps even identified with them a little. I went and explained to my son the little I know about Judaism and the Orthodox and Meah She'arim and Poland. I told him that everyone once dressed that way there, that is, the Jews in the villages and towns and even in the cities, and that's how they looked and that's how they lived. But with all these stories about Judaism, I forgot to tell you the strange dream I had last night.'

'In my dream I saw Jerusalem, and there was a road going out of it and on the road there was a long column of people. There was a war, I didn't know which one, and everyone had to leave Jerusalem. There were a lot of people walking there, whole families, men, women and children, all of them dragging bundles with their hands or on their shoulders, but they were marching very quietly, very slowly, without any uproar – not like in the films about the Holocaust, where everyone is running in panic and pushing one another. Here, on the contrary, everyone was walking in an orderly way, without any tension. Gradually the city emptied out, and at the entrance to the city, at the side of the road, there were two older men with beards, dressed in black like the ultra-Orthodox from Meah She'arim. And they tore the lapels of the clothing of everyone passing by – the shirt lapels of the men, and the dress lapels of the women, but they tore everyone's clothing, one by one. That's all. That's the dream.'

Yoel stopped talking, leaving us all in a state of shock. The impact of this apocalyptic dream hit us like thunder. Was it a dream about the third destruction of Jerusalem? Another Holocaust? In Poland Yoel's parents' home was destroyed and they had to wander on the roads, hungry and cold, and even lost their infant daughter who died of starvation before their eyes, at the side of the road. There they were humiliated and persecuted, but here Yoel had succeeded in building himself a refuge in Jerusalem. Was he predicting in this dream that he too, like his ancestors, would be sentenced to go into exile?

This is indeed the picture that seems to be painted in Yoel's dream. But if we go into it more deeply and examine its details carefully, we will be able to distinguish an important difference. Yoel's exiles are not pushed on their way but walk 'very quietly, very slowly, without any uproar'. It's important to Yoel that the refugees from the second Holocaust should not be humiliated and trodden into the ground, but should march quietly and honourably and bear proudly their identity as human beings; they remain together in families, and do not lose their human image. Moreover, the old men, who look 'like the ultra-Orthodox from Meah She'arim', tear a mourning rent in the garments of the people as they go out, according to Jewish custom. As we heard from him earlier, Yoel is still having trouble adopting Jewish tradition and identifying with his Jewish roots. On the one hand he still rejects them, but on the other he's already beginning to feel 'a bit more rooted here, or a bit more belonging'. And indeed, in the dream it seems clear that he accepts the tearing of the garments, which is a concrete Jewish symbol of participation in mourning. Yoel's indecision is nearing its end, and his Jewish identity is already quite strong, and so his fear of a second Holocaust is interwoven with a feeling of belonging to the Jewish people. Yoel does not feel certain that his and his family's wanderings have already ended. During its short history the State of Israel had experienced several wars, and the fear of another war that might end in defeat and the capture of Jerusalem remains in his heart, as in the hearts of many others. This is clearly reflected in his dream, but from this point on his fate is connected to the fate of the people in his city, and his identification with them is complete.

At the last stage of therapy the 'memorial candles' make use of many motifs connected with their personal and collective identity. The feeling of belonging to a community of some sort, to the Jewish people and even to humanity in general arises mainly in symbolic form, as in the tearing of the garments in Yoel's dream.

Baruch, for example, already saw himself at the beginning of therapy as a flagbearer, as someone with a role to play in public service, but at that time his sense of mission was permeated by motifs of extermination and death. Now, with the course of therapy almost completed, the 'memorial candles' are becoming filled with optimism, and sometimes they even tend to ascribe to themselves superhuman strength or almost messianic missions. The self, which is becoming consolidated and defined in a balanced way in the real world, now seems to be liberating great psychological powers which were hitherto invested in the difficult struggle for psychological survival. It is these powers bursting out into consciousness that grant the 'memorial candles' the feeling of superhuman strength. This feeling contains the explanation for the improvement occurring in their functioning at work and in life in general. As mentioned, even before they began therapy many of the survivors' children had excelled in creativity or achieved impressive intellectual accomplishments. Now that new psychological powers are being liberated within them, these creative talents are becoming stronger. This is also true of the feelings of uniqueness and mission they have had since childhood. Their sensitivity towards the past is now directed at a new horizon. The past is not a dead weight arousing anxiety and fear but a source of light and warmth having a deeply moving link with the present, which can be experienced as part of the reality of life.

The new pschological powers are reflected symbolically in the dreams of the survivors' children, as we can see from the following dream of Ariela's, which she related to me at one of our individual sessions.

'I'm together with my mother on a ship of illegal immigrants [to Palestine under the British Mandate]. The ship is jammed with people. At a certain moment we're ordered to jump into the sea. Something is apparently about to happen, and the ship is in danger. We jump into the sea and I see my mother sinking down very deep into the water. I, on the other hand, am not only not sinking in the water, but I find myself simply walking along on the surface of the water.' Ariela stopped talking for a moment and grinned. 'It sounds funny, it's like Jesus walking on the water in the Sea of Galilee. At any rate, I'm walking along quite easily on the water and following my mother, who has touched the bottom of the sea and is now beginning to float upwards very slowly. Notice that I don't hurry to dive in after her in order to rescue her, as I would always do before, throughout my life, out of some sense of responsibility towards her, as if I always have to protect and rescue her. Somehow I'm trusting that she'll find her way up by herself. At any rate, I wait patiently for her. Not that I turn my back on her and leave her, God forbid – on the contrary, I'm standing there with open arms to receive her when she finally reaches the surface.'

Nira too had a dream in which she found superhuman powers within herself.

'We're escaping from the camp and they're running after us, but we're a group of young people and we run and reach a wide river. We get into rowboats, two in each boat. In the boat in which I'm rowing my mother is sitting with me. Her face is my mother's face but her body is that of a twelve-year-old girl. I am rowing against the stream but I'm not getting tired. I find tremendous powers within myself. Suddenly I see that this girl, who is actually my mother, is dying of hunger and will soon be dead. I decide that I must stop at any cost in order to give her something to eat and drink before she dies. Somehow I stop and there's a sort of kiosk in which an older woman is selling things. She tells me that all she has is milk and I start giving my mother the milk to drink, cup after cup, but she doesn't recover. Finally this woman tells me that there's nothing more to do, the girl is dead.'

Nira stopped talking, continuing only after a long while: 'Later in the dream there was a totally different scene. I was on a beautiful, sunlit beach, and I was walking there with some boy. It was clear that we were a couple because we had so much joy and love. That's it, that's the whole dream. I woke up with a feeling of joy and optimism. Nice, isn't it?'

Nira and Ariela are coming to terms with acceptance and separation in their dreams. As we have heard, Nira's mother spent the war years in Holland in a small, dark hiding-place, and there – as it seemed to Nira – she died inside, emotionally. For many years Nira has exchanged roles with her mother – she has been holding her emotionally, giving her milk to drink in the language of the dream, in a desperate attempt to revive the parts of her psyche that had died in the hiding-place. The older woman in Nira's dream apparently represents the nanny who brought her up from infancy and was a most important figure for her during the years when her mother was too depressed to take care of her. The woman in the dream provides the milk needed to revive the baby-mother, but she is also the one who tells Nira that the child is dead and there is no way to revive her. The figure of the nanny, both authoritative and holding, which Nira internalized many years before, now blended with the figure of the therapist, who convinced her that there was no more point in trying to revive ego parts that had been dead for so many years, and that it would be better to make peace with her mother's sad state, to separate from her and to go out into the world, in order to be able finally to live her own life.

The most interesting motif in Ariela's and Nira's dreams is the immense, almost supernatural power they find in their bodies – one walks on water like Jesus, while the other rows upstream in the river. Not only does Ariela not sink in the water like her mother, but she also knows already that there's no point in trying to rescue her sinking mother, and it's enough to wait for her until she touches bottom and floats up again. She now trusts her own powers and even her mother's powers; she already knows how to live her life and how to hold her mother in a new way, more balanced and more appropriate to the reality of life.

Another dream that tells us about the new powers awakening in the psyches of the survivors' children is one of Mordechai's, which also takes place on the water.

'I'm on this sort of flat raft, poling along calmly in the middle of the sea. My brothers are also poling the same sort of rafts, and also some other people, each one on his own raft. It seems to me that these people are the members of the group. At a certain moment I turn my head back and I see a large group of dolphins pursuing us. They are getting very close, making these high waves in the sea. The dolphins and the waves together overturn the rafts, one by one. I become tense, and I continue poling with all my might, but there's a big dolphin pursuing me and finally he manages to overturn my raft as well. However, I'm already very close to shore and a big wave throws me onto the shore. I know that I'm the only one who has survived, and that I have a very important task to perform. In the dream I'm not exactly sure what the task is, but the sense of a mission for the sake of all the others is very clear.'

Mordechai has indeed had a mission imposed on him in the role of the only child of his parents, who had lost their families. Mordechai's first association to the dream was of the prophet Jonah who was swallowed by the great fish and then spewed out onto the land. God had given his prophet Jonah a mission, but what was the mission that his individual and family history, and perhaps even the history of his people, had given Mordechai? Perhaps this is the task of the 'memorial candles' who succeeded in overcoming death, the heritage of their parents, and finding their own paths.

Mordechai escaped from that journey filled with adventures and difficulties onto a safe shore. His parents went through the seven circles of Hell during the Holocaust, but finally found their way to a sheltering land. Mordechai too wandered for many years on the shaky raft of his life, until he succeeded in reaching a safe shore by his own powers and started a new life.

In the dreams presented here the motif of water stands out. Water is a universal archaic symbol. At the creation God separated the land from the water; the water which had covered the entire earth receded and the land was born out of it. The foetus spends nine months in the amniotic fluid in its mother's womb; during the birth process it comes out of the water. Water is a universal archaic symbol, a kind of chaos out of which life is born. The water in the dreams does indeed inspire a sense of danger and threat, but the 'memorial candles' are born out of it with strengthened psyches. Their parents' Holocaust, as well as the 'private Holocaust' undergone by each of the 'memorial candles' during their childhood and adolescence, is hinted at in the background of the dreams. Mordechai wanders about on the little raft among the waves with a group of dolphins pursuing him. Ariela and her mother slip off a ship resembling a jammed ship of illegal immigrants to Palestine, and Nira rows upstream, escaping from threatening figures. But now the new powers that have developed in the 'memorial candles' are revealed. The ego and superego of the 'memorial candles' have become stronger during the course of therapy and have enabled the development of more mature identification mechanisms, which were first activated towards the therapist and the group, and later towards other figures as well. These identification mechanisms, which were used to strengthen the ego, have enabled the 'memorial candles' to achieve fuller integration of the parts of their selves by encountering and separating over and over again from the parts that belonged to objects (generally the parents) that had been internalized and assimilated into their internal world. These parts, which consisted mostly of their parents' guilt feelings, depression and unworked mourning, as well as the terrors of the Holocaust, gradually disappear from their internal world and are replaced by emotional and mental attachments to the world of reality; this is the psychological birth of the survivors' children, a new self is consolidating. Now all that remains for them to do is to continue building their lives out of a sense of uniqueness and mission, since they have been given the lifework of establishing intergenerational continuity.

The feelings of mission and continuity that filled his heart were realized by Itzhak in his planting a grove of trees in the Jerusalem hills in memory of the members of his family who perished in the Holocaust – a tree for each of them. The real trees he planted symbolize the cut-off family tree; they constitute a memorial for those people for whom he himself has ceased to serve as a 'memorial candle'.

'Yesterday I visited the grove,' said Itzhak. 'Sometimes I feel the need to be alone there. There I feel calm and I can think about many things. I saw that some of the pines were slightly yellow and I felt sad. I was afraid they might die. I sat down and cried. I spoke to my grandfather, my father's father, and also to my grandmother and grandfather on my mother's side. My grandmother – I think her name was Penina, but I'm not completely sure. Not even a picture has remained from her. Recently, when I've been talking to Nurit about the preparations for our wedding, I don't know why, but in spite of my happiness I feel a lot of sadness. I think about all those who won't be able to share the happiness of our wedding. But yesterday in the grove I suddenly thought that they had a life before the camps, and they had a large family around them, warm and supportive. There was life. My father had many friends in Poland whom he left behind. I don't always feel as close to my friends as my father felt towards his. When I looked at the pines yesterday I thought that I did this for myself, but actually it's also for my father and mother. The first time in my whole life that I saw my father crying was when I brought him to the grove and he saw the pines I planted with my own hands. He hugged me and put his head on my shoulder and cried and cried like a child. I felt so much warmth inside. I was so proud that I could be strong for him and give him such a true feeling of closeness and warmth inside.'

'The most terrible thing for my parents was their thoughts about what they had gone through, and also about my grandmother and grandfather – about the fact that my grandfather died in Sobibor.

He didn't suffer very much before he was sent to the gas chambers. Whenever my father couldn't sleep, these thoughts would go round and round in his head: "Did they suffer or not? What really happened to them? How did they die?"'

'I talked to my grandfather yesterday. I told him about my problems, about how it isn't always easy for me to get along with people. I presented Nurit to him and I asked him if she seems nice to him, and I also asked him what to do when things are difficult for me. I imagined that I was sitting on his lap and he was caressing me. My father was never able to hug me or to caress me. Mostly he was very detached and closed up within himself.'

Itzhak started to cry and the tears stopped him from talking. After a long while he continued emotionally:

'In general I had a very good feeling yesterday. I felt the bond transmitted from my grandfather to my father, and from him to me. Actually, my mother did sometimes succeed in giving me some warmth, but that's something else. It's masculine warmth that provides confidence. That's what my father couldn't give me, that's what I felt being transmitted to me from my grandfather in the grove yesterday.'

When he approached the end of his therapy, Itzhak asked me not to hold the last session in the therapy room where we had been meeting for over six years, but to hold it in the grove he had planted. We went to the hill plot together, sat among the trees and talked for a long time. Itzhak was very moved and his emotionality infected me – we alternately laughed and cried. He began jumping from place to place and showing me the trees he had planted, one after another, repeating the name of the person in whose memory he had planted each tree and what the person's place was in the family fabric. When I asked him why it was so important for him that I come with him to the grove for our last session, he answered:

'You and the group have been with me for years on this long journey. Together we went through all the periods of depression with the terrible memories of death, and the long, difficult process when I gathered together all the pieces of my mosaic that had been scattered and hidden within myself. You helped me begin to connect with the family figures who had disappeared and to combine them into something that finally allows me to feel like a whole being. This grove is the end of the journey for me. It symbolizes the completion of two circles: the circle of my inner development and my family circle – finally I felt clearly its exact place within myself. During all these years you and the group played a very important role in the excavation work, in finding lost parts and cleaning them of the layers of dust and mud that had accumulated on them. Afterwards you also helped me to find the place where each part belongs and gradually join them together to complete the picture. You know, sometimes I think the work of therapy is very similar to the work of an archaeologist. Bringing you here to the grove now is the last part that was still missing for completing the circle of therapy. I felt that it was important for me to actually show you the trees and introduce you to my family, since you already know them so well. Being here together really completes the circle.'

The circle has indeed been completed. When the mists of death disperse from the psyches of the 'memorial candles', a clear and sharp family picture is revealed: great cities teeming with life and towns in the heart of prewar Europe; extended families gathering together on happy, festive occasions or at times of sadness and death; and babies, children and young people who are none other than their parents before they were enveloped by the smoke of the crematoria. Then the 'memorial candles' find their place in the chain of the generations, and, as links in this chain, their task in transmitting the family heritage to the coming generations. Afterwards Itzhak can come to the pine grove with his little children and read to them from the book of life.

NOTES

1. A Jewish winter festivity roughly corresponding to carnival, celebrating the rescue of the Jews of Persia as recorded in the Book of Esther.
2. It should be mentioned that in recent years there has been an increasing number of tours of young Israelis, not necessarily the children of survivors, to the remnants of the concentration camps, ghettoes, and Jewish communities of Eastern Europe. Some people see this as an expression of both a personal and a national need to put an end to the denial and repression of the traumatic past.
3. A Jewish religious primary school.
4. The book of Pentateuch.
5. A Jewish religious secondary school, usually attached to a synagogue.

Bibliography

Ackerman, N.W. (1967) 'Prejudice and scapegoating in the family'. In G.H. Zuk & I. Boszormenyi-Nagi (Eds), *Family Therapy and Disturbed Families*. Palo Alto: Science and Behaviour Books, 48–57.

Aleksandrowicz, D. (1973) 'Children of concentration camp survivors'. *Yearbook of the International Association for Child Psychiatry and Allied Professions, 2,* 385–94.

Appelfeld, A. (1971) *The Skin and the Shirt.* (In Hebrew) Tel Aviv: Am Oved.

Appelfeld, A. (1983a) *The Shirt and the Stripes.* (In Hebrew) Hakibbutz Hameuhad.

Appelfeld, A. (1983b) *Tzili: The Story of a Life.* (Trans. Dalya Bilu) New York: E.P. Dutton.

Axelrod, S., Schnipper, O.L. and Rau, J.H. (1980) 'Hospitalized offspring of Holocaust survivors: Problems and dynamics'. *Bulletin of the Menninger Clinic, 44,* 1–14.

Barocas, H. (1971) 'A note on the children of concentration camp survivors'. *Psychotherapy: Theory, Research and Practice, 8,* 189–90.

Barocas, H. and Barocas, C. (1973) 'Manifestations of concentration camp effects on the second generation'. *American Journal of Psychiatry, 130,* 820–1.

Bell, N.W. and Vogel, E.F. (1960) 'The emotionally disturbed child as the family scapegoat'. In N.W. Bell & E.F. Vogel (Eds), *The Family.* Glencoe: Free Press.

Benedek, T. (1956) 'Psychobiological aspects of mothering'. *American Journal of Orthopsychiatry, 26,* 272.

Bergman, M.V. (1982) 'Thoughts on Superego pathology of survivors and their children', in M.S. Bergmann and M.E. Jucovy (Eds), *Generations of the Holocaust.* New York: Basic Books.

Bergmann, M.S. and Jucovy, M.E. (Eds) (1982) *Generations of the Holocaust.* New York: Basic Books.

Bettelheim, B. (1943) 'Individual and mass behaviour in extreme situations'. *Journal of Abnormal and Social Psychology, 38,* 417–52.

Bettelheim, B. (1960) *The Informed Heart.* New York: Free Press.

Bion, W.R. (1961) *Experiences in Groups and other Papers.* London: Tavistock.

Blitzer, J.R. and Murray, J.M. (1964) 'On the transformations of early narcissism during pregnancy'. *International Journal of Psychoanalysis, 41,* 77–89.

Bluhm, H.O. (1948) 'How did they survive? Mechanisms of defense in Nazi concentration camps'. *American Journal of Psychotherapy, 211,* 3–32.

Bowen, M. (1960) 'A family concept of schizophrenia'. In D.D. Jackson (Ed.), *The Etiology of Schizophrenia.* New York: Basic Books.

Bowlby, J. (1951) *Maternal Care and Mental Health.* Geneva: World Health Organization.

Caleffi, P. (1955) *La personalità distrutta nei campi di sterminio.* Venice: Universita Popolare.

Chodoff, P. (1963) 'Late effects of the concentration camp syndrome'. *Archives of General Psychiatry, 8,* 323–33.

Cohen, E.A. (1954) *Human Behaviour in the Concentration Camp.* London: Free Association Books.

Colman, A. (1969) 'Psychological state in first pregnancy'. *American Journal of Orthopsychiatry, 39,* 788–97.

Danieli, Y. (1980) 'Families of survivors of the Nazi Holocaust: Some long and short term effects'. In N. Milgram (Ed.), *Psychological Stress and Adjustment in Time of War and Peace.* Washington DC: Hemisphere Publishing.

Davidson, S. (1972) 'The treatment of Holocaust survivors'. In S. Davidson (Ed.), *Spheres of Psychotherapeutic Activity.* Jerusalem: The Medical Department, Kupat Cholim Center.

Davidson, S. (1980) 'Transgenerational transmission in the families of Holocaust survivors'. *International Journal of Family Psychiatry 1,* 95–112.

Deutsch, H. (1946) The *Psychology of Women.* New York: London Research Books.

Devoto, A. and Martini, M. (1981) *La violenza nei lager.* Milan: Franco Angeli Editore.

De Wind, E. (1968) 'The confrontation with death: Symposium on psychic traumatization through social catastrophe'. *International Journal of Psychoanalysis, 49,* 302–5.

Dor-Shav, N.K. (1978) 'On the long-range effects of concentration camp internment of Nazi victims'. *Journal of Consulting and Clinical Psychology, 46,* 1–11.

Dreyfus, G. (1984) 'On the problem of identity and Jewish definition'. (In Hebrew) *Ma'amarim 1984–1985.* Haifa: G. Dreyfus.

Ehrlich, S. (1987) 'Narcissism and object love: Towards a metapsychology of experience'. (In Hebrew) *Sihot, 1,* 83–94.

Eitinger, L. (1961) 'Pathology of the concentration camp syndrome'. *Archives of General Psychiatry, 5,* 371–9.

Eitinger, L. (1962) 'Concentration camp survivors in the postwar world'. *American Journal of Orthopsychiatry, 32,* 367–75.

Epstein, H. (1979) *Children of the Holocaust.* New York: G.P. Putman's Sons.

Erikson, E.H. (1959) 'Identity and the life cycle'. *Psychological Issues, 1.*

Ferreira, A.J. (1960) 'The pregnant mother's emotional attitude and its reflection upon the newborn'. *American Journal of Orthopsychiatry, 30,* 553–62.

Fogelman, E. and Savran, B. (1970) 'Therapeutic groups for children of

Holocaust survivors'. *International Journal of Group Psychotherapy, 29*, 211–36.

Foulkes, S.H. (1984) *Therapeutic Group Analysis.* London: G. Allen & Unwin.

Frankl, V.E. (1947) *'Ein Psycholog erlebt das KZ '.* Vienna: Jugend und Volk.

Freud, A. (1967) 'Comments on trauma'. In S. Furst (Ed.), *Psychic Trauma.* New York.

Freud, A. and Dann, S. (1951) 'An experiment in group upbringing'. *Psychoanalytic Study of the Child, 6,* 127–69.

Freud, S. (1921) 'Group psychology and the analysis of the ego'. Standard Edition, Vol. 18. London: Hogarth Press (1955).

Freud, S. (1923) 'The ego and the id'. Standard Edition, Vol. 19. London: Hogarth Press (1961).

Gill, M. and Klein, G. (1964) 'The structuring of drive and reality: David Rapaport's contribution to psychoanalysis and psychology'. *International Journal of Psychoanalysis, 45,* 483–98.

Gampel, Y. (1982) 'A daughter of silence'. In M.S. Bergmann & M.E. Jucovy (Eds), *Generations of the Holocaust.* New York: Basic Books. 120–36.

Gampel, Y. (1987) 'Aspects of intergenerational transmission'. (In Hebrew) *Sihot, 2,* 27–31.

Grossman, D. (1986) *See Under: Love.* (Trans. Betsy Rosenberg) New York: Farrar Straus Giroux.

Grubrich-Simits, I.G. (1979) 'Extremtraumatisierung als Kumulatives Trauma'. *Psyche, 33,* 991–1023.

Hazan, Y. (1977) 'Clinical symptoms of Holocaust survivors as a possible explanation for social phenomena'. (In Hebrew) Unpublished seminar paper. Jerusalem: The Hebrew University of Jerusalem.

Hazan, Y. (1987) '"The second generation of the Holocaust" – a doubtful concept'. (In Hebrew) *Sihot, 1,* 104–8.

Heller, D. (1982) 'Themes of culture and ancestry'. *Psychiatry, 45,* 247–61.

Hopper, E. and Kreeger, L. (1980) 'The survivor syndrome workshop'. In C. Garlans (Ed.), *Group Analysis.* London: The Trust for Group Analysis, 67–81.

Jackson, D.D. (1957) 'The question of family homeostasis'. *Psychiatric Quarterly Supplement, 31,* 79–90.

Jung, C.G. (1946) 'Psychology of the transference'. *Collected Works,* Vol. 16. London: Routledge & Kegan Paul.

Jung, C.G. (1952) 'Symbols of transformation'. *Collected Works,* Vol. 5. London: Routledge & Kegan Paul.

Kaplan, D.M. and Mason, B.A. (1960) 'Maternal reaction to premature birth'. *American Journal of Orthopsychiatry, 30,* 539–52.

Kernberg, O. (1975) *Borderline Conditions and Pathological Narcissism.* New York: J. Aronson.

Kestenberg, J.S. (1972) 'Psychoanalytic contributions to the problem of children of survivors from Nazi persecution'. *Israel Annals of Psychiatry and Related Disciplines, 10,* 311–25.

Kestenberg, J.S. (1982) 'Survivor-parents and their children'. In M.S. Bergmann and M.E. Jucovy (Eds), *Generations of the Holocaust.* New York: Basic Books, 83–102.

Khan, M.M.R. (1963) 'The concept of cumulative trauma'. *Psychoanalytic Study of the Child, 18*, 286–306.

Klein, H. (1968) 'Problems in the psychotherapeutic treatment of Israeli survivors of the Holocaust'. In H. Krystal (Ed.), *Massive Psychic Trauma.* New York: International University Press, 233–48.

Klein, H. (1971) 'Families of Holocaust survivors in the kibbutz: Psychological studies'. *International Psychiatry Clinics, 8*, 67–92.

Klein, H. (1973) 'Children of the Holocaust: Mourning and bereavement'. In E.J. Anthony & C. Koupernik (Eds), *The Child in His Family,* 393–409.

Klein, H. (1987) 'Living in the shadow of the threat of death – forty years after the Holocaust: Therapeutic aspects'. (In Hebrew) *Sihot, 1*, 94–8.

Klein, M. (1948) *Contributions to Psycho-Analysis 1921–45.* London: Hogarth Press.

Krystal, H. (Ed.) (1968) *Massive Psychic Trauma.* New York: International University Press.

Krystal, H. (1978) 'Trauma and affects'. *Psychoanalytic Study of the Child, 33*, 81–116.

Krystal, H. and Niederland, W.G. (1971) *Psychic Traumatization: Aftereffects in Individuals and Communities.* Boston: Little, Brown & Co.

Last, U. and Klein, H. (1974) 'Cognitive and emotional aspects of the attitudes of American and Israeli youth towards the victims of the Holocaust'. *Israeli Annals of Psychiatry and Related Disciplines, 12.*

Levi, P. (1947) *Se questo e un uomo.* Turin: Francesco de Silva.

Levi, P. (1986) *I sommersi e i salvati.* Turin: Einaudi.

Lifton, R.J. (1967) *Death in Life: Survivors of Hiroshima.* New York: Randon House.

Lifton, R.J. (1980) 'The concept of the survivor'. In J.E. Dimsdale (Ed.), *Survivors, Victims and Perpetrators.* New York, Washington and London: Hemisphere Publishing, 113–26.

Lipkowitz, M.H. (1973) 'The child of two survivors: A report of an unsuccessful therapy'. *Israeli Annals of Psychiatry and Related Disciplines, 2*, 363–74.

Mahler, M. and Furer, M. (1972) *Symbiose und Individuation.* Stuttgart: Klett.

Masterson, J. & Rinsley, D. (1975) 'The borderline syndrome: The role of the mother in the genesis and psychic structure of the borderline personality'. *International Journal of Psychiatry, 56*, 163–78.

Meissner, W.W. (1970) 'Thinking about the family: Psychiatric aspects'. In N.W. Ackerman (Ed.), *Family Process.* New York: Basic Books, 131–70.

Mitscherlich, A. (1979) 'Die Notwendigkeit zu Trauern'. In Maerthesheimer (Ed.), *Kruezfeuer: Der Fernsehfilm Holocaust.* Maerthesheimer.

Niederland, W.G. (1964) 'Psychiatric disorders among persecution victims: A contribution to the understanding of concentration camp pathology and its after-effects'. *Journal of Nervous and Mental Disease, 139*, 458–74.

Niederland, W.G. (1968) 'Clinical observations on the "survivor syndrome"'. *International Journal of Psychoanalysis, 49*, 313–15.

Nilsson, A. (1970) 'Paranatal emotional adjustment: A prospective investigation of 165 women'. *Acta Psychiatrica Scandinavia*, Suppl. 220.

Rakoff, V. (1966) 'Long term effects of the concentration camp experience'. *Viewpoints, 1*, 17–21.

Rakoff, V. (1969) 'Children and families of concentration cap survivors'. *Canada's Mental Health, 14*, 24–6.

Rotenberg, M. (1987) *Re-biographing and Deviance.* New York: Praeger.

Rottman, G. (1974) 'Untersuchungen uber Einstellung zur Schwangerschaft und zur fotalen Entwicklung'. In H. Grabner (Ed.), *Geist und Psyche.* Munich: Kindler Verlag.

Russel, A. (1974) 'Late psychological consequences in concentration camp survivor families'. *American Journal of Orthopsychiatry, 44*, 611–19.

Sandler, J. (1960a) 'On the concept of the superego'. *Psychoanalytic Study of the Child, 15*, 215–21.

Sandler, J. (1960b) 'The background of safety'. *International Journal of Psychoanalysis, 41*, 352–6.

Satir, V. (1968) *Conjoint Family Therapy.* Palo Alto: Science and Behaviour Books.

Semel, N. (1985) *A Hat of Glass.* (In Hebrew) Tel Aviv: Sifriat Poalim.

Shoham, S.G. (1985) 'Valhalla, Golgotha and Auschwitz'. (In Hebrew) *Zemanim, 17*, 21–4.

Sigal, J. (1971) 'Second generation effects of massive trauma'. *International Psychiatry Clinics, 8*, 55–65.

Sigal, J. (1973) 'Hypotheses and methodology in the study of families of Holocaust survivors'. *Yearbook of the International Association for Child Psychiatry and Allied Professions, 2*, 411–16.

Sigal, J., Silver, D., Rakoff, V. and Ellin, B. (1973) 'Some second generation effects of survival of the Nazi persecution'. *American Journal of Orthopsychiatry, 43*, 320–7.

Silvermann, M.A. (1986) 'Identification in healthy and pathological character formation'. *International Journal of Psychoanalysis, 67*, 181–92.

Smith, M.E. (1968) 'Maturational crisis of pregnancy'. *Dissertation Abstracts, 28*, 3354–5.

Stern, M. (1959) 'Anxiety, trauma and shock'. *Psychoanalytic Quarterly, 34*, 202–18.

Titchener, J.L. (1967) 'Family system as a model for ego system'. In G.H. Zuk & I. Boszormenyi-Nagy (Eds), *Family Therapy and Disturbed Families.* Palo Alto: Science and Behaviour Books, 96–105.

Trossman, B. (1968) 'Adolescent children of concentration camp survivors'. *Canadian Psychiatric Association Journal, 12*, 121–3.

Verny, T. and Kelly, J. (1981) *The Secret Life of the Unborn Child.* London: Sphere Books.

Wiesel, Elie (1972) *One Generation After.* New York: Bard Books.

Winnicott, D.W. (1965) *The Maturational Processes and the Facilitating Environment.* New York: International University Press.

Zwerling, I. (1982) 'A comparison of parent–child attachment and separation in American Holocaust survivor families'. Presented at a meeting of the American Mental Health Association for Israel (AMHAI), Chicago.

Name index

193–4, 215–16
Hazan, Y. 36, 125, 127
'Hedva' 137–8
Heller, D. 31–2
'Henia' 69
Hopper, E. 148, 149

Isaac 116–16
'Itamar' 199–201
'Itzhak' 71, 74, 77, 80, 151–2, 183–4, 244–8, 256–8

Jackson, D.D. 29
Jesus 116, 252
Jonah 254
Jung, C.G. 114, 132

Kelly, J. 58
Kernberg, O. 78
Kestenberg, J.S. 10, 54, 94, 145
Khan, M.M.R. 77
Klein, G. 39
Klein, H. 8, 13, 19, 22, 57, 62, 88, 99, 118, 123, 209–10
Klein, M. 72, 92
Korczak, J. 116
Kreeger, L. 148–9
Krystal, H. 10, 15, 54, 58, 62

Last, U. 209–10
'Leah' 12, 16–17, 244
Levi, P. 4–5, 15–16, 183, 197, 246
Lifton, R.J. 11, 23, 88
Lipkowitz, M.H. 67, 118

Mahler, M. 41, 79
'Malka' 70, 72, 82
'Martha' 175–6, 178, 200–1, 235–6, 237
Martini, M. 14
Masterson, J. 78
Meissner, W.W. 31–2
'Menahem' 32–4, 36, 37–8, 44, 46, 106–7
Mengele, J. 139
'Michal' 169–74
'Mina' 10–11
'Mira' 121
'Miriam' 45, 46, 122–3, 136–7, 219, 233, 244–8

Mitscherlich, A. 99
'Mordechai' 69–70, 169–70, 243–4, 247–8, 254–5
Moses 46, 249
Murray, J.M. 66

'Nahum' 109–10, 150–1, 153
'Naomi' 67
'Nehama' 28–9, 184–5
Niederland, W.G. 14–15, 125, 127
'Nira' 118, 169–74, 182–3, 253–5
'Nurit' 82–3

'Ora' 187, 189, 193
'Orna' 165–7

'Penina' 135–6, 137

'Rachel' 218
'Rahel' 186–8
Rakoff, V. 27, 67
'Raphael' 140, 146–8
Rau, J.H. 32
'Rina' 242–3, 247
Rinsley, D. 78
'Rivka' 160–4, 219
'Roni' 45, 100–1
Rotenberg, M. 116
Rottman, G. 59
Russel, A. 27, 58, 118, 122–3
'Ruth' 91–2, 98, 189–90, 192, 205, 217–19

Sandler, J. 86, 153
'Sara' 117–18
Satir, V. 29
Savran, B. 148
Schnipper, O.L. 32
Semel, N. 48, 63–7, 95, 101–2, 118–21, 123, 144
'Shimon' 70, 73
Shoham, S.G. 115–16
'Shulamit' 24
Sigal, J. 27, 67, 118, 123
Silver, D. 27
Silvermann, M.A. 153
Smith, M.E. 66

Titchener, J.L. 29
Trossman, B. 27, 122, 145

Subject index

abandonment 10–12, 66, 79, 81–2; of relatives 89
achievers 77
adaptation 8, 14, 17
adolescence 12–13, 53, 194–5
age of group members 2
aggression 84, 132–3, 139, 141, 147
aggressor: attraction to 188; identification with 133, 145; role 40; and victim 114–49
alliance 145
anger 11, 54, 123–5, 139, 214
anxiety 57, 86, 117, 139–41; perpetual 15, 18
apathy 10, 79
appearance 202–8
archetype theory 114, 132
armour, psychological 16
arousal, hyper- 15

belonging phase 158
birth of children: family situation 31; importance of 26–7; see also childbirth, pregnancy
body image 54, 57, 61
boundaries 82, 84, 125, 158, 192, 214
bravery, disappearance of 16
breast-feeding 68–70, 72–4

career choice 125–6, 127
causality, perception of 15
childbirth 67–9
children: as symbols 27, 29; importance of birth 26–7; loss of 63–4; role 29

clinging 79, 117
closeness, expressing 246
closing-off, psychic 116, 144–5, 154
communication channels in family 29
community, loss of 20–2, see also roots
compartmentalization 13
compensation process 77
'concentration camp syndrome' 18
conformity 16
continuity 21–2, 34, 48, 55, 63, 94, 256
control 129, 139, 143, 181
cross symbol 33–4
crowd, disappearance in 14–15
crying 71–2, 100, 127, 172–3

daughters 31–2, see also father, mother
death camps, life in 14
death: culture 148; feelings of 214; identification with 88–113; images 88–94; topic of 103–4
deceit 63–4
defence mechanisms: of survivors 8, 13, 17, 19; of survivors' children 80, 87, 103, 156
defences 52, 78, 145
denial 13, 19
dependence: discouraging 79; on children 10, 42; on captors 10, 15; on parents 42; on partner 55, 181